The Skilled Helper

A Model for
Systematic Helping and
Interpersonal
Relating

The Skilled Helper

A Model for Systematic Helping and Interpersonal Relating

Gerard Egan

Loyola University of Chicago

Brooks/Cole Publishing Company
Monterey, California

A Division of Wadsworth Publishing Company, Inc.

ISBN: 0–8185–0133–2
L.C. Catalog Card No.: 74–82756
Printed in the United States of America
10

Production Editor: Lyle York
Interior & Cover Design: Linda Marcetti
Illustrations: Creative Repro Photolithographers, Monterey, California
Typesetting: Datagraphics Press, Inc., Phoenix, Arizona

Preface

This book has been written primarily for those who will be learning about helping by practicing the skills that constitute the helping process. Since helping is an art, it is learned by doing. Extensive reading in theories of counseling and psychotherapy has limited value unless it is integrated into an experiential learning process. Traditionally, helper-training programs have been overly cognitive. Too often, students have been able to discuss theories and research findings but have not been able to translate them into effective helping. This book, therefore, is addressed not so much to the "student" as to the "trainee."

The Skilled Helper presents a three-stage helping model and a helper-skills training program designed to increase the reliability of the helping process. It is not an introduction to different theories of counseling or a detailed presentation of any one theory. Rather, it presents a practical model for *doing* counseling. This model, while primarily practical, is not atheoretical. It is based on learning theory, social-influence theory, behavior-modification principles and practice, and skills-training and problem-solving methodologies. It points out three principal stages in the helping process and the skills the helper needs to implement each stage. There is a substantial amount of evidence (see the references in the Introduction) that the skillful use of this model does increase the reliability of the helping process. This text is an attempt to integrate skills-training, social-influence, and behavioral approaches to helping and to establish a training *technology* that applies both to helper training and to the helping process itself.

I would like to thank Don Dinkmeyer, President, Communication and Motivation Training Institute, Coral Springs, Florida, Allen E. Ivey of the University of Massachusetts, Richard L. Bednar of the University of Kentucky, Ronald R. Schmidt of American River College, Sacramento, California, Frank C. Noble of Arizona State University, and Bruce R. Fretz of the University of Maryland for their reviews of the original manuscript of this book. Their comments were most helpful. I would also like to thank the students in the counseling psychology program at Loyola. Their enthusiasm and responsiveness to experiential learning and their critical comments continue to make a learner of me. For this I am very grateful.

Gerard Egan

Contents

Chapter three: Attending   55

Chapter four: Stage I: Helper response and client self-exploration   73

I. The helper skills of Stage I   75

II. Helping as social influence: The experience of the client   106

III. Self-exploration   114

Chapter five: Stage II: Integrative understanding/dynamic self-understanding   127

I. Dynamic self-understanding: Client goal for Stage II   128

II. Helper skills in Stage II   133

Chapter six: Stage III: Action programs   182

Chapter seven: Epilogue   233

Bibliography   240

Index   251

Introduction

1. The developmental model is designed to increase the reliability of helping.
2. This model is based on
   a. the work of Carkhuff and others, who espouse systematic skills-training approaches to helping and helper training,
   b. social-influence theory, and
   c. learning theory and the principles underlying the maintenance and change of behavior.
3. This model has been developed for all who are involved in the wide variety of helping professions.
4. The importance of psychological theory (for instance, personality theory) is not denied. The personality theory upon which the developmental model is based is eclectic.
5. Values are bound up in the helping process. One expresses a value simply by choosing a particular helping system.
6. The skills discussed in this book are primarily the skills of effective interpersonal relating.
7. Group training is the preferred approach to both the education of helpers and the treatment of helpees.
8. The terminology used in this text is varied; it attempts to avoid role connotations.
9. A training manual accompanies the text. It is one step in the entire systematic training process.

Norman Kagan (1973) suggests that the basic issue confronting the helping professions is *reliability,* not validity.

Not, can counseling and psychotherapy work, but does it work consistently? Not, can we educate people who are able to help others, but can we develop methods which will increase the likelihood that *most* of our graduates will become as effective mental health workers as only a rare few do? It is my basic premise that attempts to validate therapy derived from personality theories have failed, not because of the inadequacy of the theories, but because the average practitioner has not been adequately educated to implement the theory. This is not to deny that better theories are needed but rather to assert that there is enough truth in extant ones to ameliorate the critical mental health problems of our world if only we could translate their implications into effective action with greater consistency [p. 44].*

The developmental model of helping presented in the chapters of this book is designed precisely to increase the reliability of the helping process.

The parentage of the developmental helping model

The model presented in these pages is both old and new, both simple and sophisticated. A good model must integrate the best helping techniques into a goal-oriented, *systematic* scheme with, as Aristotle suggests, "a beginning, a middle, and an end." A rudimentary form of such a model has long existed in the common sense of man, but, as is the way with common sense, it has generally been ignored. This rudimentary helping model is a three-stage developmental one; that is, it has "a beginning, a middle, and an end," all in dynamic relationship with one another. I was in high school when this model was first formally presented to me as "Think. Judge. Act." That is: explore the problem, understand its ramifications and demands, and then act to solve it. In a helping context it takes this form: establish the kind of relationship with the person who comes for help that will enable him to explore the problematic in his life freely; then help him to see the problem objectively and understand the need for action; and, finally, help him to act. The model, as it appears in the chapters of this book, has three major interrelated sources.

1. The work of Carkhuff and other systematic skills-training systems. It has been the genius of Robert Carkhuff and his associates (see, for example, Carkhuff, 1969a,b, 1971, 1972a,b,c,d, 1973; Carkhuff & Beren-

*Kagan, N. Can technology help us toward reliability in influencing human interaction? *Educational Technology,* 1973, **13,** 44–51. This and all other quotes from the same source are reprinted by permission.

son, 1967; Truax & Carkhuff, 1967) to take this "folk" model and forge it into a scientific model through extensive and rigorous research and practice. Not only does Carkhuff spell out the demands characteristic of each stage of the model, but he also both delineates the skills needed by the helper to be effective at each stage and elaborates a technology for selecting prospective helpers and training them in these skills. The "folk" model has needed a technology and Carkhuff has provided it. But he has gone further than this. Since the helping skills he outlines are basically the same skills anyone needs to live effectively as a social-emotional human being, Carkhuff suggests that the best mode of treatment is to *train the helpee directly and systematically* in the skills he needs to live more effectively. These include both human-relations and problem-solving skills. This step constitutes a revolution in the helping professions.

Although the work of Carkhuff and his associates constitutes the major influence on the model developed in these pages, Carkhuff, too, has predecessors. For instance, he owes much to Carl Rogers (1942, 1951, 1957, 1959, 1961, 1967) for the development of the first stage of his model and the skills belonging to the first stage and part of the second. But Rogers stops far short of Carkhuff's three-stage model. Of course, Carkhuff has his critics (see *The Counseling Psychologist,* 1972, **3** [3] for a sampling), but, in my opinion, his contributions to the field of helping are outstanding.

Others have developed systematic helping and helper-training systems, either independently or based in part on Carkhuff's work. For instance, Brammer (1973) presents an integrated, eclectic developmental model similar to Carkhuff's. Brammer expands the three general helping stages into eight specific ones. He is also generous in his delineation of helping skills. For instance, he identifies seven clusters of skills, which include over twenty specific skills, to promote "understanding of self and others." While this proliferation of stages and skills is bewildering to the novice, the detail and specificity are very stimulating to the experienced helper.

Ivey and his associates (Boyd, 1973; Ivey, 1971, 1972; Haase & DiMattia, 1970; Hackney, Ivey, & Oetting, 1970; Ivey, Normington, Miller, Morrill, & Haase, 1968; Moreland, Ivey, & Phillips, 1973; Wittmer & Lister, 1972) have developed systematic technologies for training helpers under the rubric "microcounseling." Their systematic training procedures are also very useful in training-as-treatment approaches to helping.

Hackney and Nye (1973) have developed a helping model that they term a "discrimination" model. This model is goal-centered and action-oriented, and it stresses skills training. The authors identify the major elements of the three-stage developmental model, although they do not put them together as systematically as Carkhuff.

Kagan and his associates (Archer, 1971; Archer et al., 1972; Archer & Kagan, 1973; Danish, 1971; Danish & Kagan, 1969; Dendy, 1971; Goldberg, 1967; Grzegorek, 1970; Hartson, 1971; Heiserman, 1971; Kagan, 1971, 1973; Kagan, Krathwohl, & Miller, 1963; Kagan & Schauble, 1969; Spivack & Kagan, 1972; Ward et al., 1972) have developed a microskills approach to counselor training.

> The general teaching strategy . . . has evolved as a sequential progression of lessons beginning with a didactic presentation of concepts, then to simulation exercises to interpersonal affective stress, to video and physiological feedback, to study of self-in-action, to feedback from clients and, finally, to understanding of and skill at dealing with the complex bilateral impacts which occur when two people are in relationship with one another [Kagan, 1973, p. 44].

Their approach is highly systematic and focuses on a technique called "interpersonal process recall" (IPR), an inquiry session in which both helper and helpee explore the experience they have had together in a practice session. A third party serves as mediator in this session.

> During the recall both interviewer and client are present. An inquirer encourages *each* one to talk about the unexpressed attitudes, intentions, feelings, thoughts, strategies and expectations he had about the other—*each participant* equally. . . . These "mutual recall" sessions afford additional possibilities for learning [Kagan, 1973, p. 49].

Kagan emphasizes skills-training technology but does not systematically outline the overall helping model into which the skills fit.

Goldstein (1973) criticizes traditional psychotherapeutic approaches for failing to be of service to the poor; he develops his own "structured learning therapy" to help poor patients acquire interpersonal and related skills as means of increasing adequacy of functioning.

In general, the literature reveals a renewed realization of the necessity of teaching skills systematically and experientially, both to prospective helpers and to people who are interested in improving their interpersonal style. I have shown concern over the goallessness and ambiguity that have characterized so much of the human-relations-training movement and have suggested that systematic skills training be integrated into these processes (Egan, 1973b). Wallen (1973) has developed a microskills approach to interpersonal-communication training.

2. Social-influence theory. While it may sound to some like a radical departure from traditional (especially nondirective) approaches to helping, to say that helping is a social-influence process is, in a sense, a statement of the obvious. *All* human interaction can be conceptualized (though certainly not exclusively) from the viewpoint of the social-influence process. As soon as I involve myself with my fellow human beings, I become both one who influences and one who is influenced (see Berscheid & Walster, 1969; Gergen, 1969; Kelman, 1967; Zimbardo & Ebbesen, 1970). I influence others both by acting (for example, when I show care for others, they are influenced to like me, respect me, and cooperate with me; when I am cynical, others are influenced to avoid and fear me) and by not acting (my silence at a meeting influences other members to think of me as impotent or unconcerned or to feel a need to "deal with" my silence). We live in a society charged with social-influence attempts. All of us from time to time involve ourselves in social-influence attempts, overtly or covertly, knowingly or unwittingly. Since the laws of social influence operate both in the transactions of everyday life and in helping situations, it is only natural to study helping and interpersonal relating from the viewpoint of the principles of social influence so that we can use these principles creatively instead of becoming their victims.

Jerome Frank (1961, 1973) was one of the first to point out social-influence elements in widely divergent approaches to helping (he uses the words "persuasion and healing") in different cultures. Strupp, in discussing "the basic ingredients of psychotherapy" (see Garfield, 1973; Strupp, 1973a,b), defines the helping relationship in terms of the kinds of social-influence processes that characterize parent-child relationships. Stanley R. Strong (1968) has developed a two-stage model of helping (quite similar to Carkhuff's) based on social-influence theory. Both he and his associates (Dell, 1973; Kaul & Parker, 1971; Kaul & Schmidt, 1971; Murphy & Strong, 1972; Roll, Schmidt, & Kaul, 1972; Schmidt & Strong, 1970, 1971; Strong, 1970; Strong & Dixon, 1971; Strong & Gray, 1972; Strong & Matross, 1973; Strong, Meland, & Keierleber, 1972; Strong & Schmidt, 1970a,b; Strong, Taylor, Bratton, & Loper, 1971) have been engaged in basic research related to that model. The model, in its simplest form, states that in Stage I the helper establishes a power base or influence base with the helpee through perceived expertness, trustworthiness, and attractiveness and in Stage II uses this influence to help the client change both his attitudes and his behavior to more constructive patterns. Carkhuff's model is basically a social-influence model, although he does not refer to it in those terms. Indeed, he emphasizes client self-determination rather than the power of the helper. Still, the skills Carkhuff sees as critical to the first stage (and, actually, to the entire model) are precisely the skills that Strong sees as the basis of the helper's power or influence—that is, the communication of respect, genuineness, and accurate empathy—which are behavioral ways of establishing the expertness and the trustworthiness of the helper.

The conceptualization of helping solely as a social-influence process leads to certain obvious problems. Social influence stresses the notion of getting the client to do something, while skills-training approaches suggest that this "something" should be, principally, training in skills that lead to more effective living and self-determination. Critics of strict social-influence approaches are afraid that the "more knowing" (that is, the helpers) will use their skills and knowledge to dominate and control the "less knowing" (that is, the helpees). London (1964, 1969) deals directly with the question of psychotherapy as a form of social control. He believes that the main ethical problem of modern behavior-control technology is the threat it presents to traditional ideas of personal responsibility and political liberty. However, since (in my opinion) it is impossible completely to avoid social-influence processes in helping, helpers should stress overt social influence, based primarily on caring, understanding, and collaboration, and directed toward helping clients learn the skills of effective interpersonal living. Otherwise helpers and helpees alike become the victims of helping as a covert social-influence process based primarily on the helper's need to control and the helpee's disorganization, suggestibility, and dependency. Although the theory and research of Strong and his associates are significant components of the model presented in these pages, I personally have some concern with what seems to be an overemphasis on control in their writings. The Carkhuff-Strong model, however, is an open, developing one, and differential emphasis on one dimension or another depends on the value systems of the various proponents.

3. Learning theory and the principles underlying the maintenance and change of behavior.   The third major influence is directly related to the first two. No helping model that ignores the basic principles of human behavior and change could be called practical. Skinner (1953) helped unleash a revolution in the behavioral sciences that has not yet abated. His work has given rise to a great deal of controversy centering around values (see London, 1969; Matson, 1973; Rogers & Skinner, 1956). Some practitioners declare themselves either "for" or "against" behavior modification in an almost political way, but this is not only an oversimplification of the important value issues but also a step backward in the science and art of helping. Since counseling is directed toward helping a client (1) maintain growthful transactions with himself and his environment, especially his interpersonal environment, (2) change those behaviors that are self- and other-destructive, and (3) acquire skills that will enable the client to live more effectively, the helper must have a thorough practical grasp of the basic principles underlying learning, unlearning, and relearning, no matter how he feels about behavior modification as a package of techniques. If the helper and/or the helpee ignore these principles, they will be ground up by them. Some clients come to helpers precisely because they have been fighting fundamental laws of behavior (for example, a teacher complains of the dependency of her pupils and yet reinforces this dependency by the way she responds to them). Some helpers unwittingly reinforce the very behavior they are trying to help the client change. While a sophisticated theoretical knowledge of these principles and a conceptualization of helping as a learning process (Bandura, 1961, 1969; Ferster & Perrott, 1968; Glaser, 1971; Murray & Jacobson, 1971) are not necessary for the average helper, a solid elementary grasp of these principles (Berkowitz, 1972; Sherman, 1973; Whaley & Malott, 1971) is most useful. Even more important is the helper's ability to use them in his own life and help others use them in theirs (Mehrabian, 1970; Patterson & Gullion, 1971; Rimm & Masters, 1974; Watson & Tharp, 1973).

This text does not pretend to be a substitute for the books mentioned above, but the developmental model outlined here is based on these behavioral principles. The student/trainee is encouraged to develop a repertory of problem-solving and behavior-modification skills based on learning principles. In the helper-training programs I direct, I have the student/trainees learn the basic principles of behavior maintenance and change experientially by engaging in a self-modification project (Watson & Tharp, 1973). In turn, the trainees use the skills of the first two stages of the developmental model to help one another implement these self-modification projects.

In summary, then, this book attempts to integrate the three major influences cited and serves as a practical introduction to a three-stage developmental model of helping that emphasizes skills training for both the helper in his training and the helpee in his treatment.

The helping professions

Who needs the kinds of skills described in these pages? The answer is simple. All of us at one time or another are asked to help and all of us are involved daily in human relationships. Many professions demand two sets of skills, one set dealing with a specific technology (such as medicine) and another in the area of human relations. The doctor doesn't face just an ulcer in Room 436; he faces a human being, perhaps scared and dependent. No doctor can merely assign the patient's humanity to chaplains, aides, or volunteers while he takes care of his body. Who are the helpers—the officially designated, paraprofessional, volunteer, and everyday helpers—who need helping skills?

chaplains	organizational-development consultants
child-care workers	ants
church workers	parents
community-development workers	peer helpers
counselors	physicians
correctional-system workers	police
family members	probation officers
friends	psychiatrists
group leaders	psychologists
hospital workers	rehabilitation workers
human-relations specialists	residence-hall directors, counselors, and assistants
interviewers	social workers
marriage partners	teachers
mental-health workers and aides	trainers
ministers	tutors
nurses	volunteers in human-services programs
	youth workers

I am sure that you could enlarge this list. Since the need for help in this world is endless, we well might ask why people do not help one another more than they do. Is it simply a question of selfishness? No one would deny that there is a great deal of selfishness, egocentricity, and noncaring in the world, but it is also probably true that many people would volunteer their services if they thought they *could* help, if they felt they had the skills needed to help. Many more would volunteer their services if there were intelligent, well-organized, community-centered programs, run by high-level helpers, that would provide training for the volunteers in whatever skills a particular program demanded. Just as psychologists have talked about the untapped potential within each individual (Maslow, 1968), we can talk about the untapped helping resources within any community.

Helpers and psychological theory

In order to read this book, the student/trainee does not need a great deal of background in psychological theory (in fact, more is needed to read this introduction than to read the rest of the book). In the past the tendency was to overload the prospective helper with psychological theory. He was schooled (often in the worst sense of the term) in personality theory, developmental psychology, abnormal psychology, and highly cognitive approaches to counseling and psychotherapy— often at the expense of skills training and experiential learning. To a large extent this is still true today. However, there is a growing body of opinions and evidence (Archer, 1971; Archer & Kagan, 1973; Carkhuff, 1968, 1969a; Carkhuff & Berenson, 1967; Carkhuff & Truax, 1965; Dendy, 1971; Goldstein, 1973; Haase & DiMattia, 1970; Hurvitz, 1970; Kopita, 1973; Lamb & Clack, 1974; Pyle & Snyder, 1971; Rappaport, Gross, & Lepper, 1973; Rioch, 1966; Suinn, 1974; Truax & Carkhuff, 1967—to name but a few) that helpers with extensive training in psychological theory and a variety of academic credentials do not necessarily help, and that the paraprofessional helper, if properly trained in helping skills, can become very effective even without extensive training in psychological theory. Indeed, if a choice had to be made between skills training and cognitive learning, it would be better to choose the former. However, it would be better if such a choice did not have to be made. The potential helper should be trained in theoretical issues in helping, developmental psychology, abnormal psychology, and personality theory; but these should have a *practical impact* on the prospective helper's ability to help. Too often, theory remains just theory, crammed into dull courses that must be suffered through as a kind of rite of passage, wasteful of human resources.

Personality theory. Frank (1961) suggests that everyone has a need to impose some kind of order or regularity on the mass of experience that surrounds him daily. According to Frank, each of us develops from our personal experiences a set of more or less explicit assumptions about the nature of the world in which we live. This is our "assumptive world," which helps us predict our own behavior and that of others. This world view, however broad or limited, does give us some degree of security. Likewise, each of us formulates, implicitly or explicitly, a set of assumptions about the nature and behavior of man. Each of us can be said to have at least an implicit theory of personality from which we work.

The personality theory underlying the developmental model of helping is not made explicit in these pages. The personality theory implicit in the model does not represent any one school, for it, too, is born of the kind of "integrative eclecticism" that Brammer and Shostrom (1968) recommend in developing theories of helping (for an example of this in the area of personality theory, see Janis, 1969). Its roots lie in self theory (Combs & Snygg, 1959; Rogers, 1959), learning theory —especially social-learning theory (Bandura & Walters, 1963; Skinner,

1953, 1963, 1971)—and self-actualization theory, which is itself "integratively eclectic" (Maslow, 1968, 1970).

A question of values

Values are essential to helping in a number of different ways. Curran (1968) notes that many people experience social-emotional crises because of conflicting values in their lives. Helping is directed, at least in part, toward the exploration of the client's value system, in order to find out whether he is being torn apart by the pursuit of values that are in some way contradictory. Rokeach (1973) has done research showing that many people have an idealized set of values ("notional" values) and a practical set ("real" values). The latter determine behavior. He describes values-confrontation as a potent tool for helping another person change his behavior.

Helpers with different value emphases choose different helping systems. For instance, nondirective and social-influence systems take different approaches to client autonomy. The former emphasizes releasing the client's potential and his ability to direct his own life, while the latter emphasizes problem-solving and having the client act in more productive ways. Breggin (Trotter, 1973) says that the purpose of therapy is not to give attention, love, affection, or support but to liberate the person to get it somewhere else. On the other hand, others see therapy—at least partially and actually, if not wholly and ideally—as "the purchase of friendship" (Schofield, 1964). Some values emphasized (at least implicitly) by the developmental model are responsibility, self-determination, caring, altruism, problem-solving (getting the work done), cooperation, interdependence, growth in interpersonal skills, development and use of human potential, self-control, discipline, helping, and living intensively. The skilled helper both knows what his own "real" values are and can help others discover, define, and implement theirs.

Helping and/or human relationships

This book focuses on helping relationships. However, the term "human relationships" appears in the subtitle. As Brammer (1973) notes, "Helping relationships have much in common with friendships, family interactions, and pastoral contacts. They are all aimed toward fulfilling basic human needs, and when reduced to their basic components, look much alike" (p. 48). To word this in a slightly different way, the skills discussed in the following chapters are *primarily* the skills of effective interpersonal relating. They belong first in everyday life and are not merely the inventions or tools of something apart from real life that is termed "helping." For this reason Carkhuff and Berenson (1967) can talk about counseling as "a way of life." The skills discussed and illustrated in this text are the skills needed in marriage, friendship, family living, and the interpersonal aspects of work situations. Therefore, although the book focuses primarily on helping and the language it uses is the language of the helping process, it also deals with the basics of interpersonal communication (and I use it in human-relations-training courses).

There is an important difference between interpersonal relating and helping, especially the helping that is carried out by professionals and paraprofessionals rather than the helping that is woven into the fabric of everyday human relating. Everyday interpersonal relationships are characterized by more *mutuality* than is the helping or counseling process. Friends help *each other,* while, in more formalized helping relationships, roles are more clear-cut: one is the helper or counselor and the other is the helpee or client. The helper might well find deep satisfaction in his helping, but he is not being helped by the client, nor is he ordinarily establishing a friendship. I believe this distinction is an important one and will say more about it as we examine the helping process more closely.

Group approaches to training and treatment

My assumption is that the best kind of helper training includes skills training and experiential learning in the context of a small group. Carkhuff (1969b, pp. 129–185) lists the advantages of group-training methods, and I have discussed groups as the locus of human-relations training (Egan, 1970, 1973a, b). As has already been noted, Carkhuff also recommends direct training of helpees in human-relations and problem-solving skills. The model presented in this book can be considered in two ways.

1. *A helper-training model.* This text provides a program for the prospective helper. The trainee learns the model and the skills needed to implement each stage of the model. He then uses the model and the skills of the model in helping others in both one-to-one and group helping situations.

2. *A helpee-treatment model.* The developmental model can also be seen as a training program for the client; as Carkhuff (1969b) suggests,

in many cases training might well be the best form of treatment or at least an essential part of the treatment process. The helper, once he has gone through the training process itself and mastered both the model and its skills, can help clients by using the same training methodology to train them directly in interpersonal-relating and problem-solving skills. In Carkhuff's model, training is the preferred mode of treatment and group training is the best form of training. In this second use of the model, the trainee learns not only a helping model but, at the same time, a training-as-treatment *methodology*. Since this second approach is much more unusual than the first, the examples in the following chapters focus principally on one-to-one helping. However, everything said about both training and helping is applicable to groups. Like Carkhuff, I believe that training is an extremely important component of treatment and that the advantages of group training and treatment make group approaches preferable.

Terminology and pronouns

How should one refer to the person who comes to another for help? Carkhuff refers to him as the "helpee." In medical circles he has always been called the "patient." Rogers (1951) uses the term "client" extensively. None of these terms seems completely satisfactory. "Helpee" can seem very patronizing. "Patient" evokes all the specters of the medical model (sickness) and connotes one who hands himself over to others to be cured; it seems too passive. "Client" is generally a good term, but there is still something overly "professional" and role-ridden about it. If counseling is essentially a role-free experience (Gibb, 1968), role-laden terms do not seem to fit. If single words fail, we can turn to phrases: "the person coming for help," "the person seeking help," or "the person you are trying to help." Perhaps there is no ideal way to designate the person who feels he must go to another person for help. In the following pages I avoid the term "patient," but I use "client," "helpee," and a variety of phrases. "What's in a name?" you well might ask. I bring up the question of terminology because I am trying to avoid what I refer to elsewhere as the "reverse halo effect" (Egan, 1970). When a person discloses the problems in his life, there is the tendency on the part of some to *identify* him with the problems he reveals, even though the problematic areas form only a part of his life, which in many other ways might be a constructive one. If the person coming for help falls victim to this process, he indeed becomes a "helpee" burdened with all the negative connotations of that term. Labels of any kind can get in the way. However, if I say "helpee" with a great deal of respect, or say "client" without locking myself up behind the protective armor of the role of "counselor," all is well.

I often speak directly to the student/trainee, using the pronoun "you." I refer to myself often enough as "I" rather than use "the author" or other cumbersome third-person circumlocutions. Throughout the book, I use "he" and "him" to include both sexes in order to avoid awkward expressions such as "he or she" and "he/she." I find such expressions distracting. Finally, my experience with trainees has taught me that high-level helping is in no way limited to males, and I have tried to achieve a balance between the sexes in my choice of examples.

Training manual

A training manual has been prepared to help the student/trainee learn to discriminate and communicate the major helping skills of this model. In my training experience such exercises have served as an indispensable link between the student's reading of texts and his actual practice of the skills with his fellow trainees in a training group.

Chapter One

Helping, Helper, and Trainee

1. A working model of helping or counseling helps the trainee make sense of the vast literature on helping.
2. A working model of helping, rather than a theory or a school, is presented here.
3. There is a crisis in the helping profession: many helpers simply do not help.
4. Many helpees have problems because they do not have the skills they need to cope with life, especially interpersonal living.
5. A high-level helper is socially intelligent, hardworking, action oriented, at home with people, and in touch with the human condition.
6. The trainer must himself be a high-level helper. Trainees tend to be inhibited or stimulated by the skills level of the training director.

Clutter or richness?

The name of the game in the literature dealing with counseling and psychotherapy is complexity—or, perhaps, clutter. If one reads the psychotherapy section of the *Annual Review of Psychology* or leafs through books that are compilations of the different "psychotherapies" (for instance, Corsini, 1973; Ford & Urban, 1963; Jurjevich, 1973; Patterson, 1973; Stefflre, 1965), he sees a bewildering number of schools and systems, approaches and techniques, all of which are proposed with equal seriousness and all of which claim a quite high degree of success. The beginner, then, needs an approach that is effective in itself and that will help him make some sense of the vast literature dealing with helping relationships. In a word, the beginner needs a practical working *model* that will tell him

> what he should do to help another in emotional distress,
> what skills he needs to do it,
> how he can acquire these skills,
> what the person coming for help must do in the helping process,
> what skills the person coming for help needs in order to involve himself
> in this process,
>> how he acquires these skills, and
> what steps or stages make up the helping process.

If the beginner assimilates such a model and the skills needed to implement it, he can view the clutter of systems, schools, and techniques as richness. He can mine from the helping literature what he needs to develop and perfect this open-ended model and acquire techniques that enable him to extend this model to ever-widening areas of human problems.

A working model of helping

This book does not deal with specific schools of counseling and psychotherapy. A school, in the sense in which it is described here, tends to be identified with a particular historical figure, as psychoanalysis is identified with Freud. A school is also usually related to a well-elaborated theory of personality, and it is from this theory that therapeutic methodology flows. Thus psychoanalysis is both a theory of personality and a system of psychotherapy. Schools often tend to be literary in their approach to man rather than more narrowly empirical. Both personality theory and psychotherapeutic practice tend to be based on clinical insights (quite often, the insights of the founder of the school) rather than on controlled research. I hasten to add that literary ways of knowing have their own validity and need not be defended; but I find certain difficulties in using literary ways of knowing (which often deal with myth and metaphor) as bases for psychotherapeutic practice. I prefer an empirical approach to counseling and psychotherapy, complemented in practice by literary approaches to man. School approaches to psychotherapy tend to be both rigid and overly vague. Thorne (1973a) sees no value in the proliferation of schools. He contends that schools arise when practitioners rediscover older facts and methods and give them new names. "Newness" and "esoteric vocabularies" are signs of schools. For Thorne, then, some schools are only fads, while others are old wine in new skins. It is my feeling, therefore, that the beginner should not approach counseling through any specific school and that he should have a practical model to help him make sense of the schools, theories, and helping technologies that exist.

The beginning helper needs a framework of at least two kinds.

1. A practical framework.   The beginner needs a framework that will tell him what to do in order to help. The helping model presented here presents a practical strategy for helping. It indicates both the *stages* through which, as a general rule, the helping process moves and the *skills* the helper must exercise at each stage of the model in order to achieve the goals of each stage. The model presented here is backed up by a great deal of empirical evidence. See the works of Carkhuff, Ivey, and Strong and their associates, cited in the Introduction, for summaries of this evidence; new evidence is appearing continually in the journals. This evidence suggests (1) that the model, if used skillfully, works; that is, it is related to positive counseling outcome (as measured by a variety of outcome criteria); and (2) that the skills called for by the model are essential to its working. Therefore, the model works *if*—if the helper has developed the skills called for by the model and if he uses these skills in the helping process. Such a helper is called a "high-level" helper and is to be distinguished from the "low-level" helper, one who has not developed the skills of the model or who has not mastered the model itself or who does not use the skills he does have in trying to help.

Why is it suggested here that the beginner start with a practical model of helping rather than with a theory or with a review of a variety of theories? Some research shows that with beginning counselors there is often a gap between their initial theoretical stance and their actual practice (Rosso & Frey, 1973). Furthermore, high-level helpers who hold to different theories often look quite similar in practice (Fiedler, 1950), while practitioners with the same theoretical outlook can look quite different in practice (Lieberman, Yalom, & Miles, 1973). I have chosen to emphasize the practice of helping in this book as more practical for the student/trainee. Theory is not ignored (see the Introduction for some of the theoretical bases of the model presented here), but most of the time it is implicit and subordinated to practice.

2. An integrating framework.   The beginner also needs a framework that will enable him to borrow ideas, techniques, and methodology from other theories and approaches and to integrate them into his own conception and practice of helping. I hope that this model provides that kind of framework, for it is both the product of the kind of "integrative eclecticism" (though I prefer the term "systematic eclecticism") urged by Brammer and Shostrom (1968) and a practical tool that will help the student/trainee begin the process of forging his own unique "systematic eclecticism" (see Thorne, 1973b). It is an open model, one that can borrow from any school or approach. It is an operational model, and, as Thorne (1973a) notes, "Operational approaches simplify the study of the various schools of psychology and differentiate their respective contributions" (p. 882).

The crisis in helping

The helping professions need help. In a series of articles, Eysenck (1952, 1960, 1965) has suggested that people in need of social-emotional help are as likely to be rehabilitated *without* psychotherapy as with it. Carkhuff (1969a, b, 1972c; Carkhuff & Berenson, 1967) sees a more grim picture. Counseling is not a neutral process: it is for better *or for worse.* If the distressed person finds a skilled helper, he is likely to improve— that is, to begin to live more effectively according to a variety of outcome criteria. However, if he is involved with a "low-level" helper, it is quite likely that he will get worse. Even more grim is Carkhuff's finding that the *average* experienced counselor in one research project was a "low-level" helper.

There are many helping professions: those associated with the ministry, social work, psychiatry, counseling, teaching, psychology, law, and so on. There is some evidence that these professions are usually staffed by relatively low-level helpers—that is, helpers who rate low in the core skills of the helping process such as genuineness, concreteness, accurate empathic understanding, and respect. For instance, a national study of Roman Catholic priests (Kennedy & Heckler, 1971) indicated that some 70 percent of those studied fell into a category entitled "underdeveloped." Indeed, one of the focal areas of their lack of development was interpersonal relationships. This does not mean that priests in general are poor human beings or even that they are any worse (or any better) than those who populate the other helping professions. In fact, one of the conclusions of this study was that *"the priests of the United States are ordinary men."* The problem is, however, that "ordinary men" (as defined by the study) do not usually make effective helpers.

There is an interesting parallel between the training of priests and the training of others in the helping professions. The training of the priests in the study had been highly cognitive in nature, although they were being trained for a profession that demanded a great variety of practical skills. The priests had received practically no training in human-relations skills, and what training they received was not systematic. If the various training programs for priests had been spelled out in operational terms indicating clearly and concretely the dimensions of the training process, one could have predicted that such overly cognitive training programs would do little to produce effective helpers. Seminary training, in a wry (but unfortunate) sense, was "successful," for it produced the kind of helpers it was designed to produce. The training for other helping professions is also highly cognitive in nature. Sometimes clinical-psychology graduate students move directly from a strictly academic education to internship practice, in which they are responsible for treating clients. This practice seems unethical, for the trainee has not had to demonstrate an adequate level of proficiency in basic helping skills. Carkhuff and his associates (Carkhuff, 1972d; Carkhuff & Berenson, 1967, pp. 7–11) find evidence indicating that many graduate students in the helping professions become *less* capable of helping because of the training they receive! Overly cognitive, nonsystematic training programs, run by educators who themselves lack basic helping skills— this is a devastating combination.

We need not just improved programs but a revolution in the training of helpers. There are many professional helpers with the proper credentials (degrees, licenses, and so on) but without essential skills. Carkhuff calls a helper a "functional" professional if he has the skills needed for effective helping. There is a great need for functional professionals, whether or not they have credentials.

Another sign of the need for reform in the helping professions is the tendency of many helpers to give most help to those who least need it (Goldstein, 1973; McMahon, 1964; Schofield, 1964; Shapiro & Asher, 1972; Williams, 1956). The preferred client for many helpers is what Schofield calls the "YAVIS" patient—young, attractive, verbal, intelligent, and successful. Therefore, much of the "success" experienced by such helpers is due to the fact that they choose minimally disturbed clients with optimal resources.

Ivey (1973) challenges the conservatism of the counseling profession:

> We have known for years that what we have been doing is not particularly effective (Eysenck, 1952; Bergin, 1971). Traditional approaches to counseling and psychotherapy simply don't deliver. There are also new techniques such as those discussed by Carkhuff that do deliver. Yet, what do we find in our counseling centers, community mental health centers, hospitals? We still find a predominance of the same sloppy, inefficient treatment methods that Eysenck exposed so clearly twenty years ago [p. 3].

The present crisis can be seen as either problem or plight. When it is seen as *plight,* there is a great deal of wringing of hands and the kind of criticism that does nothing but beget further criticism. However, if the present crisis is seen as *problem,* we can begin to take the steps necessary to solve it. If an extensive literature exists suggesting that present training programs do not produce effective helpers, we can design programs that do. If we see that one of the principal faults of these programs is that they do not provide systematic training in skills that have been demonstrated to be effective in the helping process (Ivey, 1971; Matarazzo, Wiens, & Saslow, 1966; Whitely, 1969), we can develop programs based on such systematic training. This book attempts to provide an introduction to such programs.

As Peter Drucker (1968) notes, *all* organizations are by their nature conservative. Even businesses change only when they must, and they have a relatively clear criterion for success or failure: profit and loss. Organizations that have no clear-cut criteria for judging success or failure—education, government, churches—can afford to be even more conservative than businesses (how do you determine whether a given university is "successful" in a given year?). The helping professions face the same problems. Professionals tend to transfer the burden of failure to the client. We haven't helped people because they are not "motivated" or because they "resist" us or because they leave therapy "too soon"—and the excuses multiply. The helping professions have to elaborate concrete criteria of success and failure and delineate the core processes that lead to success. Only then can we determine whether failure is due to an unmotivated client or to an unskilled helper.

Skills and social-emotional problems

This book presents a *skills* approach to helping. The assumptions are (1) that the helper is a skilled person, a person who is himself living effectively and who is certainly living more effectively than the client in the areas of the client's problems, and (2) that the client learns the skills he needs to live more effectively through the counseling process. One way of looking at the "crazy" behavior of the person in social-emotional trouble is this: when a person faces certain stressful life situations (for instance, a woman trying to face up to and deal with her husband's problem drinking), he or she may not have the *skills* needed to deal with the crisis and the stress. If a person does not have these skills, he falls apart in various ways. For instance, he will persist in trying ineffective solutions (for example, the alcoholic's wife yelling at him and nagging, even though it does no good), or try bizarre but ineffective solutions (for example, the wife taking an overdose of sleeping pills or shooting her husband), or simply give up (the wife taking the children and leaving him). The tendency to try "crazy" solutions to problems that call for skills is very common. Men run around with other women because they cannot communicate with their own wives, they drink because they feel they are useless, they punish their families because they cannot work things out with their boss, they take drugs because life is "meaningless." A person who does not have the skills to handle a given crisis engages in the "crazy" behavior of a man who knocks his head against a wall because he does not have the skills needed to climb it, go around it, or move back from it. Perhaps his ultimate solution is to sit catatonically at the base of the wall.

How are people helped, then? One answer is that they are helped by being trained in the skills they need to live life and meet its crises more effectively. One set of skills is of paramount importance: basic human-relations skills, the skills needed for effective involvement with others. How often is it discovered that married people do not even have the skills necessary to be decent to each other?

Anthony (1973) carried out an experiment suggesting that proficiency in human-relations skills can be used as an index of overall psychological adjustment. Pierce and Drasgow (1969) demonstrated that improvement in interpersonal functioning leads to improvement in other areas of living. When they trained severely disturbed patients directly in human-relations skills, these patients improved on a *variety* of criteria.

Why are relatively few people more than the "ordinary men" of the study on priests? One answer is that when the unskilled in human relations get together intimately with the unskilled (as in marriage and family life), no human growth takes place, or their interactions become destructive. All human contacts are for better or for worse. In growing up, the youngster has a great deal of contact with the "significant adults" in his life, whether they be parents or others, such as teachers. If these significant adults are significantly lacking in the ability to express respect, care, genuineness, and understanding, not only will the child fail to develop these skills, but he will also come to think of himself as unworthy of care (for, after all, no one gives it to him). If the same process is repeated in school, the child does not learn to prize himself any more than he did at home. He finds no effective models in human-relations skills and, more often than not, he is locked into a "parallel-learning" situation in which he communicates very little with his peers. The net result is that most children become the "ordinary men" of the study, beset, if they are fortunate, by the "psychopathology of the average" (Maslow, 1968) or, if they are less fortunate, by more serious forms of psychopathology. Where do children learn, in any systematic way, the human-relations skills that are so necessary for effective living?

Let's consider another example. John and Mary fall in love with each other. They marry and enjoy a relatively trouble-free "honeymoon" period in their marriage. Eventually, however, the problems that inevitably arise from living together in such intimacy assert themselves. If up to this point John and Mary have been sustained only by positively valenced emotional experiences with each other, then trouble begins. They find, for instance, that they cannot "communicate" with each other. The relationship deteriorates. They live in misery, or they divorce, or they end up—for better or for worse—with someone in a helping profession. Perhaps they have never learned the skills they need to live together in such intimacy. They have not learned that good human relationships demand a great deal of *work*. Some people have the good fortune to come from families in which parents possess and model high-level human-relations skills. In our example, however, John and Mary, like so many others, have not been so fortunate. Not only did they not learn these skills in the context of family life, they did not learn them anywhere else (certainly not in twelve, sixteen, or even twenty years of schooling). John and Mary do not live decently because they do not even know how: they do not have the skills of communicating understanding and respect for each other.

I am not suggesting a simplistic "lack-of-skills" behavioral model to take the place of a more esoteric (but still simplistic) medical model of psychopathology. I am suggesting that erratic and immature human behavior can often be traced in part to a lack of skills and that skills-deficit is an important component of any behavior problem. If so, then skills training, as both Carkhuff (1969b) and Ivey (1971) suggest, will be a preferred mode of treating a wide variety of behavioral problems. Most of us have probably seen couples like John and Mary transcend much of the problematic in their lives after learning basic communication/decency skills.

White (1963) suggests that *interpersonal competence* is a critical factor in the development of a sense of identity. It is utterly amazing, then, that interpersonal-skill building is left so much to chance in our society. It is also amazing that our educational systems have not filled the vacuum created in the home. There is no doubt in my mind that children should be systematically trained in human-relations skills. (Note that such training is not the same as the high-self-disclosure encounter-group approach to human-relations training that so many people fear.) Such training would demand teachers who relate to one another at relatively high levels, and, if Carkhuff's research is correct, the average teacher falls far short of this goal. What *do* children learn about human relating in school or in their day-to-day human contacts? The evidence indicates that they learn:

> how to remain superficial,
> how to build facades,
> how to play interpersonal games,
> how to hide out from themselves and others,
> how to downplay risk in human relating,
> how to manipulate others (or endure being manipulated),
> how to promote self-interest, and
> how to hurt and punish others, if necessary.

Neither caring nor the skills essential for translating care into practice are taught as a primary value. Some people claim that America is wealthy enough to take care of all those who need help—the poor, sick, aged, orphaned, disabled—but wealth means nothing, relatively speaking, in a culture that does not put high priority on caring. What does it mean when someone pays someone else who does not care for me to take care of me?

Portrait of a helper

What should a helper be, then? Ideally, he himself is striving to become Ivey's (1971) "intentional person," Carkhuff's (1969a,b) "effectively living" person, Maslow's (1968) "self-actualized" person, or Jourard's (1971b) "transparent" person. That is to say, a helper is first of all committed to his own growth—physical, intellectual, social-emotional (religiously oriented people add "spiritual")—for he realizes that he must model the behavior he hopes to help others achieve. He knows that he can help only if, in the root sense of the term, he is a "potent" human being, a person with the will and the resources to act.

He shows respect for his body through proper exercise and diet. He makes his body work for him rather than against him. He realizes that if he is to live effectively he needs a high energy level, and he knows that a poorly tended body results in loss of energy.

He has adequate basic intelligence, is aware of his own intellectual possibilities, respects the world of ideas. When it comes to intellect, he neither sells himself short nor pretends that he has more going for him than he actually has. Since ideas are important to him, he reads. He reads actively and hungrily, for he is eager to expand his view of the world. He respects good literature and the world of myth and metaphor. He respects good theory and good research, but he is a practical person, a "translator," who makes what he reads work for him. Because he is a good learner, he is a good translator. He can turn good theory and good research into practical programs that enable him to help others more effectively, and he has the skills to evaluate these programs.

Even more important, he has good common sense and good social intelligence. He is at home in the social-emotional world, both his own and that of others. He has developed an extensive repertory of social-emotional skills that enable him to respond spontaneously and effectively to a wide range of human needs. These skills are second nature to him.

A good helper knows that helping is a great deal of *work*. He attends to the other person both physically and psychologically. He knows what his own body is saying and can read the nonverbal messages of his client. He listens intently to the other, knowing that effective counseling is an intense process in which much can be accomplished if two people are willing to collaborate. He responds frequently to the other, for he is working at understanding him. He responds from the frame of reference of his client, for he can see the world through the client's eyes. He respects his client and expresses his respect by being available to him, working with him, not judging him, trusting the constructive forces found in him, and ultimately placing the expectation on him that he live life as effectively as he can. He genuinely cares for the person who has come for help; that is, he is nondefensive, spontaneous, and always willing to say what he thinks and feels, provided that it is in the best interests of his client. A good helper is concrete in his expressions, dealing with actual feelings and actual behavior rather than vague formulations, obscure psychodynamics, or generalities. His speech, while caring and human, is also lean and to the point.

A helper is an integrator. He helps the client explore his world of experience, feeling, and behavior; as the client produces data about himself, the helper helps him integrate that data in a way that helps the client understand himself and his behavior. The counselor, in this process, is not afraid to share himself and his own experiences *if* he sees that this will advance the helping process. He is not afraid to confront the client with care, to place demands on him, if these demands arise from the experience of the client and not from the needs of the helper. He is not afraid to deal openly with his own relationship with the client to the degree that it helps the client understand his own behavior and interpersonal style. But he does all these things with caution and respect, remembering that helping is for the client. He does not let himself and his needs get in the way of helping.

Action is important to the good helper. Since he is an agent in his own life—that is, one who seizes life rather than submits to it—he is capable of helping his client elaborate action programs that lead to constructive behavioral change. He knows that self-understanding is not enough and that the helping process is not complete until the client acts on his understanding. He is a pragmatist: he will draw on all possible helping resources that will enable his client to achieve his goals. Indeed, he realizes that the process of helping is developmental—that the entire process is leading to constructive behavioral change on the part of the client. Because of his wide response repertory, the helper can "come at" a problem from many different vantage points and help generate alternative behaviors. He is not bound to any single course of action. When he uses a variety of techniques in the counseling process, he is the master of the techniques he uses: he owns them; they do not own him. He follows a counseling model, but he is not afraid to diverge from it when such divergence might prove more constructive. Ultimately, he has no need of specific models or techniques, for he is living effectively, and helping is something instinctive with him.

The good counselor is at home with people. He is not afraid to enter the world of another, with all its distress; he is not intimidated by the problematic in the lives of his clients. The intimacy of the counseling process is not substitutive for him, for he is not an incomplete, needy person who feels good when he finds people with problems like his own. He can handle crises: he can mobilize his own energies and those of others in order to act forcefully and decisively. He realizes that it is a privilege to be allowed to enter the life of another person, and he respects this privilege.

He is not a man who has never known human problems, but he does not retreat from the problematic in his own life. He explores his own behavior and knows who he is. He knows what it means to be helped and has a deep respect for the helping process and its power for better or for worse. Even though he is living relatively effectively, he is always a man in process. He does not help others in order to satisfy his own needs, but he knows that "when he makes it possible for another person to choose life he increases his own possibilities of continuing to choose life" (Carkhuff, 1969a, I, xii).

This, then, is the ideal helper. The following chapters deal not only with the ideal but also with what is minimally necessary in order to be a helper who is "for better" rather than "for worse."

Portrait of a trainee

The message underlying this portrait of a helper is, obviously, that helping is a demanding profession. It is just as obvious that preparation for his profession should be just as demanding. The trainee must learn to live effectively physically, intellectually, and socio-emotionally. He certainly must learn to deal with the problematic in his own life, not just once and for all, but continually, for he is a person in process. One of the basic assumptions of helping is that the helper is living more effectively than the client, at least in the areas in which the client is having trouble. Reformed addicts or alcoholics often make excellent helpers (see Yablonsky, 1965), especially in drug and alcoholism programs. But current addicts and alcoholics are poor counselors, especially for drug and alcoholism programs.

Is a prospective helper, then, being trained or treated? This issue is important. The answer to the question is either "it depends" or "both." It depends on how effectively the trainee is living as he enters the training program. If he has unresolved problems that will interfere with his effectiveness as a helper, he should work them through during the course of the training program. Or, since effective training in the skills proposed by the model *is* at the same time effective treatment, the prospective helper is being *both* trained and treated.

Let's look at this issue in another way. What do trainees talk about when they practice the skills they are learning with one another? In his training programs, Ivey (1971) uses volunteer clients who discuss real problems with the trainees. They are usually paid, but some have refused payment because they felt that the help they received was payment enough. I would like to suggest that, in high-level training programs (that is, in programs peopled by highly motivated trainees and run by high-level trainers who are themselves effective helpers), the trainees should deal with real material in their practice interactions. The content of these interactions should be *relevant* to their interpersonal and helping styles. In the beginning, the trainees can talk about less threatening (but nevertheless real) issues until rapport and trust have been established and later move on to more critical issues. The ideal program thus will provide both training and treatment (to the degree that the latter is necessary). It is obvious, then, that trainees will not all proceed at the same pace, for some will have more problems to work out than others; but the assumption that all should proceed at the same pace is unwarranted. These are the main reasons I prefer to use real client problems, rather than role-playing, in practice sessions. The trainee in such a program learns, sometimes painfully, what it means to be a helpee. I personally would prefer to be helped by someone with such experiential knowledge.

Some words of caution. In the average university counseling class, not all of the assumptions above are met: for instance, not all members of the class will have the kind of motivation and characteristics outlined in this section; some will be in the class because they are curious about counseling; some, because they need three hours' credit. Therefore, it is best to move cautiously. The first principle is that the trainee should always be allowed to talk about what he wants to talk about; he should always be in control of his own self-disclosure and self-exploration. But even in the university class situation, the trainees should use personally relevant material in practice sessions, even though they restrict themselves to relatively safe areas such as present interpersonal lifestyle ("what I am like with others," "what my interpersonal strengths are," "what I would like to improve in my interpersonal relationships," and so on). The more real the training process, the more the trainee will benefit from it.

Since helping is ultimately about action (constructive behavioral change on the part of the client), and the helper is an agent of change in a collaborative social-influence process, the trainee, too, should be an *agent;* that is, he should reach out and actively seize the training program rather than merely submit to it. Years of education as it is generally conducted teach students to be passive; students learn to submit to education. This passivity is difficult to root out. The high-level trainee makes demands on himself. He practices trainee skills on his own, outside the classroom or training setting, until these skills become second nature to him. He reads avidly, not to do well on tests, but because he is hungry for the ideas that will broaden his horizon and that he can make work for him in the helping process.

The trainee's first responsibility is to acquire the skills that have been demonstrated effective in the helping process: attending, communicating accurate empathy, respect, concreteness, and genuineness. A second set of essential skills revolves around principles of learning and of the maintenance and change of behavior. Since these principles underlie behavior, including helping behavior, the trainee must learn them or run afoul of them. They include the nature and function of reinforcement, conditioning, shaping behavior, aversive stimuli, and others. While this book is not a text on behavior modification and the reader is expected to become more familiar with these principles from other sources, the basic laws of behavior will be mentioned frequently and the student/trainee must begin to learn their application, especially their application in the context of the model.

One personal skill that the trainee should acquire during the program is the ability to evaluate his present strengths and deficiencies in helping and human relations. The training model provides him with criteria for this kind of evaluation. In my experience with counselor trainees, I discovered early that, in general, they were not good self-evaluators: they could not give a concrete picture of their areas of strength and deficit. This skill, too, must be taught during the training program.

As the trainee masters the basic developmental model and begins to read more widely in the helping literature, he can begin to discover techniques from other helping approaches that will widen his repertory of skills and enable him to continue to develop the basic model.

The trainer

Training in the developmental model of helping presented in this book assumes that the trainers themselves are high-level helpers. If the trainer is not communicating at a level higher than the trainees, the latter will suffer, either by making little or no progress or by actually regressing to the level of the trainer. Like helping, training can be for better or for worse.

Ivey (1971) suggests that a person really possesses a skill only when he is able to teach it to another. The trainee might well aim for this target: to learn helping skills experientially in such a way and to such a degree that he could, eventually, train others. The ultimately successful trainee becomes a helper who can reproduce himself. In a sense, then, it is not enough just to be able to do counseling effectively; there is something that is even more socially productive than helping the emotionally distressed, and that is increasing the number of helpers. The best trainees become the best helpers; the best helpers make the best trainers (Carkhuff, 1972c).

Chapter Two

An Overview of a Developmental Model of Helping

1. This model is called "developmental" because it is composed of progressive interdependent stages.
2. The model can best be understood by considering the behavioral goals of the helping process. Constructive behavioral change is the primary goal.
3. The model has a pre-helping phase that stresses the importance of attending and listening.
4. The stages of the model are:
   a. Stage I: the helper responds to the world of the client in order to help him explore himself.
   b. Stage II: the helper uses the skills of advanced accurate empathy, self-disclosure, confrontation, and immediacy to help the client see a more objective picture of himself and realize his need to change his behavior.
   c. Stage III: the helper helps the client choose and implement the kinds of action programs that lead to constructive behavioral goals. He supports the client as the latter moves through the successes and failures of these action programs.
5. The developmental model attempts to provide the client with the skills he needs to help himself and perhaps to become a helper to others.
6. The helper is a source of reinforcement (and therefore motivation) for the client.
7. The developmental model serves as a guide or cognitive map for the helping process.
8. Some cautions in using this model: beginners are sometimes awkward and overly rigid in applying this model. The model provides a repertory of skills to be used as needed rather than a rigid plan for helping.
9. To master this model, the trainee needs good modeling from a high-level trainer and supervised practice.
10. Training in the developmental model is

  a. an excellent way to check out one's repertory of helping skills and to learn those skills in which one is deficient and
  b. a way of learning a training methodology that can itself be used as a basic treatment process.
11. A helper-training group is an experiential learning community based on mutuality.

Introduction

On the following page is an outline of the developmental model that will be used in our examination of the helping and helper-training processes. (Note that it is *not* the same as the "developmental-counseling" model elaborated by Blocher [1966] and Dinkmeyer [1970].) Study it for a moment. Why is it called "organic" or "developmental"?

First of all, it has progressive stages (a pre-helping phase and then three distinct stages). It *moves* somewhere. Second, as a general rule each stage is successful only to the degree that the preceding stage has been successful. For instance, if the helper's attending skills are poor, he probably will not be very successful in Stage I. Or if the helper fails to understand the world of the client in Stage I, the client will probably not explore his behavior very effectively. In such a case, the integration that takes place in Stage II will be incomplete, for it will be based on incomplete data. If the helper fails to establish effective rapport with the one desiring to be helped, the latter probably will not reveal himself as fully as is necessary; for instance, he will fail to discuss important but sensitive areas of his life for fear that he will be misunderstood or rejected by the helper. Third, the helper skills demanded at Stage II depend on and are more complex than the skills at Stage I. The skills demanded at Stage III are more complex still. One of the reasons that many counselors never get to Stage III is that their skill is not sufficient even to carry out Stage I effectively.

The completely *nondirective* counselor stays at Stage I or perhaps proceeds to the beginning of Stage II. He assumes that if he helps the client to explore his behavior and to begin to understand himself, constructive forces that are somehow lying dormant in the client will be released. The client, once these forces have been released, will go on to change his behavior and live more constructively. On the other hand, the completely *directive* counselor begins at Stage III. He listens to the client's story and then begins, almost immediately, to give the client advice. He assumes that the client does not know what to do about his problems. In a sense, the highly directive counselor sees the client as a

AN OVERVIEW OF AN ORGANIC OR DEVELOPMENTAL MODEL OF HELPING AND INTERPERSONAL RELATING

The model has a pre-helping phase and three stages:

Pre-helping or pre-communication phase: Attending

Helper's goal: Attending. To attend to the other, both physically and psychologically; to give himself entirely to "being with" the other; to work with the other.

Stage I: Responding/self-exploration

Helper's goal: Responding. To respond to the client and what he has to say with respect and empathy; to establish rapport, an effective collaborative working relationship with the client; to facilitate the client's self-exploration.

Client's goal: Self-exploration. To explore his experiences, behavior, and feelings relevant to the problematic in his life; to explore the ways in which he is living ineffectively.

Stage II: Integrative understanding/dynamic self-understanding

Helper's goal: Integrative understanding. The helper begins to piece together the data produced by the client in the self-exploration phase. He sees and helps the other identify behavioral themes or patterns. He helps the other see the "larger picture." He teaches the client the skill of going about this integrative process himself.

Client's goal: Dynamic self-understanding. Developing self-understanding that sees the need for change, for action; learning from the helper the skill of putting together the larger picture for himself; identifying resources, especially unused resources.

Stage III: Facilitating action/acting

Helper's goal: Facilitating action. Collaborating with the client in working out specific action programs; helping the client to act on his new understanding of himself; exploring with the client a wide variety of means for engaging in constructive behavioral change; giving support and direction to action programs.

Client's goal: Acting. Living more effectively; learning the skills needed to live more effectively and handle the social-emotional dimensions of life; changing self-destructive and other-destructive patterns of living; developing new resources.

problem rather than a person. Once he understands the problem sitting in front of him, he engages in a great deal of problem-solving behavior. The model we are using suggests that both of these extremes are inadequate approaches to helping. The completely nondirective counselor fails to use certain kinds of interactions (for example, helper self-disclosure, confrontation, immediacy, and the suggesting of alternative frames of reference) that can help the client understand himself more fully. Furthermore, the completely nondirective counselor is in no position to help the client through the action stages. He assumes that understanding is enough. The completely directive counselor fails to realize that, generally speaking, constructive behavioral change is based on the client's ability to understand himself, to see the "bigger picture," to place himself and his behavior in a wider context. He fails to see that it is not enough that he (the helper) understand the person in need of help. Often the overly directive person will ask the client many questions to get the kind of information that he (the helper) thinks he needs in order to solve the other's problems. Even when this process works, it is self-defeating, for the client has not learned *how* to take counsel with himself or *how* to go about handling his own problems.

Beginning with the end: The goal-directed nature of counseling

Recent eclectic approaches to helping emphasize the centrality of client goals and action programs (see, for example, Brammer, 1973; Carkhuff, 1973; Hackney & Nye, 1973; Krumboltz, 1966; Krumboltz & Thoresen, 1969; Strong, 1968; Thorne, 1973a). Thorne approaches client action from the viewpoint of learning. For him, helping means modifying the learning process and includes learning, relearning, and unlearning. Key questions are: What is to be learned? How is this learning to take place?

The person who comes for help is usually unhappy because of his behavior—either what he does or what he fails to do:

John frequently loses his temper over inconsequential matters and yells at his wife and children.

Sally cannot stop drinking even though it is jeopardizing her job.

Bill is afraid of teachers and cannot bring himself to ask them for help.

Joan gets "sick" when an available male asks her for a date.

Tom is depressed and still grieving, although his wife died two years ago.

Clara is prejudiced against Jews and is beginning to feel guilty about it.

Tony is very bright but merely squeaks by in college, not even studying the subjects he says interest him.

> Adele is anxious almost all the time but doesn't know why.
> Mike vents his rage against society by starting fires.

The behavior may be public or private, internal or external, overt or covert; but in all cases it distresses the client and/or those who come in contact with him.

Helping, according to the developmental model, is more than helping a client explore his behavior (Stage I). It is even more than helping him understand the world more objectively and see the need for action (Stage II). It is helping

> John to learn how to live decently with his family,
> Sally to stop drinking and learn more creative ways of dealing with distress,
> Bill to talk with teachers,
> Joan to get rid of her fear of closeness with a male,
> Tom to surrender his grief and find renewed meaning in life,
> Clara to get rid of her prejudice,
> Tony to decide to remain in college or leave, and, if he stays, to learn how to become involved in learning,
> Adele to get rid of her anxiety, and
> Mike to find more constructive ways of venting his anger and of confronting a hostile environment.

Some counselors and counseling systems do not place this kind of emphasis on client action. They stress Stage I or II or a combination of the two. Other counselors and counseling systems tend to minimize the importance of Stages I and II and proceed almost immediately to behavior-modification and problem-solving programs (Stage III). In the developmental model, constructive behavioral change on the part of the client is central and therefore the whole model is behavioral. Stages I and II exist for two basic reasons: *value,* as an expression of respect for the person of the client, as a way of prizing him; and *action,* to prepare the client to engage in constructive behavioral change. Stages I and II are essential, but they are not to be overemphasized or to become ends in themselves. These stages help the client establish rapport with the helper, reduce his anxiety, increase his self-confidence, explore his values, increase his motivation, and pull together the data and resources he needs to launch an intelligent goal-directed action program. Stages I and II guard against setting goals prematurely.

This choosing to emphasize action is, perhaps, a decision based on certain values; others may conceive of counseling differently, based on different sets of values. Too often, in my estimation, counseling "loses the name of action." The counselor listens to the client, tries to understand him, is warm and accepting—but nothing ever happens. Sally goes on drinking, Clara remains prejudiced, and Mike ends up in jail. Some counselors excuse their own ineptness by throwing up their hands and saying, "The client was not motivated. He really didn't want to change." Others say, "Well, the client still has the same presenting symptoms [anxiety, rage], but he can live with them more comfortably." Still others say, "The client terminated counseling too soon." If listening and understanding are not enough to help the client change, the helper must do more. The helper, then, must exercise a great deal of agency in the helping process in order to help the client become an agent in his own life.

Person-centered rather than problem-centered counseling

This assessment might sound overly pragmatic. It needs to be made, however, because the average counselor does not err by being too pragmatic or too action-oriented. Still, the counseling process should center on the person rather than on the person's problems. As the counselor moves with the other through the helping process, his problems might well change. Drinking might prove to be just a symptom, a man's way of drowning his sense of inadequacy. Poor communication in marriage might mask adolescent lifestyles. A girl might fail in college in order to punish overly rigid parents. The "presenting" problem is often not a problem at all. The client pushes a safe problem out front to see how the counselor handles it. Only after trust has been established is he willing to discuss what really bothers him. The good counselor, although he is constantly sensitive to self-defeating patterns of behavior in his clients and to the ultimate necessity of behavioral change, still prizes his clients for themselves and not because they are problems to be solved.

Relevant to person-centered counseling is another question: is it possible to help a person you don't like? I prefer to see this issue as one of respecting rather than liking. A good helper works at respecting his client, and he can help someone if he respects him. In a similar way, a good helper does not work at being liked or loved by the client. He is satisfied if he gains the client's respect.

An overview of the skills needed in the model

On the following pages, the stages of the model pictured at the beginning of this chapter are spelled out in greater detail. The skills both helper and client need to progress through the various stages successfully are described briefly. These skills will be explained fully in subsequent chapters. Without them, the counselor simply is not a "skilled helper."

The pre-helping phase

This phase refers only to the counselor and not to the person coming for help.

Helper's skills: Attending

The skills needed by the helper are summed up in the word *attending*.

> The helper, by his very *posture,* must let the client know that he is "with" him, that during the time they are together he is completely "available" to him. This is *physical* attending.

> The helper must *listen* attentively to his client. He must listen to both the verbal and the nonverbal messages of the person he is trying to help.

>> *Verbal:* he has to listen attentively to the words of the client, however confused they might be.

>> *Nonverbal:* he has to listen to the messages that are carried in the client's tone of voice, silences, pauses, gestures, facial expressions, and posture.

In a word, the helper has to keep asking himself: What is this person trying to *communicate*? What is he saying about his feelings? What is he saying about his behavior?

Although attending skills are easy to learn, attending carefully to another is work that demands a great deal of effort on the part of the helper.

Attending involves *pre-helping* skills. Mere attending does not in itself help the client, but, unless the counselor attends both physically and psychologically to the person in need, he will not be able to help him. "Pre-helping" does not mean "unimportant."

Stage I: Responding to the client/client self-exploration

The person in trouble presents himself for help. The helper first of all *attends* to what the client is saying: then he *responds* in a way that helps the client explore his behavior (his feelings, his attitudes, what he does, what he fails to do, what is constructive in his life, what is destructive, and so on). What skills does the helper need in order to facilitate his client's self-exploration?

Helper's skills

Accurate empathy (primary level): the helper must respond to the client in a way that shows that he has listened and that he *understands* how the client feels and what he is saying about himself. In some sense, he must see the client's world from the client's frame of reference rather than from his own. It is not enough to understand; he must *communicate* his understanding.

Respect: the way in which he deals with the client must show the client that he respects him, that he is basically "for" him, that he wants to be available to him and work with him.

Genuineness: his offer of help cannot be phony. He must be spontaneous, open. He can't hide behind the role of counselor. He must be a human being to the human being before him.

Concreteness: even when the client rambles or tries to evade real issues by speaking in generalities, the helper must ground the helping process in concrete feelings and concrete behavior. His language cannot be vague counseling language.

Client's skills

Self-exploration: if the counselor is effective, he will help the client explore the feelings and behaviors associated with the problematic areas of his life. This search will be as concrete as possible and will gradually deepen as the person in need comes to trust the helper and his skills.

Some comments on Stage I and its skills

Each of these stages and the skills needed at each stage will be spelled out in much greater detail in separate chapters. The skills of Stage I are crucial. If the helper does not have them, he simply cannot help, for the skills of Stages II and III build on them. The ways in which empathy, respect, and genuineness are expressed may change somewhat as the helper moves deeper into the helping process, but the need for these skills never disappears.

Stage I can also be described as a social-influence process. If the helper is going to influence the life of the client, he has to establish a basis for this influence. During Stage I, if the helper is really sincere and skillful, the client comes to see him as an *expert* in some sense of that term, for he sees the counselor responding helpfully; he learns to *trust* him, for the counselor is acting in a way that engenders trust; and, generally speaking, he is *attracted* to the helper, for he sees him as an ally, a person he can respect, one who can help him find his way out of the problems besetting him. In a word, the skillful counselor establishes good *rapport* with the client in Stage I. He does so by presenting himself for what he is (or should be): an effectively living person who sincerely wants to help. Such a helper engages in a social-influence process in that he becomes a *collaborator* with the client in the latter's attempts to rid himself of his misery and live more effectively.

Self-exploration, while absolutely necessary, is not an end in itself. A person cannot act intelligently without understanding himself, his goals, his needs, and his failures. But he cannot understand himself unless he is willing to explore his feelings and his behavior. Many counselors and clients bog down at this stage. They explore endlessly without ever reaching the kind of understanding that leads to action.

Stage II: Integrative understanding/ dynamic self-understanding

As the person seeking help explores the various problem areas of his life, he produces a great deal of data that is useful, generally speaking, only to the degree that it can be pieced together to reveal behavioral themes in his life. The helper, as he begins to see these themes and view isolated data in a larger context, helps the client see this bigger picture as well. What skills does the helper need to make this integration and to help the client make the same kind of integration for himself?

Helper's skills

All the skills of Stage I.

Accurate empathy (advanced level): the helper must communicate to the client an understanding, not only of what the client actually says but also of what he implies, what he hints at, and what he says nonverbally. The helper begins to make connections between seemingly isolated statements made by the client. In this whole process, however, the helper must *invent* nothing. He is helpful only to the degree that he is accurate.

Self-disclosure: the helper is willing to share his own experience with the client *if* sharing it will actually help the client understand himself better. He is extremely careful, however, not to lay another burden on the client.

Immediacy: the helper is willing to explore his own relationship to the client ("you-me" talk), to explore the here-and-now of client-counselor interactions—to the degree that it helps the client get a better understanding of himself, of his interpersonal style, and of how he is cooperating in the helping process.

Confrontation: the helper challenges the discrepancies, distortions, games, and smokescreens in the client's life and in his interactions within the helping relationship itself, to the degree that it helps the client develop the kind of self-understanding that leads to constructive behavioral change.

Alternative frames of reference: the effective helper can offer the client alternative frames of reference for viewing his behavior, to the degree that these alternatives are more accurate and more constructive than those of the client. For instance, the client might see his verbal interchanges as witty (one frame of reference), while the helper might suggest that his interchanges seem biting or sarcastic to others (an alternative frame of reference).

Client's skills

Nondefensive listening: the helper must help the client develop the skill of listening, both to what the helper himself is saying (as he shares himself or engages in immediacy or confrontation) and to the environment outside the helping sessions themselves. Since it is often painful to listen to one's environment objectively, the client needs support from the helper. Obviously the helper cannot help the client develop this skill unless he (the helper) works at developing a relationship of trust based on mutual respect.

Dynamic self-understanding: it is not enough that the client understand himself in some abstract way. Understanding must serve the cause of behavioral change. Somehow, a spirit of "Now I see what I am doing and how self-destructive it is; I've got to do something about it" should characterize Stage II.

Some comments on Stage II and its skills

The skills of Stage II will be explored and illustrated much more fully in subsequent chapters. The skills of Stage II can be deadly in the hands of a low-level counselor. Self-disclosure can become exhibitionism; confrontation can become a club; immediacy and the offering of alternative frames of reference, a power struggle. Some counselors even look upon themselves as experts in the more dramatic Stage-II skills without having mastered the skills of Stage I. Stage-II behaviors have to take place in the spirit of Stage I.

Since one of the helper's goals is to help the client listen non-defensively, he must introduce Stage-II behaviors tentatively. The counselor must constantly keep in mind that helping is for the helpee even though it is assumed that the helper is the more effectively living person in the relationship.

Stage II can also be viewed as a social-influence process. In Stage I the counselor establishes a power base (although in the case of helping, his power should come from his genuineness, his respect for the client, and his empathy, and not just from the client's perception of him as an expert). In Stage II the helper uses this power to influence the client's perception of himself—that is, to help him achieve a more realistic perception of himself, his environment, and the interaction between the two. If the counselor is not a skillful person and if he fails to base Stage-II behaviors on an accurate understanding of the client and his needs, Stage II degenerates into manipulation and control. Furthermore, while it is still true that the interaction taking place is a social-influence process, it is a destructive one. Social-influence processes, too, are for better or for worse. It cannot be overemphasized that low-level counselors often specialize in Stage-II behaviors. If they take these behaviors out of the context of the organic helping process, they do so at the expense of those who come looking for help. Counselors who tend to specialize exclusively in either Stage-I or Stage-II behaviors are usually inexpert even in their specialty. Helping is an organic, developmental process and, *as a general rule,* no given stage can be eliminated without jeopardizing the entire helping process.

Ideally, as Stage II progresses, the client sees more and more clearly the necessity for action on his part. He might well be fearful of change and he might even doubt that he has the resources necessary for change, and these fears and doubts must be dealt with if he is to act. Sometimes he must act *first* in order to see that his fears and doubts are groundless. The dynamic self-understanding sought in Stage II should not be confused with an eternal quest for insight, divorced from action. Some people think that if only they can understand themselves fully, everything will be all right. This is magical thinking. Stage II, then, should be carried out in the spirit of both Stage I and Stage III; that is, it should be based on accurate empathy, respect, and genuineness and should be oriented toward action programs.

Stage III: Facilitating action/action

The client must ultimately *act,* in some sense of the term, if he is to live more effectively.

Helper's skills

All the skills of Stage I.   As we shall see later, accurate empathy (primary level) is useful and necessary throughout the helping process. Respect, at Stage III, includes expectations that the client will not live less effectively than he is capable.

All the skills of Stage II.   As the relationship between helper and client deepens, the helper can engage more strongly and more pointedly in interactions involving self-disclosure, immediacy, confrontation, and the suggesting of alternative frames of reference. The proviso, however, is the same: these interactions must be *for* the client; that is to say, at Stage III they must be oriented toward helping him act, change, live more effectively. The helper is ready to extend himself in any reasonable and human way to help the client act.

The elaboration of action programs.   The helper collaborates with the client in the elaboration of action programs. These may include problem-solving techniques, decision-making processes, behavior-modification programs, "homework," or training in interpersonal and other kinds of skills.

Support.   As the client involves himself in action programs, fears and doubts arise, he fails at times, and, in various ways, he succeeds. Also, new problems arise. The helper must reinforce the client's successes and help him through the problems that arise from this action phase.

Client's skills

Cooperation. If the helping process is being carried out skillfully, the client will be learning cooperation throughout the process. Since the elaboration of action programs is usually a collaborative effort, the client must involve himself in planning strategy.

Risk. The client should learn how to risk himself. He must learn that, paradoxically, it is "safe" to risk himself. This means that he must first take small risks and be reinforced for success and helped to weather failure. Again, the helping process itself, from Stage I on, should be teaching the client how to take reasonable risks.

Acting. Ultimately, there is no substitute for acting. Acting has many forms. It may mean stopping some self-destructive activity (such as drugs). It may mean starting on some program of growth (such as a physical-fitness program). It may mean developing new attitudes (such as a sense of self-worth) through a variety of processes (such as an ongoing group experience). But, in general, no one should be counseled to undertake an action program unless he has the *skills* to carry out the program effectively. If he does not have them, his first action program should be training in the required skills. For instance, a client should not be counseled to "go talk things out with his wife" if he doesn't have the communication skills necessary for such a task. In this case, the priority action program for him is skills training.

Some comments on Stage III and its skills

Many counselors never get to Stage III. They assume that this stage is the responsibility of the client. Other counselors try to start with Stage III and then wonder why their clients are not cooperative. Failures are then blamed on the client. In the ideal case, once the client understands the need for action he goes out and acts on his own. But sometimes the opposite is true. For instance, in the case of a regressed psychotic person, the helper might first have to act in his behalf—to get the regressed person, through some kind of behavior-modification program, to a state in which he is able to cooperate, however minimally, in a helping program. In most cases, however, the helper and his client must *collaborate,* both in the elaboration of action programs and in working through the problems that arise as these action programs are pursued. If action programs require prior skills training, the helper can either train the client himself (if the required skills fall in the area of his competence) or have the client go to someone else who can train him. In the latter case, the helper might well maintain contact with the client and give him the support he needs to pursue the skills program.

The logic of the developmental model: Training as treatment

The ideal logic of the helping process works something like this:

The client as helpee. The helper responds to the client from the client's frame of reference. He helps the client explore his problems, his confusions, and his behavior as concretely as possible. He respects and understands the client, is genuine with him, and tries to help him understand himself and deal realistically with the issues that bother him.

The client as helper to himself. However, the goal is not just to go through this process with the client but to help the client learn how to go through this process with himself (or with the help of his friends). The counselor is trying to help the client become autonomous or independent. The helping process is really successful when the client learns how to explore his own problems concretely, when he can understand and respect himself.

The client as helper to others. The ultimate goal, in any case in which this is possible, is to train the client to help others. In other words, the helping process is most successful when through it the client learns the skills he needs to live effectively and learns them so well that he can now be a helper to others. Once a person learns to initiate with and respond to others, on at least a minimally facilitative level, he is a potential helper.

An exciting way of implementing the logic of the developmental model is to train the client directly in the skills of each stage of the model. Thus training, as Carkhuff (1969b) suggests, becomes a preferred way of treating or helping the client. Since the basic skills of helping are also the basic skills needed for effective living, training is a more direct way of helping. You, as a student/trainee, are to be trained in all the skills of the helping model. Once you master these skills, you, too, can train clients who come to you for help in these skills. Ideally, just as in your own training, this training should be done in a group. You then train clients how to be good helpees (such as how to talk about their problems concretely), but you also train them to be helpers to themselves and to one another. The problems they bring up as they practice helping are, of course, real problems in their lives. At this stage, group training in helping skills as a preferred mode of helping your clients may sound too new or too much for you to handle. However, as you move through your own training process, keep the notion of training-as-treatment alive in your mind. In the course of your own training, this idea may become more and more feasible to you.

The counselor as agent of reinforcement and client motivation

Reinforcement is part of the social-influence process. It is also, therefore, an important part of the counseling process. In general, any human activity that is rewarded tends to be repeated. If a person wants to help another extinguish a certain kind of behavior, one thing he does is to see to it that the unwanted behavior is not rewarded. For instance, if a mother rewards a little boy with her attention every time he whines, it is quite likely that he will continue to use whining as a way of getting what he wants. Therefore, one way to extinguish whining behavior in the child is to not reward it with attention. It is, however, assumed that the mother gives the boy adequate attention when he doesn't whine. Similarly, one way to encourage any particular behavior is to reward it. For instance, if a child tidies up his room and his parents notice it and express their pleasure (social reinforcement), it is more likely that he will tidy up the room again.

It is not my intention here to give any kind of detailed explanation of the principles of operant conditioning. It is important, however, to realize that what the skillful counselor does enables him "to establish himself as a potent reinforcer of the helpee's behavior so that he may direct the helpee's constructive actions" (Carkhuff, 1969a, p. 43). The counselor who is unaware of the basic principles of operant conditioning is at a distinct disadvantage, for he may be reinforcing behaviors that both he and the client would like to see extinguished, and he might be failing to reinforce constructive behaviors undertaken by the person seeking help. The counselor, as a "significant other," acts as a potent source of reinforcement throughout all the stages of the counseling process. Let's look at Stage I from the point of view of client motivation. If the client is "hurting" badly, he will usually be relatively highly motivated to seek help. In fact, social-influence theory states that the confused person, the one who feels inadequate, the one who feels helpless and perhaps hopeless, is precisely the person who is most open to influence from others. In other words, he sees any kind of help as potentially rewarding. Anything that will help relieve his pain is a potent source of reinforcement. Furthermore, if his counselor is skilled, in Stage I the client will come face to face with someone who shows in a variety of ways that he is "for" him. Being respected, not being judged, being listened to and understood by someone who obviously cares in a role-free, genuine way—all of this is highly rewarding. Therefore, if the client sees in the counseling process both the possibility of getting rid of his pain and the rewards of working with a person who cares and understands, it is quite likely (though not inevitable) that his motivation for cooperating actively in the counseling process will be quite strong. If the client comes to the counselor poorly motivated (he has been sent, he is afraid, he fears change, or he has had bad experiences with other counselors), then what takes place in Stage I (if the helper is skilled) should heighten his motivation. For instance, the skilled helper will deal with the client's hesitation with understanding: "You've been through this before, and you wonder if there is any use in trying it again." Or: "It isn't easy to come to a stranger and start talking about things that are pretty personal and painful." Or: "It's not easy to dig into your feelings and behavior and set them in front of yourself and in front of someone you hardly know." Recognition that self-exploration is often a difficult, discouraging, and painful process helps ease the client's pain and is, in some sense, a social "reward" for engaging in it.

In Stage II, advanced accurate empathy, counselor self-disclosure, and immediacy can also be reinforcing if they are appropriate and skillfully executed. For instance, if the helper tactfully shares some of his own experience in a way that does not add a further burden to the client, the client might well find this rewarding. He might feel less like a "helpee," for even a minimal amount of mutuality in the helping relationship gives him a chance to experience the counselor in a role-free way, as another human being. Even confrontation, when skillfully executed, can be reinforcing. Heavy-handed confrontation is almost always punishing, but when confrontation arises from deep understanding and strong "standing with" (caring), the client experiences primarily the helper's care and respect, and the painful dimension of confrontation becomes secondary.

In Stage III the client is doing "homework," putting into practice some of what he learned in Stages I and II. As he attempts to put a greater degree of constructive directionality into his life, the counselor remains a strong source of reinforcement. First of all, the client finds it rewarding to have the collaboration of an interested party in translating his learnings into action. Second, it is rewarding to have someone understand the pain and frustration of trying new ways of behaving. Third, it is rewarding to have someone recognize success and achievement when it does take place. For example, a client in Stage II comes to the realization that drugs, even "soft" drugs, are robbing him of energy, vitality, and a sense of direction in life. He wants to quit and needs help. The counselor suggests ways in which he can find substitute satisfactions in higher-level activities (study, work, play, helping others) and helps him develop the interests and skills he needs to do this. Second, the helper understands the pain of withdrawal and the frustrations the client experiences in his search for new sources of satisfaction, and he communicates this understanding to the client. Third, when the client does show signs of both kicking the drug habit and developing more mature satisfactions, the helper recognizes both small and large successes. Ultimately, the principal source of reinforcement for the client must be not the understanding, work, and recognition of the counselor but his own behavior. The lifestyle of the client—his work, his play, his interpersonal relationships, the energy he has to meet life, his intellectual pursuits, his living for others—must itself be the principal source of reward. Aristotle long ago noted that human activities (such as friendship) pursued in a deeply human way are deeply satisfying in themselves. To speak in the terminology of our day, they carry with them their own natural reinforcement. In the life of the client, the social reinforcement provided by the helper must eventually give way to this kind of natural reinforcement.

This idea leads me to a few words of caution with respect to the reinforcement process. First of all, as I have just indicated, the reinforcement of the counselor is ultimately no substitute for the satisfaction of a life lived effectively. Second, excessively high and excessively low levels of reinforcement are usually counterproductive. For instance, if the counselor's only reply to the client's report of success in speaking openly and caringly with an alienated son is an "uh-huh," such "reinforcement" is so low that it appears more like rejection. On the other hand, if the counselor is always indulging himself in such comments as "Gee! That's really great! You've succeeded again against all odds!"— such obviously phony (or at least inappropriate) enthusiasm and support will not be reinforcing at all. Third, the counselor should understand clearly just what he is reinforcing (or failing to reinforce). The unskilled counselor may reinforce behavior that, although it should be understood empathically, should nevertheless be extinguished. For instance, if the helper is warm and accepting whenever the client engages in self-pity ("poor-me talk"), it is quite likely that the client will continue to wallow in self-pity. One way the counselor can understand exactly what he is doing in the counseling process is to ask himself just what he is reinforcing (or failing to reinforce) and how he is doing it. Fourth, the helper should realize that, since he is a potent source of reinforcement for the client, he wields great power with him. His ability to reinforce the client is an important factor in establishing the "power base" of the social-influence process. The helper should be careful to use this power to help the client explore and develop his own (non-self-destructive and non-other-destructive) values and not as a way of forcing his own value system on him. Finally—and perhaps most important—the counselor should realize that reinforcement is a complex process that should be dealt with as carefully as possible. The client is open to a great complexity of stimuli, both within and outside the counseling process. It is impossible always to know which of these stimuli are reinforcing and which are aversive.

Using the developmental model as a guide: An example

Too often, counseling is presented to the trainee as a completely intuitive process. While it is true that the most effective helpers operate in some sense beyond all particular systems and can turn all systems to their advantage in helping the client, the beginning counselor still needs some kind of guide to help him make the counseling process more intelligible and therefore more effective. If the helper is lost in the counseling process, the client will also be lost. The developmental model provides the map the helper needs. Through it he can know what stage he is in with respect to each problem brought up by the person seeking help. Familiarity with the skills of the model helps the counselor know just how he is responding to the client at a given moment (understanding, sharing his own experience, suggesting an alternative frame of reference, helping the client elaborate some action program). Knowledge of the "map" is obviously no substitute for the skills the helper needs to make the model effective, but in learning the skills there is no substitute for knowing precisely what he is doing.

Let's use an extended example to illustrate just how the model can be used to help the counselor know just where he is in his relationship to the client and to the problems the client presents. For the sake of clarity, the example will be oversimplified; it will be too pat. But one of the principles of systematic training is to move from the simple to the more complex, from the clear to the more obscure.

Bob is a third-year college student who has just returned to school after a visit with his parents at home. He comes to one of the college counselors, quite upset. He comes on his own initiative because he is in pain. He has seen a counselor for a session or two on one or two occasions before this, but he does not feel that he was helped by these visits. He comes in and sits down with the counselor. Stage I has begun. The first problem he brings up is that he is doing poorly in studies. In no way is he achieving according to his talents. Perhaps this is a safe problem that he pushes out in front to see how the counselor will handle it, or, more importantly, to see how the counselor will relate to him. In the self-exploration stage, because he is attended to, respected, not judged, listened to, and understood, Bob produces a great deal of data concerning his problem of failure in school: poor study habits, refusal to do work, boredom, restlessness, periods of depression, poor relationships with a variety of teachers, and so on. Bob begins to trust the counselor and the counselor begins to see that Bob's problem is not just "doing poorly in school." Failing in school *is* a problem, since Bob is wasting his own time and the time of others in school, but it is not a focal problem. Failing is a symptom of a deeper malaise. The counselor who is not willing to let Bob explore himself might precipitously assume that failure in school is the focal problem and move quickly into Stages II and III in an attempt to help Bob develop a better attitude toward school and more productive approaches toward studying. However, the effective counselor, because he gives Bob wide latitude to explore his behavior, begins to see that school is not the real problem: "You seem to be saying that it's not just school that has you tied up inside." The counselor, as he begins pulling the data of the self-exploration process together (a Stage-II function), also begins to see a bigger picture. Because he has been understood and respected, Bob is now ready to deal with issues that are much more crucial for him. He tells the counselor that he has just returned from a very painful visit at home, and he begins to relate a history of parental indifference and neglect and, paradoxically, a history of parental demands that he achieve socially and scholastically. The counselor, in moving into Stage II (the "piecing together" stage), has discovered that studies are not the most important issue. Now that Bob has brought up concerns that are more "real" and pressing, the helper returns to Stage I to deal with these new concerns. He realizes that Bob eventually might need help in finding ways to improve his scholastic life (Stage III), but he first deals with the issues that seem to underlie Bob's will to fail.

Bob has always resented his parents' indifference but has never been able to deal with it directly. In his relationship with his parents over the years, he has come to learn that he is "no good." The counselor helps Bob explore his relationship with his parents and his feelings about himself. Stage I (with the new problem area) is a time, again, of self-exploration, of getting at the data in terms of behavior, attitudes, and feelings. The counselor's accurate responses help Bob make his observations more and more concrete. When Bob begins to explore his feelings and behavior freely, the helper moves once more into Stage II; that is, he begins to piece the data together into a larger perspective and, if possible, begins to relate what is happening in school to what is happening at home. For instance, he suggests to Bob that failing in school has a double payoff. It confirms in Bob's eyes that he is "no good" and it also punishes his achievement-oriented parents. The high-level counselor knows where he is and what he is doing. He realizes that he is bringing together behavioral themes in a way that will help Bob get a deeper understanding of his attitudes about himself and his behavior in school. If the Stage-II process is successful, Bob will be able to say, "Now I'm beginning to see what is really bothering me and what underlies this mess in school." Ideally, he also begins to realize his need to act, both in his relationship with his parents and in his approach to school.

In Stage II the counselor calls on other behaviors (besides advanced-level accurate empathy)—self-sharing, immediacy, confrontation, the suggesting of alternative frames of reference—*tentatively* and *to the degree* that they help Bob achieve the kind of dynamic self-understanding that is the goal of Stage II. For instance, the helper might briefly share with Bob some of his experiences with his own parents—*if* such self-sharing is to the point, *if* it keeps the focus on Bob's problem and helps him understand himself better, and *if* it does not make Bob feel burdened with someone else's problems. Or the counselor might sense that Bob's distrust of his parents has generalized to other adults and that he is having difficulty trusting the counselor, even though the counselor has acted in a way that merits trust: "You have distrusted adults so long that you're still wondering whether you can trust me. You're still not sure, and it makes you hesitant." The high-level counselor is not afraid of such "you-me" talk and engages in it to the degree that it helps the client get a deeper understanding of himself. In our example, the counselor sees that the difficulties that Bob has with adults in his day-to-day life are also asserting themselves in the interaction between him and his counselor. The helper does not engage in "you-me" talk in order to fulfill his own needs or for the sake of immediacy itself; instead he uses it to help Bob understand his feelings and behavior more fully. The counselor might also offer Bob alternative frames of reference for viewing himself and his behavior. While Bob experiences himself as worthless, the helper suggests that he has *learned* to consider himself worthless through the interactions he has had over the years with the significant adults in his life. In many respects, his contacts with his parents have been "for the worse." However, learned feelings of worthlessness are different from being worthless. Alternative frames of reference are valid and useful to the degree that they are based on an understanding of Bob. Throughout this model, nothing takes the place of accurate empathic understanding. Finally, in Stage II the counselor thinks that Bob might benefit from some kind of challenge or confrontation, but he realizes that confrontation, too, is not an end in itself and must be based solidly on an accurate empathic understanding of Bob. For instance, if Bob is using his past as an excuse for not doing anything now,—if, in effect, he is saying "My parents destroyed me in the past, so I'll destroy myself in the present," or "They made me the way I am and now I can't do anything about it"—the counselor challenges this kind of thinking. He might say, "Maybe dwelling excessively on what your parents have done to you robs you of the energy you need to take responsibility for yourself." In summary, whatever kind of interaction the helper uses with Bob—self-sharing, immediacy, the suggesting of an alternative frame of reference, confrontation, or any combination of these—he knows precisely what he is doing and what he is trying to achieve. The model lays out both counseling goals and the skills needed to achieve these goals.

If our counselor is a high-level helper, he does not remain forever digging around for data in Stage I. Even during Stage I he begins to ask himself how all the data fit together. In Stage II he pulls together the themes that have relevance for Bob—the theme of parental rejection (and its variations), the theme of worthlessness (and its concrete manifestations), and the theme of failure (as confirmation of worthlessness, as revenge). But once Bob begins to see what is happening in his life, the counselor begins to think about the kinds of action programs that will help Bob live more effectively. This is the work of Stage III. In the present example, what are the programs of Stage III? First of all, if one of Bob's problems is that he sees himself as basically "no good," the relationship with the counselor who respects and prizes him is in itself an action program. It is a program of emotional re-education. Bob also learns that it's possible to trust some adults. Another action program would include, if possible, sessions with his parents so that communication at home could become more decent. If his parents are unwilling to come, Bob must learn how to defuse and desensitize the home situation in some kind of unilateral way. In the counseling sessions, he has been exposed to interpersonal skills that will enable him to interact more decently with his parents even if they do not respond well. The counselor might take time to teach these skills directly to Bob instead of just modeling them through the counseling process. The logic of the counseling process, as we have already noted, is that Bob be respected and understood so that he can respect and understand himself and, ultimately, understand others more effectively. If Bob returns home on his next visit with at least a minimally effective dose of the basic helping skills he has been experiencing in the counseling process, it is much more likely that he will handle his interactions with his parents more creatively. These skills will also help him establish better relationships with his peers and his teachers. It is useless to encourage Bob to develop better relationships with his peers as a way of helping him establish a more realistic sense of self-worth if he does not have the basic skills to do so. If he is shy and retiring, assertiveness training can be coupled with interpersonal-skills training (an example of a kind of abbreviated training-as-treatment). The counselor does everything he can to maximize Bob's possibility of success as he ventures out to make new friends. The counselor also helps Bob elaborate action programs to make his education a more profitable and engaging undertaking—including establishing realistic educational goals, study habits, schedules, pursuit of specialized educational interests, and so on. As Bob succeeds at the first stages of these programs, he receives two kinds of support or reinforcement. The counselor provides social reinforcement whenever he sees Bob doing a good thing. But, more importantly, success itself (in studies, in developing new educational interests, in talking to his parents, in establishing friendships) is his principal natural reward.

Let's add one further complication. Bob moves with the counselor through Stages I and II in the ways we have indicated. However, as he begins to get involved with Stage III, he mentions hesitantly that sex is also problematic for him and that he is struggling with homosexual tendencies. At this point, the unskilled counselor might be tempted to say "See, that's part of the whole picture. You're also using sex to prove your own worthlessness and get back at your parents." But since this is a new (and supposedly quite delicate) problem, the counselor must first understand Bob-with-this-particular-problem. He deals with this problem using the methodology of Stage I, although he continues to help Bob launch himself on action programs related to problem areas that have already been investigated. The helper should never leap to conclusions concerning the "meaning" of any new problem the client brings up for discussion. In Bob's case, sexuality may be part of the bigger picture that he and the counselor have been dealing with, but it may also be that sexuality is the focal issue for Bob at this time in his life, is anxiety-provoking, and is absorbing most of his energy in a self-destructive way. In a word, the counselor should always deal with the person and not just with his problems.

This example of Bob is both sketchy and somewhat sanguine; that is, it may make the counseling process, which exacts a great deal of work, seem too easy. The sole purpose of this example, however, is to give the beginner some idea of how he can use the developmental counseling model to stay on top of what is happening in the counseling sessions and to give direction to the entire process.

Up to this point, much has been said about the *counselor's* use of the model to help him help the client. How much should the *client* know about the counseling model being used? As much as possible, I believe. Goldstein, Heller, and Sechrest (1966) suggest that "giving patients prior information about the nature of psychotherapy, the theories underlying it, and the techniques to be used will facilitate progress in psychotherapy" (p. 245). Counselors are often reluctant to let the client know what the process is all about. Some counselors seem to "fly by the seat of their pants," and they cannot tell the client what it's all about simply because they don't know what it's all about. Others seem to think that knowledge of psychotherapeutic processes is secret or sacred or dangerous and should not be communicated to the client. The client, then, is forced into buying a pig-in-a-poke, too often a not very succulent pig. If the developmental helping model is being used to introduce trainees to human-relations skills, the entire model should be explained fully to them before they begin the training process. In counseling situations, the client should be told as much about the model as he can assimilate. Obviously, a highly distressed client should not be told to contain his anxiety until the counselor teaches him a short course in the developmental model. But, generally speaking, the client should be given some kind of cognitive initiation into the model, either all at once or gradually, so that he can participate in it more actively. The theory is that if he knows where he is going he will get there faster. Like the counselor, he uses the model as a cognitive map to give direction to the process. In such a case, even though the counseling process remains a social-influence process, it is a collaborative one, and the client is not being influenced without his consent or cooperation. If the client is given this map at the beginning of counseling, he knows where he is going in terms of *process,* even though he does not yet have a clear idea of what the *content* of this process will be.

Some cautions

An open versus a closed model.   While the developmental model presented here is, in my opinion, the best introduction available to counseling or human-relations training—both because it gives the trainee a sense of direction in helping and relating and because it lets him know clearly the skills he must develop to be effective—still the model is only a tool. The trainee should own the model, not be owned by it. He eventually must call upon all available resources—his own experience, other systems and technologies, research, developing theories—to clarify, modify, refine, and expand the model. Any model is acceptable to the degree that it produces results.

Avoiding rigidities in the application of the model.   While the most effective helpers need no system, the beginner or low-level helper can apply the developmental model rigidly. Helping is for the client; the model exists only to aid the helping process. One rigidity is a mechanical progression through the stages of the model. But counseling does not always happen as neatly as the model, as the example given to illustrate it suggests. The phases of helping are not always as differentiated and sequential as they are presented in this book. Since the client does not present all of his problems at once, it is impossible to work through Stage I completely before moving on to Stages II and III. New problems must be explored and understood whenever they are presented. For instance, even in Stage III, the pain and frustration experienced by the client as he works at implementing various action programs must be understood, even though such understanding is a Stage-I function.

A second rigidity is the expectation that, since understanding ideally precedes action, it must always precede action. In some cases, the client will not understand his problem until he acts. For instance, the socially immature client might think that he has no problems in relating to others, simply because he has avoided any deeper contact with people. His world is filled with superficial or commercial transactions with others. However, if he is assigned homework that involves deeper contact with others, such as dating or the establishment of a friendship, his social inadequacies might well be revealed to him. Now social interaction *is* a perceived problem for him and can be treated in more conventional ways. Another example is the severely regressed person. The helper might well have to act *for* such a person by means of a behavior-modification program that will help develop in him the kind of minimal social sense he needs before his involvement in the developmental model can be considered.

A third rigidity is to try to predetermine the amount of time to be spent in any given stage. A general rule is that the helper should move as quickly as the resources of the client permit. The client should not be penalized for the helper's lack of skills in Stages II and III. The beginning helper often dallies too long in Stage I, not merely because he has a deep respect for the necessity of accurate empathic understanding but because he either does not know to move on or fears doing so. High-level clients may be able to move quickly to action programs. The helper, obviously, should be able to move with him.

The problem of being a "stage-specific" specialist.   Some counselors tend to specialize in the skills of a particular stage of the model. Some specialize in primary-level accurate empathy; others claim to be good at immediacy and confrontation; others want to move to action programs immediately. The person who so specializes is usually not very effective even in his chosen specialty. For instance, the counselor whose specialty is confrontation is often an ineffective confronter. The reason for this is obvious. The model is organic; it fits together as a whole. Stage I exists for the action programs of Stage III, and Stage II depends on Stage I. Confrontation is poor if it is not based solidly on an accurate empathic understanding of the client's feelings, attitudes, and behavior. The most effective counselors are those who have the widest repertory of responses and who can use them in a socially intelligent way. Such a repertory enables them to respond spontaneously to a wide variety of client needs. Counseling is for the client; it is not a virtuoso performance by the helper.

Awkwardness.   The beginner can expect to be awkward. A person needs a great deal of practice and experience to be able to put all this technique together skillfully. Indeed, if the counselor is not living effectively himself, he will always be awkward and artificial in his execution of the developmental model. But the trainee's awkwardness or the practitioner's lack of skill should not be mistaken for deficiency in the model. The model is only as rigid and artificial as the person using it.

One problem with a microskills approach to helper training is that the trainee finds it difficult to pull all the skills together into an integrated whole. Three factors help the trainee achieve this integration.

1. Extended practice in individual skills.   If the skills are being taught and practiced in a regular classroom situation, the "violin-lesson" analogy can be invoked. Through reading and in the classroom, the trainee gets a conceptual grasp of the skill. The teacher/trainer models the skill and then introduces the student/trainees to the skill in an experiential way. The student/trainee then gets some minimal practice within the classroom itself, equivalent to a violin lesson. In the case of the violin, once you have had a lesson, it is necessary to go home and practice a great deal if you want to become skilled. Indeed, it would be silly to return for another lesson without having practiced in between. The same holds true for you, the student/trainee. Once the classroom "lesson" is over, it is essential to practice the helping skills outside; practicing poses no problem, however, since helping skills are basically the same as human-relations skills. You can sincerely and genuinely practice accurate empathy in your daily interpersonal life. Most people find it rewarding to talk to someone who communicates understanding. In my experience, the progress of trainees who want violin lessons but no practice is slow.

2. Modeling of extended counseling sessions by high-level helpers.
Trainees need to watch someone who can "put it all together." Live
sessions (with volunteers), good films, and videotapes all help. All of
these seem more useful than written transcripts in giving trainees an
"ah-hah" experience—"Oh, that's how it's done!"

3. Supervised practice with extended sessions. Ultimately, the beginning helper has to try to help. I suggest that trainees begin by having
more and more extended sessions with one another before trying to help
actual clients. Everyday life also offers opportunities for extended, al-
beit informal, helping. Feedback from supervisors, trainee-observers,
and trainee-clients is essential.

A core approach: A final caution. This book presents a core approach
to helping; it describes skills that are useful in almost any approach to
helping. However, in no way does it exhaust the ways of helping. While
this approach should help the helper deal with a wide variety of problems, he eventually must acquire specialized sets of skills to deal with
specialized problems—juvenile delinquency, alcoholism, sexual devia-
tion, psychosis, family problems, and so on.

Systematic training

The skills-training model proposed in this book is a *systematic* approach to training. Trainees move from the simplest skills, such as
attending, to the most complex, such as the elaboration of action programs, in collaboration with the client. It is crucial that the trainee
master the simpler skills, for the more complex skills are based on them.
Even if you feel that you already possess some of the skills of the model,
there are still advantages to your moving systematically through the
training program: (1) you can use the training program to check out your
skills systematically; (2) you will be learning not just skills but a methodology, which is both a method of training *and* a method of treatment;
and (3) you can use the practice sessions as an opportunity to examine
some of the problematic in your own life, especially that which might
interfere with your being an effective helper.

As you add more and more skills to your repertory (or sharpen the
skills you already possess and relate them to the helping model), you
will find that you can be more spontaneous in the helping process,
drawing more and more easily from a storehouse of helping behaviors.

There is some tendency in the beginning to see systematic training
as too regimented. Most of us are not used to systematic training. The
skills we have (for example, athletic skills) have been learned haphaz-

ardly. As a result, we fail to actualize the potential we do have and fail to achieve the skills level of which we are capable. Systematic skills training indeed demands discipline, but, preferably, discipline in the service of development rather than for the sake of regimentation.

Mutuality in training groups

Ideally, the members of a helper-training or counseling group (in the training-as-treatment model) are not merely disparate individuals trying to learn skills and/or to grapple with the problematic in their lives. These groups function most effectively if the members work at forging themselves into a *learning community*. While it is taken for granted that such a community could not exist without mutual respect, genuineness, and understanding, the skill most needed in such a community is what Ivey (1971) calls "direct, mutual communication" (p. 65). This skill is really a group of skills:

> The skill(s) focused on in this study is one in which two individuals attempt to share with each other their experience of the other.... They are to react to the experiences they have (or have had) with each other. They are to share personal feelings with each other and to respond to these shared feelings with new and past reactions to these feelings [Higgins, Ivey, & Uhlemann, 1970, p. 21].

In terms of the developmental model, these skills are those emphasized in Stage II: advanced accurate empathy, self-disclosure, immediacy, confrontation, and the suggesting of alternative frames of reference—all in the service of helping one another grow. In both helper-training and training-as-treatment groups, mutual evaluation, feedback, and response are extremely important. These training groups, then, are by their very nature human-relations-training groups, for the members are establishing and developing relationships with one another, although these relationships are temporary and in a sense pragmatic and cannot be termed "friendships" in the ordinary meaning of that word (see Egan, 1973a, pp. 19–31). In a word, helper-training and counseling groups are most effective if a great deal of *mutuality* is developed, each member caring not only for his own learning but also for the learning of his fellow members. Group trainees (whether helpees or prospective helpers) partake in a kind of mutual give and take that does not characterize one-to-one helping. But the ability to engage honestly and skillfully in this kind of give and take is the hallmark of mature human relationships. Mutuality, then, is one of the primary advantages of a group approach to both helper-training and helping itself.

Chapter Three

Attending

1. The helper is a socially intelligent person: he can both understand others and act wisely in social situations.
2. The discrimination/communication distinction: a good discriminator knows what's going on in himself, in others, and in interactions between people; a good communicator can use this understanding in order to act in a facilitative way in social situations.
3. A rating scale is an instrument of discrimination.
4. A good helper is a good attender: his attending helps him to
   a. be a more effective discriminator,
   b. communicate respect to the client,
   c. reinforce the client, and
   d. establish a power base with the client (social-influence theory).
5. Physical attending means facing the other squarely, maintaining an open posture, maintaining good eye contact, leaning toward the other, and remaining relatively relaxed and at home with the intensity of this position.
6. Psychological attending means listening to both the verbal and the nonverbal messages of the client.
7. The effective helper also listens to his own verbal and nonverbal behavior as he interacts with the client.
8. The actively attending helper gives the client cues that he is present; these cues encourage the client to talk.
9. Good attending should be taught early in the life of training groups.
10. Don't focus on any one of the elements of attending so closely that attending itself becomes unnatural. Own attending; don't let it own you.

Social intelligence: The discrimination/communication distinction

A good helper is a perceptive helper. He attends carefully to the other person and listens to both his verbal and his nonverbal messages. He clarifies these messages through his interaction with the client and acts constructively on the results. He is also in touch with his own thoughts and feelings and with how they interact with those of the client. In sum, a good helper is socially intelligent.

Social intelligence

As early as 1920, E. L. Thorndike differentiated "social" intelligence from two other forms of human intelligence, "abstract" and "mechanical." His definition of social intelligence included two factors: the ability to *understand* others and the ability to *act* wisely in social situations. Chapin (1942), in his work with social intelligence, emphasized the second factor—the social-participation, action, or "functional" dimensions of social intelligence. He distinguished social intelligence from social insight, defining the latter as the ability of an individual to assess a social situation from the frame of reference of the participants in the situation rather than from his own. Thorndike considered such insight part of social intelligence itself. Sometimes social intelligence is called "interpersonal competence" (Foote & Cottrell, 1955; Weinstein, 1969). Weinstein sees in such competence the "ability to manipulate the responses of others" (p. 755) and therefore relates social intelligence to social-influence processes. While interpersonal competence in terms of "control," "manipulation," or "management" suggests a noncollaborative social-influence process that does not appeal to me, the socially intelligent helper nevertheless does greatly influence the client. The implications of attending as a social-influence process will be discussed later in this chapter.

The history of scientific inquiry into the definition and measurement of social intelligence need not concern us here (for that, see Walker & Foley, 1973), but the basic division of social intelligence into (1) the ability to understand social situations and (2) the ability to act on this understanding is an important one for anyone interested in helping or training in interpersonal skills.

The discrimination/communication distinction

Carkhuff (1969a) calls the ability to understand the various components of a social situation "discrimination"; Gazda (1973) calls it the "act of perceiving." A person can be a good discriminator in a number of ways. For instance:

He understands what is happening inside himself (for example, the helper is in touch with his feelings of frustration or hostility or affection when working with a client).

He perceives what is happening in his environments (for example, a father sees his two children vying for his affection; a teacher is aware of how administrative infighting affects the emotional tone of the school).

He perceives what is happening in the "world" of the other person; that is, he understands others from *their* frame of reference and not just from his own (even though he is happily married, he has a feeling for the alienation experienced by the married couple coming for help).

He sees ways in which others are living effectively and patterns of behavior that are self- and other-destructive (in talking to Sheila, he discovers that she can face crises and tolerate a great deal of distress without falling apart, while John tends to disintegrate quickly in the face of stress).

He knows what kinds of challenges might help others (he sees that it might be helpful to point out to Mary that she plays the game of "poor little girl" in her interactions with men).

He sees what kinds of action programs might benefit others (he sees that Terry must learn how to be less defensive and apologetic when talking to people in positions of authority).

On the other hand, the ability to *act* in a facilitative or helping way in social situations is called "communication" (Carkhuff, 1969a). A good communicator can translate his perceptions, insights, and discriminations into effective interpersonal transactions. He is not just an understander, he is a doer. I use the term ("agent") (which is the opposite of "patient") to refer to a person who exercises initiative in his own physical, intellectual, and social-emotional growth and in his interactions with others (see Egan, 1970, pp. 359–362). A good communicator, then, exercises agency in a number of ways:

He communicates to others the fact that he understands them from their frame of reference (for example, he tells Bill that he sees the pain he experiences when his wife becomes withdrawn and uncommunicative).

He uses his understanding of what is functional and dysfunctional in the lives of others to help them uncover areas that need concrete exploration (he tells Mary that he experiences her as "helpless little girl" in their relationship and that this prevents more satisfying adult-to-adult interaction).

His being in touch with himself allows him to reveal himself to others whenever this is appropriate (he shares with an alcoholic his own painful but successful struggle with alcoholism).

He challenges others with care and understanding (he urges a husband to explore the ways he is contributing to the deterioration of his marriage).

He collaborates with clients in the elaboration and implementation of action programs (he gives Jane some training in basic interpersonal skills; he helps George decide to remain in college, to choose a major in keeping with his talents and interests, and to develop a disciplined approach to study).

In a word, the good communicator is an agent rather than an observer, however acute, in his interactions with others. Just because a person is a good discriminator or perceiver does not mean that he is automatically a good communicator. On the other hand, a good communicator must be a good discriminator, for a good communicator is one who acts on *accurate* discriminations. High-level counselors and people, in general, who live interpersonally productive lives are good communicators. Reading books like this one will help the trainee become a good discriminator, but training in discrimination is not enough. Watching counselors in action and learning to distinguish good responses from bad ones is also very helpful, but it is not communication training. Although reading and observation are essential, one can no more become a good counselor through extensive reading than one can read and observe his way to expertise in skiing. On the other hand, the helper who acts without understanding—for example, the counselor who hopes to blast his client into action with confrontational broadsides —is even more dangerous than the counselor who understands but cannot communicate well.

Let's consider an example.

> *Client:* My husband and I are really getting along much better now. Not only that, but I got the job I wanted. I never thought it would happen, but so many changes for the good have taken place over the last six months. I just wonder if it can last!

A good discriminator will see that this woman is elated, that life has been good to her, and that things seem almost too good to be true. But unless he can communicate this to her, he remains merely a good discriminator, and good discrimination is not enough to help. However, if he is a good communicator, he might say:

> *Helper:* Things are going so great that life seems almost too good to be true!

The good communicator does not allow his understanding or perception to remain locked up inside himself.

The following pages will be filled with many examples to help you learn how to distinguish good counseling from bad, good human relations from bad. However, the only way to learn effective communication is by communicating. Therefore, you must *practice,* starting from the simplest forms of attending and progressing to the elaboration of complex action programs. There is no substitute for systematic practice in both learning and using these skills.

A rating scale as an instrument of discrimination

Since much of the history of professional psychological helping has been tied to the "medical model" (Szasz, 1961), the helping professions have tended to use illness categories to distinguish one form of psychological dysfunction from another. What Menninger (1963, pp. 9–34) calls the "urge to classify" has persisted, so that there are now long lists of various psychiatric disorders. Menninger does not use the cumbersome categorizing system of the American Psychiatric Association. Instead, he talks of the "coping devices of everyday life" (p. 125) and "five orders of dysfunction" (chapters 8–11). James and Jongeward (1971) use an extremely simple classification system: they talk of "winners" and "losers" in life and describe the characteristics of each. One advantage of the James-Jongeward classification is that it includes the distinction between those who are living effectively and those whose lives are disorganized to a greater or lesser extent.

Carkhuff (1969a,b) uses a simple five-point scale as a discrimination tool. The scale measures overall psychological functioning, global helping ability, and competence in individual helping and human-relations skills. Generally speaking, the midpoint of the scale (3) refers to basic adequacy (minimally effective functioning).

Suppose that overall interpersonal functioning is being rated. A person rated "3" is living an adequate interpersonal life; that is, he is exercising the skills of the developmental model at acceptable levels. A person rated "1" would be beset with severe disorganization in interpersonal functioning (for example, he might be very withdrawn, engage in bizarre behavior that disrupts interpersonal contact, and so on).

A person rated "4" would manifest high-level functioning in interpersonal skills, and a "5" would manifest very high degrees of creativity and agency in interpersonal living. When Carkhuff uses this scale to rate competency in individual skills, he describes what each point on the scale means for each skill (1969b, pp. 315–329). Once a person becomes familiar with the scale and the criteria underlying it, such statements as "John is functioning at about 3.5 as a helper" will be fairly clear, meaningful, and useful.

We will use a six-point adaptation of this scale as a training instrument.

In rating, either the words or the plus and minus symbols can be used. Let's apply this scale to an interchange between two people.

(– – –)	/	(– –)	/	(–)	/	(+)	/	(+ +)	/	(+ + +)

very poor   poor   inadequate   adequate   good   very good

> *Mary:* I don't think it's just my imagination. I feel that you have been ignoring me lately. Maybe "ignoring" isn't a good word. You've been withdrawing from people in general. I don't know what to do about it.

Here are some of John's possible responses and their ratings:

> (– – –) Why don't you shut up and leave me alone!

This is a very poor response because it is completely alienating.

> (– –) You've got other friends. Why not spend more time with them?

This is a poor response because it ignores Mary's feelings and the point she is trying to make; it offers advice without understanding.

> (–) Yeah. I know.

Inadequate, for it is not concrete and does not respond to specific issues.

> (+) This is really bothering you, isn't it?

Adequate, for it deals at least minimally with Mary's distress.

> (++) You see me moving away from you, and that really bothers you.

This is a good response because it recognizes not only Mary's feelings but the reasons underlying these feelings.

> (+++) My running away from things also mean running away from you, and that hurts. And you feel helpless because you can't get to me and I don't respond.

This is a very good response, accurate and full.

Since rating scales are a kind of shorthand, those who are rating must understand clearly the criteria they are using to rate. These criteria will be spelled out in detail as we examine the different kinds of responses in subsequent chapters. In general, it will be sufficient for our purposes to use just four categories: adequate (+), inadequate (–), good (++), or poor (– –).

One important criterion states that a response must be not just good in itself but also appropriate in its context. For instance, a helper might reveal something about his own experience (for example, he might talk about his own successful bout with alcoholism) in order to help a client understand himself better and begin looking for ways to handle this problem. However, if the helper reveals himself too soon (before establishing a solid relationship with the client), he might distract or scare the client with his self-disclosure. Such a response, although good in itself, is rated low because it is not helpful right here and now. The ultimate criterion for rating any response is whether the client is helped by it or not.

While trainees should learn how to rate one another's responses and overall helping ability, they should also learn how to explain their ratings in terms of behavior. For instance "I rated you inadequate in attending because you fidgeted so much with your hands and legs that you distracted the client" is a concrete, useful statement. The skills of the developmental model will be operationalized—that is, spelled out in terms of specific behaviors—to enable the student/trainee to learn concrete rating criteria.

Attending: Physical and psychological presence

Helping and other deep interpersonal transactions demand a certain intensity of presence. But this presence, this "being with" another person, is impossible without attending. Attending seems so simple a concept to grasp and so easy to do that it might be asked why a separate chapter is devoted to it. But, as simple as attending is, it is amazing how often people fail to attend to one another, even in so-called "helping" relationships. In Chapter 2, attending was referred to as a pre-helping skill and a pre-helping phase. These descriptions are somewhat misleading. Attending does not precede helping in time. Rather, it is an absolutely necessary condition for helping and, as such, must take place throughout the helping process.

Lack of attending in human relations is quite common. How many times has someone said to you: "You're not even listening to what I'm saying!"? Or someone reads a magazine while you are talking to him, or it becomes obvious that the person at the other end of the telephone conversation is eating lunch, reading, or engaging in some clandestine activity that prevents him from giving his complete attention to you. When a person is accused of not attending, his answer is, almost predictably, "I can repeat word for word everything you've said." Since this reply brings little comfort to the accuser, attending must certainly be more than the ability to repeat someone else's words. You don't want the other person's ability to remember what you have said. You want him. You want him to be present to you in a much fuller way than he is. You want more than physical (or electronic) presence. You want psychological presence. If lack of attending is disruptive of ordinary human communication, it is disastrous in helping. For this reason, the proponents of a skills/social-influence model of helping emphasize the importance of attending and teach it as a skill.

An experiment involving attending

An engaging example of the impact of attending behavior is given by Ivey and Hinkle (1970; also see Ivey, 1971, pp. 93–94). At a prearranged signal, six students in a psychology seminar switched from the traditional student's slouched posture and passive listening and note-taking to attentive posture and active eye contact with the teacher. In the nonattending condition, the teacher had been lecturing from his notes in a monotone, using no gestures, and paying little or no attention to the students. However, once the students began to attend, the teacher began to gesture, his verbal rate increased, and a lively classroom session was born. At another prearranged signal later in the class, the students stopped attending and returned to typical passive student's posture and participation. The teacher, "after some painful seeking for continued reinforcement," returned to the unengaging teacher behavior with which he had begun the class. In the nonattending condition, the teacher paid no attention to the students and the students reciprocated in kind. Both students and teacher got what they deserved: reciprocated inattention. But simple attending changed the whole picture.

The goals of attending

The whys of attending will become clearer as we describe the anatomy of attending. But even now we can relate attending to some of the components of the helping process that we have already examined.

Discrimination. Discrimination has been described as a factor in social intelligence and a necessary component of communication. Just as good communication demands good discrimination, so the ability to discriminate demands being perceptively present to people and to the contexts in which people interact. The effectively living person attends to all the environments that constitute the context of his living: the immediate interpersonal environment, his own internal environment, and his wider social environments (organizational, neighborhood, civic, international). His awareness is high. Attending, therefore, involves the skill of listening to words, sentences, and ideas, to nonverbal behavior, to interpersonal situations, to the voices of particular cultures and to cultural differences, and to trends in society. Whoever constantly puts filters between himself and the "messages" coming from his multiple environments is not good at attending, fails to discriminate, and, ultimately, communicates poorly. Attending to another person is both a communication in itself (it says "I think it's important to be totally with you") and the basis for all effective communication.

Respect. Mehrabian (1970), in discussing the importance of respect and liking in the social-influence process, deals with respect principally in terms of attending behaviors: facing the person, looking him in the eye, listening without interruption, and appearing slightly less relaxed than one actually is (see pp. 64–74). As we shall see in Chapter 4, respect plays a cardinal role in all kinds of human interactions, including counseling. The person who must share another person's attention with a magazine feels, to one degree or another, that at the moment he does not have the reader's respect or regard.

Reinforcement. We have already said a few words about the ubiquity, complexity, and necessity of reinforcement in the helping process. Attention is a potent reinforcer. Erikson (1964) speaks of the effects of both nonattention and negative attention on the child:

> Hardly has one learned to recognize the familiar face (the original harbor of basic trust) when he becomes also frightfully aware of the unfamiliar, the strange face, the unresponsive, the averted . . . and the frowning face. And here begins . . . that inexplicable tendency on man's part to feel that *he has caused the face to turn away* which happened to turn elsewhere [p. 102. emphasis added].

Perhaps the averted face is too often a sign of the averted heart. At any rate, most of us are very sensitive to others' attention (or inattention) to us. And, since this is so, it is paradoxical how insensitive we can be about attending to others.

Lassen (1973) studied one of the factors involved in attending, physical proximity, in initial psychiatric interviews. Interviewers sat either three, six, or nine feet from the client. Client anxiety during the interview was measured both behaviorally (through speech disturbances) and through self-report. Client anxiety increased with the distance of the interviewer. The helper who is present both physically and psychologically by means of high-level attending is ordinarily seen as supporting, reassuring, consoling, sincere, and genuine. His presence can be very reinforcing for the client.

Social influence. Since attending is reinforcing, it is an important element in the social-influence dimension of the helping process. Effective attending helps the counselor establish a power base with the client by showing him as interested and caring. Attending also contributes to the social-influence process in that it places demands on the client. "If I am with you fully, invest myself in you, and work with you, all of this demands a response on your part." Counselors who are afraid to put demands on the client are ordinarily poor attenders. Differential attention is another factor in the social-influence process. For instance, helpers ignore the "crazy talk" of severely disturbed clients and attend to (and thus reinforce) only their communications that make sense. In counseling sessions, the helper ordinarily gives more attention to some of the client's themes than to others. Obviously, the helper tries to stick with themes that are most important in the life of the client, but he does often control the direction of the interaction by choosing to attend to some things and not to others. If he is a helper who accurately understands the client's world from the client's frame of reference, his differential attending will most likely help the client deal more concretely with important issues.

Since the way the helper attends to the client can have great influence on him, it is necessary to lay bare the anatomy of attending.

Physical attending

Physical attending means doing certain things and not doing other things. First of all, it means getting rid of whatever might distract the helper from giving his attention to the client. The physical environment in counseling can be too strikingly beautiful (fine pictures on the wall, windows with vistas) or too uncomfortable and ugly (a cold room, uncomfortable furniture). The environment for both training and counseling should be a comfortable *work* (not relaxation) environment that easily allows the participants to give their attention to one another. If the furniture is too comfortable, it is more appropriate to lounging than to interpersonal work. A friend of mine held a human-relations-training group in his apartment one semester. One of the participants, in a paper that included criticisms of the course, reported being distracted by the comfort and elegance of his apartment. It was conducive to relaxation, not to work. Counselors who sit behind desks are not fully available to their clients. Moreover, the desk emphasizes his role in a process that should be essentially role-free. In my opinion, there should be no physical objects between the counselor and the person who has come to him for help.

One caution. Some people blame their inability to work in human-relations-training programs on their environment. In the case cited above, the trainee was placing some of the blame for his nonparticipation on the overly comfortable surroundings. Counseling and human-relations trainees sometimes blame their nonparticipation on the classroom setting, calling it "too impersonal" or "antiseptic." Training should take place in the best setting available, for the setting does affect the process; but highly motivated people can work even in adverse settings.

Positively (and more personally) speaking, physical attending means that the interactants should adopt a posture of *involvement* with one another. In counseling, the helper can control his own behavior. He should attend to his client even if his client engages in nonverbal behavior indicating withdrawal (looking at the floor, slouching). Specifically, physical attending means:

Facing the other squarely: this is the basic posture of involvement. It says: "I am available to you." Turning to the side lessens one's involvement.

Maintaining good eye contact: the helper should look directly at the client. Some helpers balk at the notion; they say that this will frighten the client, who will feel that he is being "stared down." However, there *is* a difference between staring a person down (which is a power function and implies a great deal of rigidity) and working at eye contact, which is facilitative of deeper involvement. Watch two people (or watch yourself) intensely involved in conversation. Their eye contact is almost uninterrupted. The *interaction* is so important and so engaging that they do not reflect on just how much time they spend looking directly at each other.

Maintaining an "open" posture: crossed arms and crossed legs are often at least minimal signs of lessened involvement. An open posture is a sign that the helper is open to what the client has to say to him and open to communicating directly to the client. It is a nondefensive position.

Leaning toward the other: this is another sign of presence, availability, or involvement. In your everyday environment, find examples of people who are involved with one another in serious conversation. Note how often people lean toward one another naturally as a sign of involvement.

Remaining relatively relaxed: relative relaxation says to the client: "I am at home with you." Mehrabian (1970), as we have seen, suggests that a person appear a bit less relaxed than he actually is in a social situation in order to show liking and respect. I see the picture differently. If the counselor faces the client squarely, maintains good eye contact, keeps an open posture, and leans forward during the interaction, he is involving himself in a way that puts a demand on both himself and the client. This position of involvement has a kind of tension about it. However, since the person who is living effectively *is* relatively comfortable with involvement and intimacy, he will be relatively relaxed, even in this attending position. Trying to seem less relaxed than one really is is not very genuine, and it smacks of the kind of manipulation that I object to in the social-influence process. In counseling there should be a balance between productive tension and relaxation. The helper who is relaxed, although intense and hard-working, can give himself the "living space" he needs in order to listen and respond fully. The overly tense helper tends to leap in too quickly with a response, and this tendency lessens his ability to be accurately empathic. I have watched Carl Rogers in a film in which he is counseling an actual client. I was struck by how he was both intense and relaxed. He did not leap in to respond to the client every time the client paused. He gave himself time to formulate what he wanted to say, and I believe that his being relaxed and at home in the counseling process helped him to take the time he needed to respond with respect, care, and understanding. The counselor who is tense and tight will almost inevitably infect his client with his own malaise.

If the helper faces the client squarely with an open posture, maintains good eye contact, and leans forward in a relatively relaxed way, he is in a classic attending position, which says much about his desire to become involved with the client. The five-point scale can be used to get a picture of attending. One drops to a 4 or a 3 in attending by lessening some of the features of the 5 position,—that is, by turning slightly away from the other, breaking eye contact more or less frequently, crossing arms or legs in some fashion, or lessening the degree of leaning toward the other.

Some people maintain that a 5 position may scare the client, that it is "too much." First of all, this should not be assumed unconditionally. This position may be disturbing to the low-level *helper* (and not to the client), since it demands too much involvement of him. But, since helping is for the client and not for the comfort of the helper, the high-level helper will assume an attending position proportioned to the needs of the person coming for help. Attending, like other responses, must be both good in itself (a 5 attending position is good in itself) and good in the situation (beginning with a 5 position may be too much for a particular client). The helper must certainly maintain a minimally facilitative attending position (adequate but not constant eye contact, sitting at a slight angle to the client, sitting straight or leaning only slightly toward the client), but he can move gradually to more intense attending as the relationship between him and the client grows. If the posture the helper assumes places some demands on the client, these demands are not out of order, for helping is a demanding process. The high-level helper does not adopt any rigid formula for attending. He flows naturally with the helping process and adopts whatever posture is called for at any given moment of the interaction. He can move in and out of a 5 position as the situation demands. For instance, he can move out of a 5 position (back to a 4 or a 3) when the client moves off on inconsequential tangents (the helper withdraws reinforcement) or move into a 5 position when the client comes up with something that merits more attention (his attending reinforces the client's behavior and adds force to his words: "Great! Now you're talking very concretely about your behavior."). Or, when he wants to demand more of the client, he moves forward and says: "Where do *you* want to go in this relationship?"

If the counselor is comfortable with helping others, his body and movements will not be rigid. Although he will not engage in distracting movements and sounds—fitful breaking of eye contact, keeping his hand in front of his face, nervous arm and leg movements, unnecessary sounds such as nervous laughter, clearing his throat, habitual use of words such as "okay" or "well"—he will not be afraid to use his body to communicate. Strong, Taylor, Bratton, and Loper (1971), in a study of nonverbal counselor behavior, discovered that the counselor who remains too still (perhaps rigid) is seen as precise, reserved, thoughtful, serious, orderly, controlled, cold, aloof, and intellectual. On the other hand, the counselor who is physically active (not in a fitful, nervous way but in a way that indicates nonverbal reinforcement of what he is saying) is seen as friendly, warm, casual, and carefree (relaxed and role-free), and therefore more attractive. I suggest that a counselor who is both intense and relaxed (the 5 position) is seen as both serious and friendly, thoughtful and available, controlled and free.

A 5 position is a demanding position, but counseling is demanding work. Helping should not be identified with a relaxed, informal interpersonal situation (although the latter certainly has its own value). The physical demands of these two kinds of interpersonal situations are different and should not be confused. The helper should become aware of the importance of the body in human interaction. The high-level helper knows, at least instinctively, what he is doing with his body. He knows that his body has impact value in the relationship. He is aware that his body does communicate, and he uses it to communicate, but he does not become its victim.

Psychological attending: Listening as the core of attending

Attending is a manner of being present to another; listening is what one does while attending.

Listening to the other's nonverbal behavior.   We are only beginning to realize the importance of nonverbal behavior and to make a scientific study of it. Take the case of the ordinary smile:

> To illustrate the complex, intricate nature of this medium [facial expressions], let us consider a very simple form of facial expression—an ordinary smile. One of the most common instances is the "simple smile," a mere upward and outward movement at the corners of the mouth. It indicates inner bemusement; no other person is involved. The "upper smile" is a slightly more gregarious gesture in which the upper teeth are exposed. It is usually displayed in social situations, such as when friends greet each other. Perhaps the most engaging of all is the "broad smile." The mouth is completely open; both upper and lower teeth are visible.
>
> Yet without other facial movements, particularly around the eyes, smiles would not really mean what they seem to mean. For appropriate warmth, the upper smile is usually enhanced by slight changes around the outer corners of the eyes. Even the smile is not always an entirely convincing expression of broad surprise or pleasure unless it is accompanied by an elevation of the eyebrows. Other emotional expressions also depend upon a delicate use of the eye area. In a sad frown, the eyebrows will ordinarily be drawn down at the outer ends. By contrast, they will be depressed on the inside in an angry frown [Saral, 1972, p. 474].*

The face and the body are extremely communicative. Even when two people are silent with each other, the atmosphere can be filled with messages.

Mehrabian (1971) reports on research he and his associates have done in the area of nonverbal behavior and on inconsistent messages such as like/dislike.

> One interesting question now arises: Is there a systematic and coherent approach to resolving the general meaning or impact of an inconsistent message? Indeed there is. Our experimental results show:
>
> Total liking equals 7% verbal liking plus 38% vocal
> liking plus 55% facial liking
>
> Thus the impact of facial expression is greatest, then the impact of the tone of voice (or vocal expression), and finally that of the words. If the facial expression is inconsistent with the words, the degree of liking conveyed by the facial expression will dominate and determine the impact of the total message [p. 43].

Both nonverbal behavior (bodily movements, gestures, facial expressions) and paralinguistic behavior (tone of voice, inflection, spacing of

*Excerpt from "Cross-cultural generality of communication via facial expressions," by Tulsi B. Saral, is reprinted from *Comparative Studies,* Vol. 3, No. 4 (Nov. 1972), pp. 473–486, by permission of the publisher, Sage Publications, Inc.

words, emphasis, pauses), should be listened to by the helper, for he must respond to the client's total message and not merely to his words. Indeed, as Mehrabian's research illustrates, nonverbal and paralinguistic cues can contradict the overt meaning of words. For instance, tone of voice can indicate that a verbal "no" is really a "yes." The high-level helper, since he listens to all cues and messages, is ready to respond to the total communication of the client. While only a few basic dimensions of human feelings and attitudes are conveyed nonverbally—like, dislike, potency, status, responsiveness—they are extremely important qualifiers of verbal messages.

Nonverbal behaviors are often carriers of the emotional dimensions of messages (for example, the client kicks his feet, maintains a half-smile, wrings his hands, grimaces, or folds his arms over his chest) and, as such, constitute a more primitive and less easily controlled communication system. Nonverbal behaviors are usually open to a number of interpretations. How, then, does the helper know what they mean? The high-level helper listens to the entire context and does not simply fix his attention on details of behavior. Nonverbal behavior helps punctuate and color the interaction; it confirms or denies the message carried by the words; it adds feelings not contained in the words themselves. The high-level counselor is aware of and uses the nonverbal communication system, but he is not seduced or overwhelmed by it. (See Gazda, 1973, pp. 89ff; Knapp, 1972; and Mehrabian, 1971 for fuller treatments of nonverbal behavior.)

Some trainees hesitate, in the early stages of counseling, to label feelings unless the client states them explicitly. The client can show that he is angry by both content and manner of expression without saying "I am angry." Feelings are carried by verbal content, tone of voice, gestures, and all the elements of nonverbal behavior. Many of these feelings are what Gazda (1973) calls "surface" feelings (p. 68), and it is perfectly legitimate for a helper to call these feelings to the attention of the client. However, if feelings are indistinct or too deeply buried or camouflaged, the helper should be hesitant to attribute them to a client. High-level attending or "being with" the client is absolutely necessary for high-level discrimination.

Listening to the client's verbal behavior. Effective attending makes the counselor an *active* listener. He not only hears the words and sentences but hears the ways the words and sentences are being modified by nonverbal and paralinguistic cues. What is the helper listening for? Feelings and content. He wants to know about the experience and behavior of the client and the feelings that suffuse them. His ability to listen underlies his ability to understand the client from the client's frame of reference. Good listening supplies him with the building blocks of accurate empathy. The defensive person finds it difficult to listen, for he keeps hearing things he does not want to hear. He develops the skill of selective listening to keep his anxiety in line. For instance, he hears another person when he talks superficially but not when he talks personally or intimately. He hears praise but not criticism. Or vice versa. He hears parts of sentences, but disturbing words are left out. Obviously, the helper should not be a selective listener. If selective listening is part of the client's problem, the counselor should help him develop the skill of total listening. The first step in this process is the helper's modeling total listening.

The counselor's ability to listen to himself

Norman Kagan and his associates (Kagan, 1971; Kagan, Krathwohl, et al., 1967; Kagan, Krathwohl, & Miller, 1963; Kagan & Schauble, 1969) are proponents of systematic training in counselor education. One skill they emphasize is the ability of the counselor to listen to himself during the counseling interview itself. Let's say that the following interaction takes place during the counseling session.

> *Client:* I just tighten up whenever anyone tries to get too close to me. I can talk about myself easily enough—that is, if I do most of the talking —but when there's a dialogue, I stumble around.
> *Counselor:* Even verbal closeness frightens you.
> *Client:* Yes, I really resent it when I think that people are prying into my life. It's more like preying. I have a right to my own private thoughts, even from my husband. But there are those who dig away at you until they get what they want and you feel naked.

Kagan interviews the counselor trainee after a short practice session with a client. In the interview he tries to get the trainee to recall as much as possible about how he felt and what was going on in his mind during the interview—things the trainee did not verbalize during the counseling session. For instance, in the example above, the trainer would want to know what the trainee was thinking about, how he was reacting to the client, what feelings and thoughts came up that he did not express or verbalize. The trainee might say something like this:

> *Trainee:* I was not sure whether the client was talking about me or not, but, after all, I was asking her to talk intimately about herself. I felt a bit put off, but I was afraid to deal with the issue directly. I didn't want to put her on the defensive. She also seemed to say that I shouldn't respond to her too frequently, that I should keep my distance. All of this bothered me somewhat during the rest of the interview.

The purpose of such recall is to teach the counselor to listen to himself, not just after the interview is over but during the interview itself. If he knows just what is happening inside himself while he is talking with the client, he can use what he "hears" openly and directly in the interview itself. Just as listening to the client's experience, behavior, and feelings provides the raw materials for accurate empathy, so the counselor's attending to and listening to himself provides the raw material for _immediacy_—that is, the ability to discuss with the client what is happening in the here-and-now of the client-counselor relationship. This interaction ordinarily belongs to Stage II; it presumes the establishment of some kind of relationship between counselor and client. Suppose that trainee and client are in Stage II. Let's return to the example and see what the trainee might have said next had he been listening to himself during the interview with the client.

> *Trainee:* You resent others' prying into your life, but, in a sense, that's what we are doing here. I don't know whether you are including me among the "pryers."
> *Client:* You've been tactful enough about it, but I keep wondering whether you think I'm some awful kind of person. You don't come out and say so directly, but I wonder.
> *Trainee:* You have a right and a need to be respected, even when you are exploring the shadow side of yourself.
> *Client:* Yes! And I do think you respect me. But I guess I'm saying "Be careful with me."

This kind of immediacy or direct mutual talk helps clear the air. It is possible, however, only if the helper develops the ability to attend to and listen to himself. Immediacy will be discussed in greater detail in Chapter 6, which deals with Stage II.

"Minimal encourages to talk" as attending behavior

Phillips, Lockhart, and Moreland (1969; see also Hackney & Nye, 1973, pp. 57ff) use the expression "minimal encourages to talk" to indicate ways the counselor encourages the client to explore his feelings and behavior. They include such things as "um-hmmm," repetition of one or two of the client's words, one-word questions, nods of the head, and a variety of gestures and body postures (leaning forward, moving closer). To me these expressions are like interjections or signs given by the counselor to indicate that he is attending. The fact that he is being listened to attentively, as signified by these encouragements, reinforces the client's self-exploratory behavior. Obviously, the counselor should not do these things mechanically, for he would seem phony; neither should he overdo them. They should not be allowed to take the place of communications of accurate empathy. If used properly, they will help the client explore himself; but, when he does, the helper must respond with understanding.

Training groups and training-as-treatment

Attending is basically a simple skill, easily learned and easily taught. It is a skill that members of human-relations-training groups should learn quickly and directly. In training groups, members who are not involved in a particular interaction tend to "take time out," signaling this by lapsing into nonattending behaviors (slouching, little or no eye contact, folded arms and legs). A few nonattenders seriously affect the tone of the group: it becomes much more difficult to do interpersonal work in such an environment. In training groups composed of helpees, good attending behavior should be taught early in the life of the group. Since it is an easy skill to learn, the client/trainees benefit in two ways. They have the satisfaction of learning an important skill, and they receive further reinforcement as they interact with attentive fellow trainees.

Training-as-treatment, at this stage, means teaching clients how to attend physically to one another and how to develop the skills of active listening. Specific exercises for these skills are found in the Training Manual.

A final caution

Aspects of helping are presented here in bits and pieces. The low-level helper will fasten selectively on this bit or that piece. For example, he will become intrigued with nonverbal behavior and make too much of a half-smile on the face of his client. He will seize the smile and lose the person. The high-level helper, on the other hand, can integrate all the pieces. He makes the skills—from attending on—his own and does not become their victim. With respect to attending, the high-level helper is fully present to the client and completely open, encouraging a natural flow of data from the client, from himself, and from the interaction. He marshals these data and translates them into helping behavior.

Chapter Four

Stage I: Helper Response and Client Self-Exploration

I. The Helper Skills of Stage I
 1. Primary-level accurate empathy is distinguished from advanced accurate empathy in that
    a. the goal of such empathy is to communicate to the client that the helper understands his world from the client's perspective;
    b. such empathy deals both with feelings and with the behaviors and experiences underlying these feelings; and
    c. such empathy helps establish trust and rapport and increases the level of the client's self-exploratory behavior.
 2. The beginner may experience certain problems in communicating primary-level accurate empathy: inaccuracy, feigning understanding, allowing the client to ramble, premature advanced accurate empathy, spending too much time communicating primary-level accurate empathy, jumping in too quickly, using language that is not in tune with the client's, and longwindedness.
 3. A helper who is similar in background to the client can often communicate accurate empathy more effectively than one quite removed from the client's background.
 4. Genuineness must be communicated to the client through certain behaviors: refusing to play the role of counselor, being spontaneous, being oneself, being nondefensive, and being ready to share oneself if it helps.
 5. Respect, too, must be expressed behaviorally: being "for" the client, being willing to work with him, regarding him as unique and self-determining, assuming his good will, attending, suspending critical judgment, communicating accurate empathy, making a census of the client's resources, being appropriately warm.
 6. The helper must be concrete in his responses in order to help the client be concrete in his self-exploration.

    a. Concreteness means dealing with specific feelings, specific experiences, and specific behaviors in specific situations.
    b. The helper can get the client to be more concrete by using probes and open-ended questions.
    c. Concreteness is most important at this stage (self-exploration) and, later on, in the elaboration of action programs.

II. The Experiences of the Client at Stage I
   1. The client's disorganization makes him more open to social-influence processes.
   2. The helper who is an expert because of his skills as well as because of his role and reputation will establish a strong power base with the client.
   3. If the helper is trustworthy in role, reputation, and behavior, he will quickly establish rapport with the client. Such rapport is a source of social influence.
   4. A third source of influence is the helper's "attractiveness." The helper will be attractive if he is seen as similar to and compatible with the client.
   5. The helper can help the client muster his motivational resources. The client's motivation to participate in the helping process will be high if
    a. he is in psychological pain,
    b. the issues dealt with in the helping sessions are of intrinsic importance to him, and
    c. the helper places reasonable demands on him—demands consistent with his needs and resources.
   6. We are all open to social-influence processes. Such processes are "bad" only if they are used to control, manipulate, or otherwise harm the client.

III. Self-Exploration
   1. The helper's skills in Stage I are directed toward the client's self-exploratory behavior, focusing on concrete problem-related information, solution-oriented resources, and client goals, assumptions, and values.
   2. The severity of the client's problems can be gauged by the degree of distress they cause him, their uncontrollability, and their frequency.
   3. Obstacles that stand in the way of the client's exploring himself fully are the questions of confidentiality (especially in groups), fear of disorganization, shame, and fear of change.
   4. Since the core of dysfunctioning is generally interpersonal, the best mode of treatment in Stage I is to train the client in the interpersonal skills that the helper himself uses in Stage I: <u>attending, primary-level accurate empathy, concreteness, genuineness, and respect.</u>
   5. Helping is an intense process. Certain pitfalls should be avoided:
    a. The temptation to stay too long in Stage I, pursuing insights that are unrelated to action; and
    b. the temptation to apply the developmental model too rigidly.

This chapter has three sections. Section I deals with the skills the helper needs to respond effectively to the person who presents himself for help and to help him explore his problems. These are also the skills that constitute the basis for mature interpersonal relationships. Without them mutuality is impossible. Section II deals with the client's experience of helping as a social-influence process. What makes him trust the helper (or his fellow group members in group counseling) and moves him to collaborate with the helping process? Section III discusses the process of self-exploration itself and some of the obstacles to it.

I. THE HELPER SKILLS OF STAGE I

The first task of the helper is to respond to the person who comes for help. However, as Brammer (1973) notes, the average client enters a helping relationship with certain misgivings, for a number of reasons:

1. It is not easy to receive help.
2. It is difficult to commit one's self to change.
3. It is difficult to submit to the influence of a helper: help is a threat to esteem, integrity, and independence.
4. It is not easy to trust a stranger and be open with him.
5. It is not easy to see one's problems clearly at first.
6. Sometimes problems seem too large, too overwhelming, or too unique to share easily [p. 57].

How, then, is the helper to respond to a person experiencing such fears and doubts? He should try to understand the client and communicate this understanding to him as genuinely, caringly, and concretely as possible. The ability to communicate accurate empathy, genuineness, respect, and concreteness constitutes the skills of Stage I. These are the skills that will help create for the client the climate of psychological freedom he needs in order to explore himself and the problems in his life. As Brammer (1973) notes, attending and listening encourage the client to drop his guard and become vulnerable; that is, attending and listening are social-influence processes. Therefore, the helper must go far beyond listening. He has to know how to support the client during the painful process of self-exploration and how to help the client move toward the resolution of his problems.

The order of presentation of these skills here is somewhat arbitrary. However, since the communication of accurate empathic understanding plays such a basic role throughout the developmental model, I will start with this cardinal skill.

Primary-level accurate empathy

Carkhuff (1969a) distinguishes two levels of accurate empathic understanding. At an "interchangeable" level, the helper communicates his understanding of the client's experiences and feelings that are more or less readily available to the client's perception; at an "additive" level, the helper probes more deeply, communicating understanding of feelings, experiences, and motivations that the client expresses in implicit ways and that are not so readily available to the client's awareness. I use the term "primary-level" accurate empathy for the former ("interchangeable") and "advanced" accurate empathy for the latter ("additive"). The ability to communicate advanced accurate empathic understanding, a skill used, for the most part, in Stages II and III, will be treated in the next chapter. Even before examining primary-level accurate empathy, a skill needed in each stage of the model, let's take a look at accurate empathy in general.

Accurate empathy in general.   A person is accurately empathic if he can (1) *discriminate:* get inside the other person, look at the world through the perspective or frame of reference of the other person, and get a feeling for what the other's world is like; and (2) *communicate* to the other this understanding in a way that shows the other that the helper has picked up both his *feelings* and the *behavior and experience* underlying these feelings. As Mayeroff (1971) puts it:

> To care for another person, I must be able to understand him and his world as if I were inside it. I must be able to see, as it were, with his eyes what his world is like to him and how he sees himself. Instead of merely looking at him in a detached way from outside, as if he were a specimen, I must be albe to be *with* him in his world, "going" into his world in order to sense from "inside" what life is like for him, what he is striving to be, and what he requires to grow [pp. 41–42].

If a person comes to me, sits down, looks at the floor, hunches over, and haltingly tells me that he has just failed two tests, that his girl friend has told him she doesn't want to see him anymore, and that he might lose his part-time job, I might begin to respond to him by saying:

Counselor: You're really feeling miserable—your world has all of a sudden begun to fall apart.

I see his depression *(feelings)* and begin to understand what underlies this depression *(experience)*, and I communicate to him this understanding of his world. This is accurate empathy. Or, if a friend tells me that she has just finished nurse's training and has been accepted as a

nurse in a local hospital—a dream she has had since she was a little girl
—I say:

> *Friend:* You're really bursting with joy! It's great to accomplish what you
> set out to do.

This, too, is accurate empathy. One thesis of this book is that accurate
empathy is a pragmatic value both in counseling and in all the deeper
interactions of life.

> *Primary-level accurate empathy.* Primary-level accurate empathy
entails communicating *initial basic* understanding of what the client is
feeling and the experiences underlying these feelings. This is the kind
of accurate empathy proportioned to Stage I of the developmental
model. In this response, the helper merely tries to let the client know
that he understands what the client has *explicitly* expressed about
himself. The counselor, in his own words and in his own way, communicates this understanding to the client. He does not try to dig
down into what the client is only half-saying, or implying, or stating *implicitly*. This degree of accurate empathy belongs, generally,
to Stage II. Let's take a look at a few examples of primary-level
accurate empathy.

> *Client:* I really think that things couldn't be going much better. I have
> a new job. My husband and I are getting along better than ever—even
> sexually, and I never expected that. I guess I'm just waiting for the bubble
> to burst.
> *Counselor:* It's really exciting when things are going so well. It seems
> almost too good to be true.

> *Client:* I've been to other counselors and nothing has ever really hap-
> pened. I don't even know why I'm trying again. But things are so bad that
> I guess something has to be done, so I'm trying it all over again.
> *Counselor:* You're uneasy because you're not at all sure this is going to
> work, but you feel you have to try something.

> *Client:* I have a vague feeling that I could do something more with my
> life. I'm successful enough by ordinary standards, but what does that
> mean? It's about time I took a good look at my values because I have the
> feeling I'm not really living up to them.
> *Counselor:* You have some gnawing doubts about the quality of your life.
> And so it's time to take a harder look at your life—especially your value
> system.

In these interchanges the helper says what could have been said by the
client. In Stage I the counselor generally does not go beyond primary-
level accurate empathy.

The immediate goals of primary-level accurate empathy.   When joined with respect and genuineness, primary-level accurate empathy helps dramatically to establish rapport with the client, it breeds trust and openness crucial to Stage I, a time of relationship-building. Second, research (Carkhuff, 1969a,b) shows that such empathy has a particular effect on the client: *it raises the level of his self-exploration,* which is the principal client goal of Stage I. Therefore, the counselor has an excellent criterion for judging the quality of his Stage-I responses: to what degree does his response help the client move forward in the process of exploring his feelings and behavior? Study the following interchange.

> *Client:* I don't think I'll make a good counselor. The other people in the program are much brighter than I am. I'm beginning to see my deficiencies more and more as I move through these practice sessions, and I don't really know whether I have what it takes to help someone else. Maybe I need to work more things out for myself.
> *Counselor:* You're felling pretty inadequate and it's really getting you down—enough to make you want to give up.
> *Client:* And yet I know that "giving up" is part of the problem. I'm not the brightest, but I'm not absolutely dumb. And I have been picking up some of the skills in the practice session. I'm like a kid: I want everything right away.

When the counselor "hits the mark," the client moves forward and begins to explore further dimensions of his problem. In a sense, there is no such thing as an empathic response beautiful in itself. It is beautiful to the degree that it works.

Advanced accurate empathy.   A better understanding of primary-level accurate empathy can be gleaned by comparing it with advanced-level accurate empathy (a Stage-II skill, explained in detail in the next chapter). Advanced accurate empathy gets at not only what the client states and expresses but also what he *implies* and leaves unstated or not clearly expressed. For instance, Peter explores his feelings and behavior to a certain point but seems to skirt delicate issues at the core of the problematic in his life. He also shows signs of fatigue and frustration during the counseling sessions. The counselor puts all of these clues together and says:

> *Counselor:* Peter, it seems that you are skirting some of the issues that bother you the most, and perhaps running away is more work and more depressing than facing them squarely. It's very painful for you to put yourself squarely on the line.

This is not primary-level accurate empathy because Peter has never overtly expressed these ideas, even though they have shown themselves covertly during the counseling sessions. Again, the ultimate criterion for advanced-level accurate empathy is the response it elicits in the client.

> *Peter:* I knew that had to be said sooner or later! I don't know what I'm afraid of. It's stupid of me to invest my time in counseling and then not make good use of my time.

Peter moves ahead. The issue is now out in the open where it can be dealt with more creatively. However, if advanced accurate empathy is used too early in the counseling process, it can frighten the client off or make him regress. He may deny the counselor's statements, even when he knows they are true. The rapport that has been building up suffers a setback. In Stage I, it is inefficient to confuse, scare, or anger the client by premature responses of advanced-level accurate empathy. When the client begins to explore himself rather freely, the counselor can begin to move from Stage I to Stage II.

Some common problems in communicating primary-level accurate empathy

Many of the following problems affect the beginning helper, but they are by no means restricted to the beginner.

Failure to achieve accurate empathy.   There are any number of ways the helper can fail to be accurately empathic. I'll use an example to point out some common failures. The client, obviously nervous, says:

> *Client:* What seems to be really bothering me is a problem with sex. I don't even know whether I'm a man or not and I'm about to graduate from college.

What are some examples of poor responses to such a client? First of all, the counselor might say nothing, as if what the client has said is not worth responding to. Or he might say:

> *Counselor A:* What problems are you having with sex, John?

Again, he fails to respond to John's nervousness, and his response also implies that there has been nothing to respond to.

> *Counselor B:* Many people struggle with sexual identity throughout their lives.

This is a cliché. It misses completely the feelings of the client and deals only with the content of his statement, even then only in the vaguest way. The impact of such a response is: "You don't really have a problem at all, at least not a serious one."

> *Counselor C:* This sexual thing is probably really just a symptom, John. I bet something else is really bothering you.

This is a corruption of a misplaced attempt at advanced accurate empathy. The counselor fails to respond to the client's feelings and also distorts the content of the client's communication. The response implies that what is really important is hidden from the client.

> *Counselor D:* Let's take a look at your sexual development, find out where you stand, and see how accurate your information about sex is.

Counselor D also ignores the client's feelings and jumps to a quasi-action program with overtones of sex education. It will be quite useful to find out where the young man stands in his sexual development, but the counselor is going about it in the wrong way.

> *Counselor E:* Don't you see, John? Sexual immaturity is just another part of the whole picture we have been looking at in your life. You're trying to hang onto your childhood and its safety.

This is another premature use of advanced accurate empathy, an attempt to pull things together into a bigger picture. Such attempts are ordinarily inappropriate during Stage I. Furthermore, this particular stab at advanced accurate empathy is a psychodynamic interpretation of highly questionable validity.

> *Counselor F:* Sexual maturity is an important—and disturbing—issue for you at this time of your life.

Counselor F responds with primary-level accurate empathy. He recognizes that the client is disturbed and that concern for his sexuality underlies his anxiety. This is the kind of Stage-I response that is likely to strengthen the rapport between client and counselor and stimulate further self-exploration.

Inaccuracy. If the counselor's response is inaccurate, the client can let him know in a variety of ways: he may stop dead, fumble around, go off on a new tangent, tell him "that's not exactly what I meant." He may even try to understand the counselor and get *him* back on the right track.

Client: My wife doesn't always butt into my life. There *are* times, even at home, when she makes attempts at being cooperative in our approach to raising the kids or managing the budget.

Counselor: You feel frustrated about her interference, nonetheless. It's lousy that she tries to exercise so much control.

Client: Well, yes and no. Take the kids. I get along great with them. I'm about as close to Tom, the oldest, as a parent could be.

The counselor is not accurate. He misses the point, and the client, caught off guard by his inaccuracy, goes off on a tangent. Perhaps this counselor was trying to play a game of "catch-up." His response would have been excellent had he given it one or two interchanges previously, but it does not fit here. "Catch-up" and good will are no substitutes for on-the-spot accuracy. What can the counselor do about inaccuracy? He must learn to pick up client cues that indicate that he has been inaccurate and then work to get back with the client. The counselor in the example above should have said something like this:

Counselor: The picture isn't totally negative, then. There are times when your wife is not overcontrolling. She can even be quite cooperative.

Client: When she cooperates, things are really great! Life hums. At least that's the way I see it. I think we should both talk to you. I don't think I'm giving you a biased picture, but it's possible.

An accurate reponse elicits a far more productive statement from the client. He begins to explore the possiblity that there are two sides to the picture.

Feigning understanding. Sometimes it is difficult to understand what the client is saying even though one attends to him quite fully. He is confused, distracted, in a highly emotional state; all these conditions affect the clarity of what he is saying about himself. On the other hand, the counselor himself might become distracted and fail to follow the client. At such times the counselor should not feign understanding. This is phony. Genuineness demands that he admit that he is lost and then work to get back on the track again. "I think I've lost you. Could we go over that once more?" If the counselor is confused, it is all right for him to admit his confusion. "I'm sorry. I don't think I got straight what you just said. Could we go through it a bit more slowly?" Such statements are signs that the counselor thinks it is important to stay with the client. They indicate his caring. Admitting that one is lost is infinitely preferable to such clichés as "uh-huh," "ummmm," and "I understand."

If the counselor feels that he does not quite understand what the client is trying to express, he should be tentative in his responses and give the client room to move. He will then feel free to correct the counselor or give him a clearer picture of what he means.

> *Counselor:* You seem to be saying that your students don't trust you because your emotions change so much from day to day. Is it something like that?
> *Client:* That's partly it. But I also think that the mood of the class changes from day to day, so there are many days when my emotions and theirs just don't seem to mix.

This client feels that he has room to move. The counselor's tentative response helps him clarify what he means. Brammer (1973) calls this process of checking with the client whenever you are confused or unsure "perception checking" [p. 86].

Parroting. Accurate empathy is not parroting. The mechanical helper corrupts primary-level accurate empathy by simply restating what the client has said.

> *Client:* I feel pretty low because all my children have left home, and now I'm lonely, with nothing to do.
> *Counselor:* You feel low because the children are gone, you're all alone, and you have nothing to do.

The high-level counselor is always looking for the core of what is being expressed by the client, and he becomes expert in ferreting out this core and communicating it to the client. The good response gets at the essence of (the "meat," that which gives meaning and potential direction to) what the client has expressed. It is not just a paraphrase or a repetition. The high-level counselor tries to communicate *understanding* rather than just regurgitate what the client has said. Only then can the client move more deeply into exploring himself.

Client rambling. As a general rule, the client should not be allowed simply to ramble. Rambling destroys the concreteness, the focus, and the intensity of the helping experience. Furthermore, if the helper punctuates the client's ramblings with nods, "uh-huhs," and the like, he merely reinforces the rambling. Monologues on the part of either helper or client are not ordinarily helpful. Therefore, the counselor should respond relatively frequently to the client, without interrupting what is important or making the client lose his train of thought. Frequent use of accurate empathy gives a great deal of direction to the counseling process. While it is true that the client should explore those issues that have greatest relevance for him (this is another way of saying that the client's *needs* determine the direction of counseling), still, the high-level helper will be quickly in touch with these needs (often more quickly than the client) and thus be in a position to help him get in touch with these needs.

Note that the skillful use of even primary-level accurate empathy is in itself an expression of two dimensions of the social-influence process: (1) *establishing a base of influence:* the power of the helper is increased because he is seen as more and more understanding and trustworthy; and (2) *the use of influence:* the helper responds frequently but selectively to what the client has to say. This selectivity makes the interaction more focused and concrete and therefore more directional.

Obviously, there are times when the client will speak at greater length—for instance, in the beginning, when he pours out his story for the first time. If this seems best, the counselor should attend to him as well as possible, both physically and psychologically. He should also be asking himself what seem to be the important themes—both feeling and behavioral—in what the client is saying. At the end, however, it is impossible for the helper to respond all at once with accurate empathy to everything the client has said. He needs, therefore, some way of getting back to the most salient issues and exploring them further. Some of the following expressions can be used at the end of a long monologue on the part of the client.

> *Counselor:* This whole thing has really hit you hard. Let's see if we can't get at it bit by bit.
> *Counselor:* There's a lot of pain and confusion in what you've just told me. Let's see if I have understood what you've said.
> *Counselor:* You've said quite a bit. Let's see if we can zero in on what's upsetting you.

While the client is speaking, the counselor can keep asking himself such questions as: What is really bothering this person? What is he trying to communicate to me? What is blocking him? In what ways is he grappling with life ineffectively? The high-level counselor will focus on the feelings and behavior that have the deepest meaning for the client. If these are not clear, the counselor must go back over the ground covered, bit by bit, until the real issues surface.

Getting ahead of oneself. The counselor can retard the process by getting ahead of himself, moving on too quickly to Stages II and III before doing the work of Stage I adequately. For instance, he introduces advanced-level accurate empathy too soon (thus confusing or threatening the client), confronts without laying down a base of understanding and rapport, or gives advice (premature Stage-III directionality). These premature responses sometimes indicate a lack of respect for the client ("I want to move ahead at a pace that pleases me, not one that is good for him"). Helping, even though it is directed by the helper as the person who is living more effectively, is always *for* the helpee.

Dawdling in Stage I.   On the other hand, the counselor might feel very comfortable in Stage I and tend to remain there. He constantly encourages the client to explore himself further and further until his self-exploration becomes so rarified as to be meaningless. It no longer contributes substantially to the problem-solving stage of the counseling process. Here, helping degenerates into a game that might be termed "insight hunting." Insight into one's feelings and behavior certainly plays an important part in the helping process, but it should never be allowed to become an end in itself.

Empathy of tone and manner.   If a client speaks animatedly with the helper, telling him of her elation over various successes in her life, and he replies in a flat, dull voice, his response is not fully empathic—even though what he says might well be accurate in identifying her feelings and the experiences underlying these feelings.

> *Client:* This week I tried to be more understanding with my son. Instead of yelling at him when he did something wrong, I tried to focus on other kinds of interaction with him. When he talked, I just tried to understand what he was saying and let him know that I did. You know, it worked! I don't mean that it was a technique and that I was phony. I was just with him in a different way!
> *Counselor:* This was a new and very rewarding experience. And all from trying to be with him in a simple, understanding way.

The counselor's response is fine on paper, but if he delivers it with little enthusiasm, he is not really being "with" his client.

Jumping in too quickly.   The beginner often jumps in too quickly when the client pauses, "too quickly" because he has not yet formulated his response. He can give himself time, especially if the time is seen as caring about what he is going to say. Overeagerness does seem awkward. Most beginners have to practice waiting when the client pauses. During the pause, the helper asks himself: What are the feelings here? What are the real issues? This does not mean that the counselor should lose his spontaneity. He should speak up any time he thinks he can help the client, even if he has to interrupt him. A spontaneous interruption can be a very helpful intervention. The high-level helper interrupts or pauses in a non-self-conscious way. He is so "with" the client that he does not have to ask himself whether he should speak or remain quiet.

Language.   The helper is most effective when his language is in tune with the language of the client. Consider the following example.

> *Ten-year-old client:* My teacher thinks I'm crazy. She started to do that right from the first day of class. I don't fool around any more than anyone else in class, but she gets me anytime I do. I think she's picking on me because she doesn't like me. She doesn't yell at Bill Smith and he acts funnier than I do.
> *Counselor:* You're perplexed. You wonder why she singles you out for so much discipline.

The counselor's response is accurate in a sense, but it is not the kind of language that communicates understanding to a 10-year-old. The following response would have much more meaning for the child:

> *Counselor:* You're mad because she picks on you and doesn't seem to like you much at all.

The helper's choice of words reflects his ability to assume the client's frame of reference.

The beginner often finds himself using stilted language and over-used formulas in responding to the client. For instance:

> *Counselor:* You feel sad because your friend won't talk to you.

In practice sessions, such formulas as "you feel ... because ..." are useful, for they remind the trainee to focus on both the feelings and the underlying experience of the client. After a while, however, they lose their usefulness because they simply are *not* the helper; that is, he does not usually talk that way and sounds stilted when he does so.

> *Counselor:* You're really lonely. She was the only friend you had.

This gets at the core of the client's feelings and experience in a way that is more human than the "you feel ... because ..." response. As the trainee grows more skilled and more comfortable with the counseling situation, he will find himself more capable of using language that is both "his" and in tune with the language of the client. One more caution. He should not adopt a language with which he is not comfortable just to be on the client's "wavelength."

Counselor: Unless you find some bread, man, that cat's going to leave you dead.

If the counselor is a white middle-class person who ordinarily does not talk like this, he will probably sound ludicrous. He can use informal language without adopting every bit of argot he runs across.

Longwindedness.   Longwindedness is another pitfall the beginner should avoid. The helper's responses should be relatively frequent but also lean and trim. In trying to be accurate, the beginner may become longwinded, sometimes speaking *longer* than the client in trying to elaborate an interchangeable response. This often happens when he tries to respond too quickly. He realizes that his first few sentences have not hit the mark, so he keeps on talking in hopes of eventually hitting it.

Client: I have never been very spontaneous in social situations. Since I'm shy, I kind of stand off to the side, at least figuratively, and wait to see how I can get into the conversation. As a result, the conversation often passes me by by the time I'm ready to say something. Then I'm not even at the same place in the conversation as the others. I've been inside myself and don't know what's been going on.

Counselor (jumping in right away): You're really shy and that cuts down on your spontaneity. It shows up especially when a group is standing around talking. You are listening all right: you know what people are saying. But then you begin to ask yourself, "What should I say? I shouldn't stand around here dumb." But by the time you think of what to say, it's just too late. No, it's worse than that. Now you've lost the thread of the conversation and it's twice as hard trying to get back in. Your shyness backfires on you in more than one way.

However accurate this response might be, it is certainly not facilitative. It places the focus on the counselor's attempts to understand rather than on the client's self-exploration. The result is that the client is smothered by all that the helper has to say, becomes lost and confused, and finds it difficult to move forward. If the helper continually asks himself "What is the core of what this person is saying to me?" he can make his responses short, concrete, and accurate.

Indigenous helpers.   If accurate empathy is important, it is important for a client to choose a helper who is likely to understand him. A counselor who shares the client's socioeconomic, educational, and other background variables is likely to understand the client more thoroughly than a helper who is quite distant from the client on these variables. Therefore, if a client has a choice of two high-level helpers, he would do best, generally, to choose the helper whose situation is closest to his. Someone in the army would do better with a high-level army helper. A nun would probably do better with a high-level helper who has the religious background to understand her environment. High-level helpers who have little in common with certain populations would do better to train counselors indigenous to these populations rather than try to counsel them themselves. For instance, high-level counselors might train ex-addicts, reformed alcoholics, ex-prisoners, men and women from religious orders, army personnel, and ghetto residents to become counselors to clients in these situations (Mezz & Calia, 1972; Weitz, 1972).

Responding to feelings or content. In the examples given so far illustrating the *right* thing to do, the counselor responded to both feelings and content each time. Ordinarily, this is the best kind of response. However, at any given time, one or the other might be more important. For example:

> *Client:* This week I tried to get my mother to see the doctor, but she refused, even though she has fainted a couple of times. The kids had no school, so they were underfoot almost constantly. I haven't been able to finish a term paper for a class in English literature. And I don't have much energy today to talk to you.
> *Counselor:* It's been a lousy week.

Here the counselor chooses to respond only to the feelings of the client because he believes that what is uppermost in her consciousness is that all these things have contributed to her present feelings of frustration and irritation. The emphasis with another client might be quite different:

> *Client:* My dad yelled at me all the time last year about my hair. But just last week I heard him telling someone how nice I looked, hair and all. He yells at my sister about the same things he ignores when my younger brother does them. Sometimes he's really nice with my mother and other times he's just awful—demanding, grouchy, sarcastic.
> *Counselor:* He seems pretty inconsistent to you, doesn't he?

In this response the counselor focuses on the content, for he feels that this is the client's message. The point of these two examples is that the counselor should use any kind of accurately empathic response that will help the client explore himself more thoroughly. The principal question is still "What is the *core* of the client's remarks?"

If the client is easily threatened by discussion of his feelings, Hackney and Nye (1973) suggest that, in responding, the helper start by emphasizing content and proceed only gradually to deal with feelings. This plan constitutes a process of desensitization for the client. Furthermore, the authors suggest that one tentative way of getting at the client's feelings is to have the helper say what he might feel in similar circumstances.

> *Client:* My mother is always trying to make a little kid out of me. And I'm in my mid-thirties! Last week, in front of a group of my friends, she brought out my rubber boots and an umbrella and gave me a little talk on how to dress for bad weather.
> *Counselor:* If she had treated me that way, I think I would've been pretty angry.

The goal of Stage I is to help the client explore himself and his problems. Sometimes the helper will achieve this goal more quickly if, in the beginning, he moves slowly.

Questions.   Low-level counselors ask too many questions and try to substitute questions for accurate empathy in their efforts to get the client to explore himself. Often their questions are closed rather than open-ended.

> *Closed question:* Are you having problems with your wife?
> *Open question:* In what ways does your wife irritate you?

Closed questions can be answered laconically with "yes" or "no." Since these answers do not help, the counselor tries again, often asking a different closed question. Sometimes questions are not questions but are disguised statements.

> *Counselor:* Did you get angry when your husband ignored you?

The counselor probably means to say: "You got angry when your husband ignored you." The question can be answered with "yes" or "no," while the statement, especially if it is an example of accurate empathy, calls for further self-exploration.

A question is one kind of probe. Probes are quite useful in a helping model based in part on social-influence theory; they add to the directionality of the process and place legitimate demands for concreteness on the client. But care should be used in asking questions. If the question is a good, open-ended one, it should yield information that needs to be understood by means of accurate empathy. Questions that merely pile up information that is neither understood nor used are counterproductive. Information is not an end in itself. Once the client is prompted to talk through the influence of the helper, he deserves to be understood.

Summary rules for the use of primary-level accurate empathy

1. Attend carefully, both physically and psychologically, to the messages transmitted by the client.
2. Listen especially for basic or core messages.
3. Respond fairly frequently, but briefly, to these core messages, but be flexible and tentative enough so that the client has room to move (to affirm, deny, explain, clarify, or shift emphasis).
4. Be gentle, but don't let the client run from important issues.
5. Respond to both feeling and content unless there is some reason for emphasizing one or the other.
6. Move gradually toward the exploration of critical topics and feelings.
7. After you have responded, attend carefully to cues that either confirm or deny the accuracy of your response. Does the client move forward in a focused way?
8. Note signs of client stress or resistance and try to judge whether these arise because you have lacked accuracy or have been too accurate.

Requiem for accurate empathy?

Gendlin and Rychlak (1970) claim that behavioral-oriented engineers can manipulate clients to health and happiness without "tender interpersonal relations" such as empathy and genuineness and that, since such behavior modification programs are successful, graduate training in empathy is not really needed. London (1972) believes such "ideological" statements useless and urges a pluralistic *technology* in the helping professions. I find at least two problems with the statement of Gendlin and Rychlak. One is a question of value, the other of fact. First, I find no value, generally, in the manipulation of others. More positively, I do find value in taking time and effort to enter another person's life and to try to understand him. If there is a choice, I prefer not to manipulate people into anything, even health and happiness. Second, no one who has been either a counselor or a client in a high-level helping process would term primary-level accurate empathy, advanced accurate empathy, or the various forms of genuineness as particularly "tender." To portray these dimensions of the helping process as "soft" is to miss the intensity, and often the pain, of the helping process. Furthermore, if "health" includes healthy interpersonal relationships, I would hate to live in a society that downgraded the value of accurate empathy and genuineness. Pity the society that sees understanding and genuineness as expendable luxuries. Accurate empathy and genuineness are skills, tough to master, and strong in their impact.

Some people are involved in a controversy over the very existence of accurate empathy and, if it does exist, over whether it (almost in and of itself) "cures" or not (Chinsky & Rappaport, 1970; Rappaport & Chinsky, 1972; Truax, 1972). For our purpose, accurate empathy is what is described in this chapter and the next. No claim is made that it "cures." Claims *are* made that it is effective in helping the client explore his feelings, attitudes, experience, and behavior and come to a better understanding of himself. Another way of stating this is that high-level use of accurate empathy (and the other skills of Stage I) *increases the probability* that the client will explore himself and the problematic in his life in a more concrete, focused, and directional way. Whether these claims are justified or not the reader will have to decide for himself—partially by reading the somewhat scanty research literature on empathy but most of all by experiencing the effects of accurate empathy in the helping process itself. In the area of accurate empathy, clinical evidence is still the strongest.

Genuineness: A behavioral approach

Genuineness, as it is discussed here, refers not to a moral or metaphysical property or quality but to a set of counselor behaviors essential to a high-level helping process. Accordingly, a trainee can *learn* to be genuine. To do so, he needs, first of all, a behavioral understanding of what it means to be genuine. The moral quality of being genuine is important—it is assumed here that it is a human value that should be pursued—but these pages deal more with genuineness as part of a communication process. In helping relationships, it does little good to *be* genuine if this genuineness is not translated into behavior.

Rogers and Truax (1967) describe genuineness under the rubric "congruence" and relate it to therapy:

> In relation to therapy, [congruence] means that the therapist is what he *is*, during the encounter with the client. He is without front or facade, openly being the feelings and attitudes which at the moment are flowing in him. It involves the element of self-awareness, meaning that the feelings the therapist is experiencing are available to him, available to his awareness, and also that he is able to live these feelings, to be them in the relationship, and able to communicate them if appropriate. It means that he comes into a direct personal encounter with his client, meeting him on a person-to-person basis. It means that he is *being* himself, not denying himself [p. 101].

The genuine person is one who, in his interactions, is basically himself. He is at home with being himself and therefore can comfortably be himself in all his interactions. This means that he does not change when he is with different people; that is, he does not constantly have to adopt new roles in order to be acceptable to others.

The behaviors that constitute genuineness

Being genuine has both positive and negative implications; it means doing some things and not doing others.

Professional role.   The genuine helper does not take refuge in the role of counselor. Relating deeply to others and helping are part of his lifestyle, not roles he puts on or takes off at will. Counseling at its best is role-free. What about all this talk, then, of counseling and psychotherapy as a "profession"? Doesn't "profession" imply "role"? Carkhuff (1971) makes a distinction between "credentialed" and "functional" professionals. Credentialed professionals are those who have degrees and certificates indicating that they have successfully completed a variety of training programs and on whom the sponsoring agency, often a university, is willing to put some kind of stamp of approval—often a degree. Functional professionals, on the other hand, are those who possess the skills discussed in this book. Functional professionals may or may not be credentialed; credentialed professionals may or may not be functional. Since the skills described in this book are also the skills needed for high-level interpersonal living, it does seem somewhat odd to call someone who possesses them a "professional."

Gibb (1968) maintains that counseling should be role-free and that counselor trainees should go through an experiential training program in which they can learn to become role-free. What does he mean? He says that the trainee should learn how to

> express directly to another whatever he is presently experiencing,
> communicate without distorting his messages,
> listen to others without distorting their messages,
> reveal his true motivation in the process of communicating his message,
> be spontaneous and free in his communications with others rather than use habitual or planned strategies,
> respond immediately to another's need or state instead of waiting for the "right" time or giving himself enough time to come up with the "right" response,
> manifest his vulnerabilities and, in general, the "stuff" of his inner life,
> live in and communicate about the here-and-now,

strive for interdependence rather than dependence or counterdepen-
dence in his relationships with others,
learn how to enjoy psychological closeness,
be concrete in his communications, and
be willing to commit himself to others.

What Gibb espouses in no way makes the counselor the kind of "free
spirit" who inflicts himself on others. Indeed, "free spirit" helpers can
even be dangerous (Lieberman, Yalom, & Miles, 1973, pp. 226–267).
Being role-free is not license; freedom from role means that the counselor should not use the role or facade of counselor to protect himself,
to substitute for effectiveness, or to fool the client.

Spontaneity.   The genuine person is spontaneous. Many of the behaviors suggested by Gibb are ways of being spontaneous. The high-
level helper, while being tactful (as part of his respect for others), is not
constantly weighing what he says. He does not put a number of filters
between his inner life and what he expresses to others. He is assertive
in the helping process without being aggressive. I find that one of the
cardinal problems with trainees is that they are afraid to assert themselves. Some want to settle for a caricature of "nondirective counseling"
because this is what they are most comfortable with. Since they do not
move out and meet others spontaneously in their day-to-day lives, to
do so in counseling seems foreign to them. Many trainees need a kind
of assertiveness training to teach them experientially that it is all right
to be active, spontaneous, free, and assertive.

The spontaneous person is free but not impulsive. If he weighs what
he says, he does so out of concern for the client and not for his own
protection. He is not constantly looking for rules to guide him in his
relationship with his client. He is like a basketball player. He does learn
some basic rules but, more importantly, he learns basic skills. The basketball player who has laboriously learned a number of moves uses
them whenever they are called for. In the same way, the high-level
counselor has many responses in his repertory. His ability to call on a
wide variety of responses allows him to be spontaneous.

Nondefensiveness.   The genuine person is nondefensive. He has a
feeling for his areas of strength and his areas of deficit in living and
presumably is trying to live more effectively all the time. When a client
expresses negative attitudes toward him, he tries to understand what
the client is thinking and feeling, and he continues to work with him.
Take the following example.

Client: I don't think I'm really getting anything out of these sessions at all. Things are going just as poorly in school. Why should I waste my time coming here?

Counselor A: I think you are the one wasting the time. You just don't want to do anything.
Counselor B: That's your decision.
Counselor C: There's been no payoff for you here. It seems like a lot of dreary work with no results.

Counselors A and B are both defensive. Counselor C tries to understand and gives the client the opportunity to get at the issue of responsibility in the helping process. The genuine person is at home with himself (though not in a smug way) enough that he can allow himself to examine negative criticism honestly. Counselor C, for instance, would be the most likely of the three to ask himself whether he is contributing to the stalemate that seems to exist. The person who is always defending himself lest he be hurt cannot help others effectively. Trainees who feel this way have to work out their fears and misgivings before trying to help others.

Consistency. The genuine person has few discrepancies. For instance, he does not have one set of "notional" values (such as justice, love, peace) different from his "real" values (influence, money, comfort). He does not think or feel one thing but say another. At the same time, he does not dump his thoughts and feelings on others without discretion.

Client: I want to know what you really think of me.

Counselor A: I think you're lazy and that you would like things to get better if that could happen by magic.
Counselor B: Frankly, I don't find a great deal of value in such direct evaluations, but I think it's good to talk about this directly. Maybe we can take a look at what's happening between you and me.

Counselor A is literal-minded and blunt. Counselor B sees the client's petition as a desire for greater immediacy. He knows that direct, solid feedback is important, but he prefers that it take place in a human way. Low-level counselors go to extremes: they are blunt or timid. Both behaviors are usually rationalized: the former as "frankness," the latter as "tact." Tact springs from strength, not weakness. The high-level helper knows when he is tempted to hold something back for his own sake (for example, because he fears the reaction of the client) and when he is doing it for the client's sake (the client is not yet ready to hear it

—although he will have to hear it eventually, either from himself or from the counselor). The phony is filled with discrepancies: he feels things but does not express his feelings, he thinks things but does not say them, he says one thing and does another. The phony person is inconsistent.

Self-sharing. The genuine person is capable of deep self-disclosure. Self-disclosure is not an end in itself for him, but he feels free to reveal himself intimately when it is appropriate. Since genuineness as self-disclosure is part of Stage II, it will be dealt with in greater detail in the next chapter. Genuineness also expresses itself in two other Stage-II behaviors, immediacy and confrontation. These, too, will be treated in the next chapter.

Respect: A behavioral approach

Respect, like genuineness, can be considered a moral quality. However, we are interested in the kinds of behaviors that are generated by respect. Mayeroff (1971) has said that "caring is more than good intentions and warm regards" (p. 69). The same can be said of respect. When someone is interacting with you, how do you know he respects you? What are the behaviors that indicate respect? How is respect expressed in a counseling situation? These are some of the questions we will attempt to answer. Respect is expressed differently at different stages of the model. In this chapter we are interested in both a general overview of respect and the kinds of respect behaviors that are proportioned to Stage I of the model.

Toward a definition of respect

Respect is such a fundamental notion that, like most fundamental notions, it eludes definition. The word comes from a Latin root that includes the notion of "seeing" or "viewing." Indeed, respect is a particular way of viewing another person. Respect means prizing another person simply because he is a human being. It implies that being a human being has value in itself. Choosing to prize others simply because of their humanity is also a value. It is difficult to see how anyone could commit himself to helping others unless this is a value for him. But a value is a value only to the degree that it is translated into some kind of action. I ask you, "Is reading a value for you?" You say "Yes." Then I ask, "How much do you read, and what kind of books?" You say, "Well, while I see reading as valuable, I don't find much time to read. I'm too busy at work and at home. In fact, I haven't read a book this year." Reading is *not* a value for you if you do not find the time to read. Rather, seeing-reading-as-valuable is an attitude of yours. You have a favorable opinion of reading. You believe that you (and perhaps others) should read if they get the opportunity. On the other hand, reading *is* a value for the man who actually reads. He finds the time or makes the time because reading is one of his priorities. Respect, as it is discussed here, works the same way. It is not just an attitude, not just a way of viewing human beings. Respect is a value—that is, an attitude expressed behaviorally. Some values induce men to act, while others make them refrain from acting. That is, values can be active or passive. For instance, suppose that justice is a value for me. If it is a *passive* value, I do nothing to cause injustice to others. If it is an *active* value, I *do* things to see to it that justice is promoted: I am active in various civil-rights movements, I fight for more equitable tax laws, and so on. Some values, then, merely set limits on our behavior, while others galvanize us into action. Respect, I assume, is an active value for the helper. Even better, it is both active and passive: it sets certain limits for the helper in his interactions with the client, and it also stimulates him to act toward the client in certain ways.

Verbal expression of respect

In helping situations, respect is not often communicated directly in words. In the case of respect, actions literally speak louder than words. For instance, the helper seldom, if ever, says "I respect you because you are a human being," "I prize you," or "I respect you for engaging in self-exploration. You are doing a good thing." Respect is communicated principally by the way the helper *orients himself toward* and *works with* the client. "Orientation toward" and "working with" tend to merge into each other in practice, but we will look at them separately in order to get a better look at the anatomy of respect.

Orientation toward the client

In a sense, "orientation toward" comprises the attitudes that must be translated into concrete behaviors if respect is to be truly a value.

Being "for" the client. The counselor's manner indicates that he is "for" the client simply because the client is human. This is not a tender or sentimental attitude. The helper is a *caring* person in a down-to-earth, nonsentimental sense. Respect ultimately involves placing demands on the client. This being "for," then, refers to the client's basic humanity *and* to his potential to be *more* human than he is right now. Respect is both gracious and tough-minded.

Willingness to work with the client.   The helper is available to the client. He feels that he can commit himself to the client. The helper's willingness is meaningless, of course, unless he has the resources necessary to help the client. For the high-level helper, helping is a value and not just a job. Since it is a value, he is available to the client in a way in which the low-level helper is not. A low-level helper might say "This is my job." The high-level helper will say "This is worth the investment of my time and energy." Since counseling is a great deal of work, done by someone with a great deal of skill, such a statement is hardly sentimental.

Regard for the client as unique.   The individuality of others is also a value for the helper. He is committed to supporting the client in his uniqueness and to helping develop the resources that make him unique. Although he is committed to helping the client change, this does not mean that the helper is determined to make the client over in his own image and likeness.

Regard for the client's self-determination.   The helper's basic attitude is that the client does have the resources to help him live more effectively. These resources may be blocked in a variety of ways, or they may be just lying fallow. The counselor's job is to help the client free his resources or cultivate them. He expects the client to be self-determining, but in ways that enhance his humanity. He can also help the client realistically assess his resources so that the client's aspirations are realistic. Ultimately, if the client chooses to live less effectively than he can, the counselor obviously should respect his choice.

Assuming the client's good will.   The helper acts on the assumption that the client wants to work at living more effectively; that is, he wants to rid himself of behavior that is destructive of self and others and to channel his efforts into constructive behavioral change. He works on this assumption until it is demonstrated false (that is, until he finds that the client is playing at counseling, is not committed to change at all, or stays with the counselor only because he is under pressure from others). Even in such cases, the helper does not readily come to the conclusion that the client is choosing not to grow. He first asks himself whether he has contributed in any way to the failure of the counseling relationship. Too many counselors abandon clients because they are not "motivated." This judgment may help the ego of the counselor, but it is not necessarily a valid picture of the client's attitude.

Working with the client

The attitudes described above must be translated into action in order to be useful in the counseling process. How are these attitudes manifested behaviorally?

Attending.   Attending is itself a way of showing respect. It says, behaviorally, "I am with you. I am committed to your interests. I am available to help you live more effectively. It is worth my time and effort to help you." Failure to attend generally indicates a lack of respect for the client. It says, "You are not worth my time. What you say is not worth listening to. I am not really committed to working for your interests."

Suspending critical judgment.   In Stage I, respect takes the form of suspending critical judgment of the client. Rogers (1961, 1967), following Standal (1954), calls this kind of respect "unconditional positive regard," meaning that "the therapist communicates to his client a deep and genuine caring for him as a person with potentialities, a caring uncontaminated by evaluations of his thoughts, feelings, or behaviors" (Rogers, 1967, p. 102). Consider the differences in the following counselors' remarks.

> *Client:* I am really sexually promiscuous. I give into sexual tendencies whenever they arise and whenever I can find a partner. This has been the story for the past three years at least.

> *Counselor A:* Immature sex hasn't been the answer, has it? Ultimately it is just another way of making yourself miserable.
> *Counselor B:* So, letting yourself go sexually is part of the picture also.

Counselor B neither judges nor condones. He merely tries to communicate understanding to the client (understanding is obviously not synonymous with approval) so that both counselor and client can begin to see the context of the client's behavior; he knows that the client's approach to life needs to be understood. The helper is not naïve. He realizes that some of the client's experiences must be transcended and that some of his behaviors must change, but he still respects the client as the subject of these experiences. He gives the client room to move, room to explore himself. His function in Stage I is to help the client explore both his behavior and the values from which this behavior springs, and he realizes that judgmental behavior on his part would cut such exploration short.

Respect, even at Stage I, is not completely unconditional. Respect includes regard for the resources of the client. At Stage I it means regard for the client's ability to give himself to the process of self-exploration. The client might well find this process painful, and the counselor can help him through his pain; but respect also includes an assumption on the part of the counselor that the client, even at Stage I, will pay the price necessary in order to begin to live more effectively. Respect, then, places a demand on the client at the same time that it offers him the help he needs to fulfill the demand. For instance, let's assume that the client has been manifesting a great deal of resistance. He talks about superficial issues or issues that are serious but unrelated to the real problematic; he changes the subject when the helper's responses bring him face to face with more crucial issues.

> *Counselor:* I think we both realize that the most important issues have not yet been brought up in our conversation. You come close to discussing important problems, but then you draw back. I realize that exploring yourself and putting all the cards on the table can be extremely painful. Putting the cards on the table is like writing a blank check. You don't know how high a figure is going to be written in.

This counselor is both understanding and gently demanding. Effective helping is for the helpee, but it is directed by the helper.

Accurate empathy. In Stage I, the best way of showing respect is by working to understand the client: his feelings, his experience, his behavior. The communication of accurate empathy is the real work of Stage I, work that requires skill and patience. I know a person respects me if he expends time and energy in trying to understand me. All the behaviors associated with the communication of accurate empathy, therefore, are behaviors indicating respect.

Cultivating the resources of the client. Cultivation of the client's resources follows from the helper's attitude toward the uniqueness, the individuality, of the client. He looks for resources in the client and helps him identify them. He does not act for the client unless it is absolutely necessary and then only as a step toward helping the client act on his own. Consider the following example.

> *Client:* There are a lot of things I find really hard to talk about. I would rather have you ask me questions. That would be easier for me.

Counselor A: Okay. You mentioned that you got in trouble in school. What kind of trouble was it? How did it all start?

Counselor B: If I ask a lot of questions, I'm afraid that I'd get a lot of information that I might think important, but I'm not convinced that it would be important for you. Putting yourself on the line like this is really new to you, and you're finding it quite painful.

Counselor B assumes that the client does have, somewhere, the resources necessary to engage in self-exploration. He expresses his own feelings and tries to understand the client's blocking. He is willing to help the client work through his pain in order to get at the resources that the client might actually possess (that is, his ability to give direction to the self-exploration process).

Warmth. Gazda (1973) sees warmth as the physical expression of understanding and caring, which is ordinarily communicated through nonverbal media such as gestures, posture, tone of voice, touch, and facial expression. Warmth is only one way of showing respect. It is not the best way, and it can easily be misused. The helper should be initially warm, but he should not show either role warmth (standard counselor warmth) or the warmth he would accord a good friend. The client is simply not a good friend. Too many counselors become warmth machines, cranking out unconditional positive regard continuously. Such warmth degenerates quickly into an "oh-that's-all-right" kind of response that is both phony and unhelpful.

Client: I'm too easy with myself. As you can see, I've let myself go physically. I'm soft and fat. I don't read any more. And now I find myself fighting with people at work.

Counselor A: First of all, Bill, most men your age let themselves go a little. And you don't look so bad to me. Don't be harder on yourself than you should be.

Counselor B: Things aren't right physically, intellectually, or interpersonally—and you don't like it.

Counselor A translates warmth into not being too hard on the client; he even goes so far as to suggest that the client lower his standards. Counselor B expresses his accurate empathy in a sincere and appropriately warm way.

Reinforcement as respect. A helper shows respect when he reinforces all constructive action on the part of the client—when the client works at self-exploration or when he takes a tentative step in the direction of constructive behavioral change. Respect is also shown by refusing to reinforce self-destructive behavior on the part of the client.

> *Client:* I have some bad news to report. I talked about being hooked on alcohol, but I got drunk twice this week.
>
> *Counselor A:* Don't feel so bad. You can't expect to change your way of living all at once.
> *Counselor B:* You feel you let yourself down a little. And perhaps you also learned that you're not going to kick the habit just by admitting it.

Counselor A might well have reinforced the client's self-defeating behavior. Counselor B tries to pick up the client's feelings; he is not judgmental, but neither does he condone the client's behavior in any way. The client does not condone his *own* behavior, so why should the counselor?

> *Client:* I didn't have a drink all week. This is the first time this has happened since I can remember.
>
> *Counselor A:* Okay. Let's see if you can repeat that this coming week.
> *Counselor B:* Hey, this is something new, and it makes you feel good about yourself!

Counselor B communicates understanding in a positive way that reinforces what the client has done.

Genuineness as respect.   Being genuine in one's relationship with another is a way of showing him respect. Therefore, the behaviors listed under "genuineness" in the previous section also constitute ways of showing respect.

Concreteness

Self-exploration is not a goal in itself but a means to an end—*action,* action that leads to more effective living on the part of the client. Self-exploration is useful in problem-solving and action programs can be based on it. Therefore, self-exploration must be concrete. Unless problems are discussed in concrete, operational terms, it is difficult, if not impossible, to solve them. Vague solutions to vague problems never lead to effective action.

> *Problem:* The client is having difficulties in interpersonal relationships.
> *Solution:* The client should be more open to different kinds of people.

When problem and solution appear as stark as this on paper, it is obvious that neither the problem nor the solution is concrete enough and that effective action is not likely to originate from such statements. Yet the same kind of vagueness exists in many counseling situations. One of the reasons many counselors never get to Stage III or do poorly in that stage is that they have never helped the client to be concrete in the exploration of the problematic dimensions of his life.

The logic of the counseling process applies to concreteness: if the counselor is as concrete as possible in his responses to the client, the client will learn to be concrete in the exploration of his behavior. This ability will serve as the basis of his becoming more concrete in his interactions with others outside the counseling situation.

I have used the following exercise to make members of training groups aware of what it means to be concrete in discussing one's own behavior. I ask the participants to think of some personally relevant concern that they would be willing to discuss in the training sessions. I ask the trainees first to state this concern very vaguely. One student says:

> *Trainee A:* Sometimes I feel funny about myself.

This is certainly vague enough. He talks about his feelings about himself, but only in the vaguest of terms. Next, I ask the trainees to make their statements concrete.

> *Trainee A:* Sometimes, when I'm studying alone at home at night, I begin to feel quite lonely. I know the feeling is going to pass, but it makes me restless.

This statement is infinitely more concrete than the laconic "Sometimes I feel funny about myself." Why? It deals with specific feelings (loneliness and restlessness) and a specific experience (studying at home at night). Finally, I ask the trainees to make their statements as concrete as they can (still without revealing anything they would prefer not to discuss in the training session).

> *Trainee A:* Sometimes, when I'm home alone at night studying, I begin to feel quite lonely. I even begin to think that I don't have any friends— even though I know this isn't the case. I get to feeling sorry for myself. Finally, it gets to me so much that I get up and go out to a nearby tavern, not to drink my sorrows away but just to be with people.

This statement is excellent in its concreteness. The feelings are specific (loneliness, self-pity), the situation itself is concrete (home alone at night studying), and the behavioral reaction is concrete (going to the tavern to be with people). Self-exploration is most concrete if it is concrete in all these ways.

Concreteness in counseling interactions

The client is being concrete in his self-exploration when he identifies specific feelings, behaviors, and experiences or situations that are relevant to his problems—that is, the areas of his life in which he is living less than effectively.

> *Client:* I feel disappointed in myself *(specific feeling)* because when my boss yelled at me without real reason *(specific experience or situation)*, I just stood there and looked at my shoe tops sheepishly. *(specific behavior or reaction)*

Let's say that this client has difficulty being assertive in interpersonal situations. His statement, then, fulfills both conditions described above: he deals with specific feelings, experiences, and behaviors that are related to one of his problems in living. A client can be concrete or vague in any particular area.

> *Vague:* I don't feel right. *(vague feeling)*
> *Concrete:* I'm scared, very scared. My palms are sweating and my heart is thumping. *(concrete feeling)*
>
> *Vague:* My boss doesn't treat me right. *(vague experience)*
> *Concrete:* The foreman doesn't like me. He gives me the dirtiest jobs, complains even when I do my work well, and, at times, makes fun of me in front of the other workers. *(concrete experience)*
>
> *Vague:* The job never seems to get done. *(vague behavior)*
> *Concrete:* I keep putting off writing my dissertation. I do almost anything to avoid it, even things I ordinarily hate to do. I work around the house, or take the kids to a show. I even do the laundry. Yet I know I have to have it done by fall or I'll lose my teaching job. *(concrete behavior)*

It is not enough that the client deal with concrete feelings, experiences, and behavior; these also must be related to the problematic in his life. Sometimes a client will speak very concretely about something that does not really bother him, but when the conversation turns to a more delicate area, an area of life he is not handling well, the vagueness begins. His vagueness becomes a clue pointing to a problem area.

> *Client:* My son and I could get along better. It's not the ideal father-son thing, but not many people have that, I guess, these days.

There is little information here. It sounds as if this area were not worth talking about. However, perhaps the client really means something like this:

> *Client:* My son and I fight constantly. There's practically no issue we agree on—from the length of his hair to where he should go to college. It's so bad lately that we sit in silence at the evening meal. He's as bad as I am now that the feud is in full swing, but I think that I must have gotten us started on this awful spiral.

Since this kind of concreteness can be painful, it is evident why some clients take refuge in generalities.

Counselor concreteness

The next question is: how can the counselor help the client be more concrete? First of all, the helper should try to be as concrete as possible in his responses, even when the client is vague.

> *Client:* I don't know. Things are just lousy. You know how things get sometimes. Nothing seems to go right. That's the way I feel right now anyway—kind of ready to throw in the towel.

> *Counselor A:* Uh-huh.
> *Counselor B:* You're pretty discouraged right now. A number of different things are going wrong for you.

Counselor B is concrete in that he identifies the client's feelings. He still does not know the experience underlying the client's discouragement, but the words he uses to respond ("a number of different things") are somewhat more concrete than the client's, and his remark is lean and to the point. His response, then, is a kind of invitation to the client to move on toward more specific self-exploration. An "uh-huh" is also a quasi-invitation, but it is much less concrete (and evinces very little accurate empathy). In the following example, the client, a high-school principal, has been discussing his relationship with one of his teachers.

> *Client:* You can't tell what other people are going to do at times—I mean, how they are going to react to you.

> *Counselor A:* People *are* sometimes unpredictable.
> *Counselor B:* Mrs. Johnson surprised you by talking directly to the superintendent.

This client uses some of the best methods for remaining vague: he uses "you" instead of "I" and therefore does not "own" the statement, he uses "people" instead of the name of the teacher, he does not directly name the emotion experienced, and he does not specify the action that surprised him. Counselor A not only reinforces this vagueness but puts the emphasis not on the client but on the teacher ("unpredictable"). In contrast, Counselor B's response eliminates all four kinds of vagueness.

A second way to achieve concreteness is not to allow the client to ramble. If the client engages in long storytelling, he inevitably includes a great deal of irrelevant matter. Some counselors suggest letting the client talk on for a variety of reasons: that it is cathartic or that the helper's listening to a long story is a way of showing respect. Others fear that, unless the client is "given his head," he will not get to the data that are most pertinent. Perhaps there is some truth in all of this, but I still think that counseling at its best includes a great deal of dialogue. If the counselor responds frequently, especially if his responses are lean and concrete, the client can achieve a degree of direction in the counseling process that is almost always lacking in long storytelling. The counselor who is willing to listen to long stories without interrupting the client might be showing respect, but he also may be doing the only thing he can do well—listening passively.

A third possibility is to ask the client directly for more specific information, especially information that clarifies vague statements. The questions asked, however, should be relatively infrequent, open-ended, and followed by responses of accurate empathy. Questions that yield the most concrete information are those that ask "what," "how," and "with what feeling" rather than "why": "What did you do that annoyed her?" "How did she get back at you?" "How did her leaving you make you feel?"

Questions of "why" do not always work so well. "Why did you two start fighting?" If the client really does not know exactly why, he will often make up an answer to satisfy the counselor.

> *Client:* Well, I don't know exactly. I don't think she ever got along well with her father. And her mother and I never really got along either. On the surface things seemed to be all right, but they never were.

The causes of things, especially the remote causes, are seldom evident. To ask the client to come up with such causes is often to whistle in the wind. Clients can talk endlessly about causes, but such talk usually does not produce the kind of insight that leads to effective action programs. Insight-seeking in counseling is *not* the same as self-exploration. The former deals with the causes of things and the reasons behind things, while the latter deals with feelings, experiences, actual situations, and behaviors. To know the cause of something (assuming that one can get to the real cause) does not necessarily induce a client to act on his knowledge.

> *Client:* I think I am the way I am with my husband mainly because of some of the things that happened when I was a child. My husband is a lot like my father was, and I did like my mother better.

Such talk is a bottomless pit. Clients can hypothesize forever on the causes of behavior that leads to ineffective living. Deutsch (1954) notes that it is often almost impossible, even in carefully controlled laboratory situations, to determine whether event B, which followed event A in time, is actually *caused* by event A. In no way does this fact mean that a person's past does not influence his present behavior.

> This is not to deny the significance of the past in indirectly affecting behavior. However, even though the past can create a certain condition which carries over into the present, it is, nevertheless, the *present* condition that is influential in the present. Strictly considered, linking behavior with a past event is an extremely difficult undertaking; it presupposes that one knows sufficiently how the past event affected the psychological field at that time, and whether or not in the meantime other events have again modified the field [Deutsch, 1954, p. 186].

Carl Rogers (1951) had already applied such thinking to the therapeutic situations:

> It should also be mentioned that in this concept of motivation all the effective elements exist in the present. Behavior is not "caused" by something which occurred in the past. Present tensions and present needs are the only ones which the organism endeavors to reduce or satisfy. While it is true that the past experience has served to modify the meaning which will be perceived in present experiences, yet there is no behavior except to meet a present need [p. 492].

Certain schools of psychotherapy, such as psychoanalysis, put a great deal of emphasis on in-depth investigations of the past. In our model, while the past need not be avoided, it should not be the focus. Investigations of the past simply do not yield the kind of material that is useful for problem-solving and action programs.

A concluding word on concreteness

Concreteness is extremely important in counseling. Without it, counseling loses that intensity or density that marshals the energies of the client and channels them into constructive action. Low-level helpers often prefer to have clients talk in generalities. They seem to think that mere talking is enough, whatever the focus. Concreteness means that the client must risk more in the counseling interactions, but little happens without risks and without facing the crises precipitated by reasonable risk-taking. If counseling sessions are boring, both counselor and client should ask themselves just how concrete the interactions are. Inevitably, in boring sessions, the level of concreteness is low. This is true in counseling and in human-relations-training sessions.

II. HELPING AS SOCIAL INFLUENCE: THE EXPERIENCE OF THE CLIENT

Up to this point I have discussed what the counselor must do in order to establish himself as an effective helper. The ultimate criterion of effective helper communication is how the client acts on this communication. If the messages of Stage I are skillfully formulated and sent by the counselor and if they are received as such by the client, they influence the client both attitudinally and behaviorally. The first set of attitudes influenced are those that deal with the client's perception of the helper. If, in Stage I, the client experiences the helper as a person who knows what he is doing, who has his interests at heart, and who helps him explore his world from the client's own frame of reference, the client is likely to be well disposed toward the helper and therefore open to his influence. In the developmental model, the first way the client usually is influenced behaviorally is in the area of self-exploration. The client's response to a helper whom he perceives to be working *for* him is to work *with* the helper in exploring the problematic areas of his own life.

This section will summarize the client's perception of the helping process in the language of social-influence theory.

The client's experience in terms of social influence

History, both ancient and recent, provides a great deal of evidence that people suffering from a variety of emotional disturbances and a variety of physical ailments of psychogenic origin have been "cured" by their belief in the curing powers of a helper. Very often such cures have taken place in religious contexts, but they have not been limited to such contexts. In the average case, people come to see a certain person as a healer with great powers. He may be a tribal shaman or a psychiatrist of great renown. People hear that he has cured others with ailments similar to theirs. In some cases these healers do not ask for fees (although it is true that some live quite well from donations from the grateful). In other cases the healers belong to professions of relatively unquestioned integrity (such as the medical profession). In either case, people see these healers acting not in their own interests but in the interests of the afflicted who come to them. This belief enables the afflicted person to place a great deal of trust in the healer. Finally, in a ceremony that is often public and highly emotional, the healer in some way touches the afflicted person and the person is "healed." The tremendous need of the afflicted person, the reputation of the healer, and the afflicted person's trusting belief in the healer all heighten the person's trusting belief that he will be cured. In fact, if he is not cured, it is often laid to his lack of belief or to some other evil within him (poor motivation, for instance), and he not only remains with his affliction but also loses face in the community. His second state is worse than the first: he is not only ill but also an outcast.

The dynamics of such a cure are hard to explain empirically. It is obvious that elements of the healing process as described marshal the emotional energies and resources of the afflicted person. He experiences hope and other positive emotions, which he perhaps has not experienced for a long time. The whole situation both mobilizes his resources and places a demand on him to be cured. It presents the afflicted person with a *kairos,* an opportune, acceptable, favorable, legitimate time to leave his old way of life behind and take up a new one. The power of suggestion in such cases is great and even overwhelming.

The high-level helper is aware of these processes and, expecially at the beginning stages of counseling, uses them to the client's advantage. While he ultimately hopes to help the client discover and develop his own inner and environmental resources, he uses the client's faith in him (which, if he is a good helper, is not misplaced) to help him control his anxiety and mobilize whatever resources he does have in order to engage actively in the helping process. The less control the client has over his life, the more influence the helper must exert. A fairly well-integrated client will be likely to collaborate with, rather than merely submit himself to, the helping process (but he is also least in need of help). A severely disturbed person will be initially capable of little collaboration and therefore will have to be influenced the most (for example, through behavior modification programs designed to develop the resources necessary for some minimal kind of collaboration).

This process is known scientifically as the theory of social influence. This theory states, in brief, that a disorganized and disturbed person, since he is in need of relief, is open to the influence of those he sees as able to help him. The person who comes for counseling is often a person who feels that he does not have the ability to control his own life or whose abilities are inadequate or too costly. Such a person is willing to place himself in some way under the social control of the counselor, under certain conditions. What are these conditions?

The afflicted person must see the prospective helper as *expert* (one who presumably has the tools or skills needed to help), as *trustworthy* (one who will act primarily in the interests of the helpee and not in his own), and as *attractive* (one who is in some sense compatible with the client and who behaves in a way that wins the approval of the client). Once the client perceives the helper as expert, trustworthy, and attractive, he allows him to enter his life and influence what he thinks and does in ways not permitted to others.

The counselor who uses a social-influence model is willing to enter the life of the client and influence what the client thinks and does for the good of the client. Indeed, he realizes that *all* counseling involves some degree of social influence. Therefore, in a social-influence process, the helper (1) works at establishing a power base or influence base with the client by establishing himself in the client's eyes as expert, trustworthy, and attractive and by involving the client in the helping process itself, and, once he has established his power base, (2) uses it to influence the client to act more effectively in his own behalf by eliminating self-destructive behaviors and by undertaking constructive behavioral programs. We discuss the social-influence model in this section because, to a large extent, such influence is based on the *client's perception* of the helper.

There are certain human values that the helper takes as givens. For instance, he holds that it is better for a person to rid himself of self-destructive behaviors (such as excessive drinking or a self-defeating interpersonal style) and to acquire certain self-enhancing behaviors (such as the ability to cooperate or the ability to understand others from their frame of reference). Respect for the client ultimately means that he desires to see the client living as effectively as he can, and he is committed to using his influence with the client to see that this happens. However, when it is at all possible, the helper should choose to elicit the client's collaboration rather than manipulate the client to health. One of his goals is to see the client become, to whatever degree possible, an *agent* in his own life. With this caution in mind, let's now discuss helping as a process of social influence in terms of the principal elements of this process: the client's perception of the helper as expert, trustworthy, and attractive.

Expertness

What is expertness? In social-influence theory, it is the client's *belief* that the counselor has some information, skill, or ability to help him. Since the client normally does not expect the counselor to act directly in his behalf (if he is having trouble with a tyrannical employer, he does not expect the helper to sit down and talk with the employer), he assumes that the counselor possesses answers to his problems or information that will enable the client to come up with his own answers. In any case, the client believes that this information will enable him to live less painfully or more effectively.

Put somewhat simplistically, there are three sources of perceived expertness in any helper: his role, his reputation, and his behavior.

Role-expertness. Role-expertness refers to the fact that he is called a counselor or psychotherapist, that he has some professional or quasi-professional position, and that he has a variety of credentials (degrees and certificates) attesting to the fact that he is an expert. Other role-designating accouterments are offices, name plates, and titles. The client sees such a person as a "credentialed" expert. Others, such as clergymen, are also seen in helping roles.

Reputation-expertness. This term means what it says: people have given testimony that the helper is good. This testimony may come from those who have actually been helped by the counselor, or it may come from other experts who consider their colleague to be a good helper. His reputation may also come from the fact that he is associated with a prestigious institution. Evidently, a helper's reputation may or may not be deserved: it is not an absolute indication that he is a high-level helper. But his reputation for expertness does have at least an initial impact on the client.

Behavior-expertness. The counselor demonstrates high levels of helping skills. This, obviously, is the most critical form of expertness. Once the client both perceives and experiences the expertness of the helper, he will tend to marshal his energies and resources in the belief, hope, and expectation that he will be helped, and he will allow the helper to enter his life as a potent source of influence. The helper must be able to *deliver* what he promises. If the hopes of the client are mobilized only to be dashed because of the ineptness of the helper, the second state of the client is worse than the first. He might well think:

"I tried, I went to an expert, and even he couldn't help me; obviously I'm beyond help."

Strong (1968) suggests that one source of behavior-expertness is the counselor's confidence in the theory and model he uses in the helping process. This confidence means much more than blind faith in a particular system. If a counselor works hard to make any particular theory or model his own, if he really invests himself in it, his effort will be evident in his attitude and behavior. He will speak and act enthusiastically and confidently. More than that, he will work hard with the client. And, as we have already seen, working hard for and with another is an excellent behavioral way of demonstrating respect for him.

We have already suggested that the counselor share with the client the model he is using so that the client, too, may have a map to guide him through the helping process. Strong (1968) suggests that this sharing is a behavioral way of demonstrating expertness to the client.

> Less obvious, but perhaps more important, are the evidences of expertise in the counselor's behavior. Most counselors pay considerable attention to structuring the interview. They point out the roles and requirements of the client and the counselor in the interview, the sequences of the process, and events likely to occur as they work toward problem solution. Such structuring, whether explicit or implicit, gives evidence of the counselor's expertness. Since the client must perceive that the counselor knows what he is doing, explicit structuring may be more effective than implicit structuring. There is some evidence that explicit structuring does enhance counseling effectiveness (Truax, 1966). Structuring also enhances the counselor's "informational influence" (Raven, 1965). The client is provided a "rational" framework to view his problem, the means of problem solution, and the importance of his efforts and further information. He is thus more able to guide his own efforts toward problem solution [p. 221].

Of course, the helper must be able to deliver what he promises after providing such structuring.

Trustworthiness

The client might come because he has heard that the counselor is an expert. However, if he is to stay with him in any creative way—and in Stage I this means self-exploration—he must come to trust the helper. Trust does not refer principally to confidentiality. Most clients assume that the counselor will not speak about them outside the counseling situation. Trust ultimately means something like this: if I *entrust* myself to you, you will respond with care and skill to help me. You will not hurt me directly yourself and you will try to see to it that I do not hurt myself. How does the client know whether the counselor is trustworthy or not? Trustworthiness, like expertness, depends on role, reputation, and behavior.

Role-trustworthiness. In our society, people who have certain roles are usually considered trustworthy until the opposite is demonstrated. Physicians and other medical professionals usually fall into this category and, when exceptions do occur (as when dentist is convicted of molesting a patient), the scandal is greater because it is unexpected. Presumably, most of those who work in the helping professions fall into the role-trustworthy category: psychiatrists, psychologists, social workers, ministers, counselors, and so forth.

Which is a more potent factor, role-expertness or role-trustworthiness? In a behavioral study of trustworthiness, Strong and Schmidt (1970a,b) had "counselors" manifest untrustworthy behavior in simulated counseling situations. This behavior included manifestation of ulterior motives to the client ("good pay" and "finding out little things about the students"), breach of confidence (a "counselor" would talk about other [fictitious] students by name), and boastfulness and exhibitionistic behavior (a "counselor" would boast that he was good at some activity the client indicated he was poor at). These "counselors," however, possessed high role-expertness (they were given the title "Doctor") and manifested some of the "expert" behaviors described earlier. The results showed that the "untrustworthy communicators, with their extreme bragging and derogatory statements about other students, were often seen as personally involved and willing to share some of their beliefs and thoughts. ... Many of the subjects wrote that the interviewer seemed like a nice, sincere person and certainly was a real expert portraying his role in the interview!" (Strong and Schmidt, 1970, pp. 202, 203). While this study is not the definitive behavioral study of the relationship between role-expertness and role-trustworthiness, it is still disquieting to know that role-expertness has such an overriding impact on the client. What the study seems to demonstrate is that the person who is seen as an expert can, if he wants, get away with a great deal. It points out dramatically how helping can be "for better or for worse." Helping obviously *is* a strong social-influence process (whether the helper likes it or not), and this fact puts a burden both on the counselor's integrity and on his skills.

Reputation-trustworthiness. Reputation-trustworthiness refers to the helper's reputation for honesty and integrity. Present or former clients and other helpers are the usual sources of such testimony. "He's a fine man." "He can be trusted." "You won't have any worries with him." Statements such as these refer both to the helper's trustworthiness and to his expertness.

Behavior-trustworthiness.   Again, the helper's behavior is the most important source of his perceived trustworthiness. He can demonstrate that he is trustworthy by

> maintaining confidentiality;
> showing genuineness, sincerity, and openness in the behavioral ways discussed in previous sections;
> demonstrating respect by means of appropriate warmth, interest, availability, and hard work with the client;
> maintaining a realistic but optimistic outlook, expressed behaviorally—for instance, by reinforcing all constructive behavior on the part of the client; and
> avoiding behavior that might indicate the presence of such ulterior motives as voyeurism, selfishness, curiosity, personal gain, or deviousness.

Kaul and Schmidt (1971) note that one is trusted if he respects the needs and feelings of the other, offers information and opinions for the other's benefit, generates feelings of comfort and willingness to confide, and is open and honest about his motives. In Stage I, the client is much more likely to reveal meaningful life data to a behaviorally trustworthy helper, even when the client sees such information as potentially self-damaging.

Finally, Hackney and Nye (1973) suggest, as I have, that the helper respond with some frequency to the client. In their eyes, the "under-participating" counselor discourages the client from trusting him and thus reduces his potential to help the client.

Attractiveness

If there is good rapport in the helping process, the counselor is, in some sense, attractive to the client. The client finds the helper "attractive" if he feels positive about the helper, respects him, sees the helper as compatible with him in some way, and wants to be like him. It has already been mentioned that a helper, generally speaking, can understand a client more quickly and more effectively the closer he is to the experience of the client. Therefore, the more similar the helper is to the client on certain socioeconomic indexes the better, other factors (such as the skill level of the helper) being equal. This same phenomenon can be translated into social-influence theory. The client sees the helper as attractive if the helper is similar to and compatible with the client—for example, if he is an ex-addict who is now a helper counseling an addict.

The client believes that such a helper can understand him more effectively and therefore he trusts him more deeply.

If the client sees the helper as an effectively living person and as one enjoying the rewards of effective living, he (without surrendering his own identity) will want to be like the helper. If, by chance, you were to meet someone who accepted you in a nonjudgmental way, who gave you his undivided attention when he was with you and listened to you carefully, who did not patronize you but still made every effort to understand you from your frame of reference rather than his own, who felt at home both with himself and with you enough to be himself quite frankly and spontaneously, who expected you to put forth your best effort and helped you to do so—you would most likely find such a person attractive; that is, you would probably feel positive about him, respect him, and feel some kind of compatibility with him. This is attractiveness based solidly on behavior-expertness, for which there is no substitute.

Role- , reputation- , and behavior-expertness, trustworthiness, and attractiveness are highly interactive variables in the helping process. We do not yet know enough about them and precisely how they interact, but the high-level helper is instinctively aware of them and uses them in ways consonant with the values he sees as essential to helping.

Client motivation

Attitude and behavior change are facilitated when the client is highly involved in the influence process. What, then, are the sources of client motivation?

1. The motivation of the client is generally high if he is in psychological pain. The disorganization in his life makes him susceptible to the influence of the helper. He sees in the helper a potential source of relief and is even willing to pay the price for relief, which is to change his behavior. Sometimes, however, he sees the pain of being helped as worse than the pain of his disorganization and therefore refuses to ask for help. At other times, he does seek help but breaks off the relationship after experiencing enough help to make the pain tolerable.
2. The client will involve himself in the helping process more fully if he is dealing with issues of intrinsic importance to him. This fact underscores the importance of the skill of accurate empathic understanding on the part of the helper. The more in tune he is with the client's world, the more probably he will be dealing with issues that have importance for the client.
3. The amount of physical and psychological effort demanded of the client by the helping process affects his motivation. If too many demands are made too soon, he will probably stop coming for help. On the other hand, if little is demanded of him and he sees no progress, he is also

likely to leave the scene. Watson and Tharp (1973) describe helping, at least in part, as a "shaping" process, in which the helper guides the client step by *gradual* step toward more constructive patterns of behavior. They see the loss of "willpower" (motivation) at any stage of this process as due to inadequate shaping. The helper, or the client himself, becomes too demanding. The helpee is asked to take a step that is too large or for which he is not prepared, and he loses heart (see pages 239–249).

Conclusion

Since, as a helper, you cannot decide whether counseling will or will not be a social-influence process (it is!), it seems best to face all the implications of such a process and explore all its ramifications. This exploration will enable you to control the elements of the helping process more effectively.

III. SELF-EXPLORATION

Psychologists have only recently begun to study self-disclosing behavior scientifically (see Cozby, 1973), and their explorations are still in the early stages. It is difficult, then, to situate the kind of self-disclosure that is associated with self-exploration in a wider context of "normal" self-disclosing behavior. Jourard (1971a,b), among others, claims that responsible self-sharing is part of the normal behavior of the healthy or self-actualized person (Egan, 1970, pp. 190–245). Ultimately, the person who cannot share himself deeply is incapable of love. Self-disclosure, however, is never an end in itself. All of us have been bored by the person who talks endlessly about himself without every really revealing himself, or have experienced the "stranger-on-the-train/plane" phenomenon—the person who reveals many of the initimate details of his life in a chance encounter while traveling. We maintain that self-disclosure, to be growthful, must be *appropriate* in both quantity and quality. To determine appropriateness, these questions may be asked: To whom is the disclosure being made? What is the content of the disclosure? In what situation does the disclosure take place? For instance, it does not seem appropriate to reveal intimate content (such as sexual problems) to a stranger during the course of a chance meeting. Such behavior might be exhibitionistic (it has shock value), or the discloser may be venting feelings about himself in what he sees as a safe situation. If a person has no close friends, he may reveal himself to a sympathetic stranger, especially if it is likely that he will never see his confidant again.

Some theoreticians, taking a common-sense approach to self-disclosure, have hypothesized that there is a curvilinear relationship between self-disclosure and mental health: very high and very low levels of self-disclosing behavior are signs of maladjustment, while moderate (and appropriate) self-disclosure is optimal. Overdisclosure is exhibitionistic or, at least, a sign of preoccupation with self. The underdiscloser is fearful of deep human contact or feels that he has much to hide; often he pours a great deal of energy into building and maintaining facades so that the person he really is will not be discovered (see Mowrer, 1968a and 1968b, for an interesting approach to underdisclosing behavior). The overdiscloser discloses a great deal even when the situation does not call for it, while the underdiscloser remains closed even when the situation calls for self-disclosing behavior. One can overdisclose or underdisclose in either quantity or quality (intimacy) of information.

Self-exploration obviously calls for a high level of appropriate self-disclosure, at least in those areas in which the client is not living effectively. The average client comes to counseling expecting to reveal himself, even though he may be reluctant to do so. Indeed, no claims are made here that self-disclosure "cures," for it is a stage in a developmental process, but it should also be noted that, as Mowrer demonstrates, in some cases, self-disclosure can release a great deal of "healing" forces or resources in any client, and thus adequate self-disclosing behavior is predictive of therapeutic outcome (Traux & Carkhuff, 1965).

The first major influence the helper has on the client, then, usually lies in the area of self-disclosing behavior. The high-level counselor often hears, "I have never told this to anyone."

The goals of self-exploration in the helping process

Neither self-disclosure nor self-exploration is a goal in itself in the developmental model. Self-exploration is adequate and effective if it leads to the kind of self-understanding that includes a realization of the need for action. I do not urge here, then, what someone has called "the tyranny of openness." Self-exploration should be functional and pragmatic. The helper, using the skills described in this chapter, provides directionality for this process: he helps the client uncover *concrete* and *relevant* feelings, experiences, and behaviors.

If we can find a way to expand the statement of a problem to a concrete list of the specific behaviors which constitute it, one major obstacle to the solution of the problem will have been overcome. In other words, the initial ambiguity with which most people analyze their interpersonal problems tends to contribute to their feeling of helplessness in coping with them. Knowing which specific behaviors are involved, and thereby what changes in those behaviors will solve the problem, provides a definite goal for action —and having that goal can lend a great sense of relief [Mehrabian, 1970, p. 7].

Let's take a look at the difference between the self-disclosing behavior of two different clients.

> *Client A:* Things just don't seem to be going right. My interpersonal life is at a low ebb. I'm overloaded with work. And a lot of other things intervene to clog up the works. I tend to give up.

This client expresses his feelings only in a vague way, he does not delineate or own his experiences clearly, and he fails to indicate his concrete behaviors.

> *Client B:* I'm depressed, really down, and this is unusual for me. I find it hard to get out of bed in the morning and I feel groggy most of the day. I try to read, but keep putting the book down and wandering around the house. I think I should go to a movie or visit a friend, but I don't do it, I don't even want to. I have even lost my appetite. This has been the pattern for a couple of weeks now. I know why. Two weeks ago I received my dissertation back from my committee. They turned it down for the second time. And I really thought I had made the corrections they wanted before. Now I'm beginning to think I'll have to get an entirely new topic, collect new data—the whole bit. But I don't think I have the energy, the drive, the motivation to do so. Yet I don't want my graduate education to go down the drain. Maybe what bothers me even more is that when I began working on the dissertation I began to withdraw from my friends. I didn't invite anyone over to my place and I turned down their invitations to dinners and parties. I didn't even hang around after class to talk to anyone. I left as soon as class was over to get to my typewriter. Anyway, now nobody calls me up anymore or comes over. I don't blame them. Why should they? I put the dissertation before them for months. So, on top of everything else, I'm lonely. I just want to pack up and go back to New York.

This client's statement is filled with specific feelings, experiences, and behaviors. The difference in self-disclosure ability between Client A and Client B is obviously vast. The skill of the counselor must help the client bridge the gap if the client cannot do so on his own.

Fruitful areas of investigation

What should the client talk about? He should talk about both his problems and the resources or potential resources he has to handle these problems. The goal of self-exploration is not mere quantity, or even intimacy, of information. Rather, it is relevancy of information, which includes (1) problem-related information and (2) solution-oriented resources. Resource-exploration provides a positive dimension to the self-exploration process. Consider the following example.

> *Client:* I practically never stand up for my rights. If I disagree with what anyone is saying—especially in a group—I keep my mouth shut. When I do speak up, the world doesn't fall in on me—in fact, sometimes others actually listen to me.

> *Counselor A:* It's frustrating to be afraid to speak up and to get lost in the crowd.
> *Counselor B:* The times you do speak up, others actually listen—and so you're annoyed at yourself for getting lost in the crowd so often.

Counselor A misses the resource mentioned by the client. Although it is true that the client habitually fails to speak up, he does have an impact when he does speak. And this is a resource.

There are certain areas of life that are worth investigating with almost every client. The following areas or topics are so pervasive that they are relevant to almost any problem the client might mention.

Interpersonal relations.   Almost inevitably, the disturbed person is "out of community" in some sense. His interpersonal life is impoverished, he is withdrawn, or he cannot get along with family, friends, or coworkers.

> *Client A:* I'm facing this operation and I'm afraid. But I really have no one to talk to.
> *Client B:* You can't say that my wife and I ever really did get along. Things were smoother in the beginning, but they weren't right.

The counselor should help *each* client explore the interpersonal dimensions of *any* problem brought up.

Assumptions.   Frank (1961) stresses the importance of the "assumptive world" of the client. Unhealthy assumptions often underlie unhealthy behavior. For instance, Client A might be assuming that all adults are as negative and unaccepting as his parents. This assumption contaminates his interactions with adults. Client B assumes that career is central to life, that it is necessary to choose a career and let the rest of life somehow fall in place around it. She finds her career boring, and, because of her assumption, life is boring. Client C assumes that people involved in religion are hypocritical and/or stupid. Because of this assumption he cuts himself off, on principle, from people and programs that have anything to do with religion. Client D assumes that she is a boring, unattractive person because she has "just" average intelligence. She acts in accord with her assumption and actually does become a boring person. The counselor should ask himself, with some frequency, what assumptions the client has made about himself, his job, others, or the world. Assumptions that are not reflected upon can be extremely destructive. If John has one set of assumptions about the marriage contract while Jane has another, fighting will be the order of the day— until these assumptions surface and are dealt with.

Goals.   The lives of disorganized people are filled with unmet goals and aspirations, unrealistic goals and aspirations, unformulated goals and aspirations. Client A wants to go to graduate school, but he does not have the intellectual resources required. Client B thinks it is critical to be in good physical shape, but he is overweight, has poor muscle tone, and cannot kick a smoking habit. Client C knows that his present middle-class lifestyle is unrewarding, but he does not know why or what to substitute for it. Client D is headed for psychic collapse, a collapse obviously unplanned but seemingly inevitable. Client E feels "dead"; he is not going anywhere and he does not want to go anywhere. The high-level helper will use his skills to see to it that the client examine the directionality of his life, especially in areas in which the client is living less than effectively. For instance, if the interpersonal life of the client is bland and sterile and is going nowhere, the question is: does it have to be this way?

Values.   I find out what my real values are by examining how I invest myself and my resources such as my time, energy, and money. As we have already noted, values differ from attitudes: values represent *de facto* self-investment. Disorganization often stems from a conflict of values; that is, a client invests himself emotionally behaviorally in two patterns of behavior that conflict with one another. For instance, John Jones finds himself heavily invested emotionally in both his work and his family. He is uneasy both when he spends the amount of time he thinks he should spend to do his work well and when he spends leisure hours with his family. A seesaw battle is going on between these two values, and John himself seems to be the loser. The counselor can help him bring his values to the surface and then establish priorities—priorities that are shared with both his family and his coworkers. Bill Smith is a social worker. He invests himself emotionally and behaviorally in helping others. On the other hand, self-gratification and pleasure are strong values in his life. He drinks hard at times, he has a variety of social-sexual involvements, he itches to get away on short vacations. The quality of his helping suffers. The skillful counselor will help the client bring his value-investments to the surface in order to see whether there are conflicting values and to determine whether the *de facto* value system of the client represents his real priorities. For instance, once the client determines that intellectual development is one of his top priorities, with the help of the counselor he can establish a realistic schedule for reading, formal education, workshop involvement, and so on.

Problem severity.   The self-exploration process should yield a quite accurate picture of the severity of any problem area in the life of the client. Mehrabian and Reed (1969) suggest that the severity of any given problem can be determined by the following formula:

Severity = Distress X Uncontrollability X Frequency

The X in the formula suggests that these factors are not just additive: even low distress, if it is uncontrollable or very frequent, indicates a severe problem. Consider the following examples.

> *Client A:* I have been thinking about my health more than usual lately. When I wake up in the morning I sometimes feel a bit of pain in my chest. And at times there are some pains in the joints of my fingers.
> *Client B:* The other night I thought I was going to die. I was lying in bed and couldn't sleep. Then, all of a sudden, I had this tremendous pressure in my chest. I was sure I was going to die. I broke into a cold sweat. Even after the pressure subsided, I was agitated. When I did finally get to sleep, I tossed and turned. When I woke up, I felt as if I'd been drugged.

Client B's distress is obviously greater than A's. Client A might wonder whether these symptoms preoccupy him too much or whether they are indicative of some health problem; but B, it seems, suffered a rather severe anxiety attack (on the supposition that there is nothing wrong with his health).

If a client intimates that he cannot control some kind of distressful behavior, the counselor should consider this a sign of heightened severity of his problem.

> *Client A:* I don't like the fact that I have a bad temper. Just yesterday the kids were playing on the porch after supper, making a racket. I was trying to read the paper. I let it go on as long as I could, but I finally got up, broke up their game, and sent them packing off to bed. I blow up once in a while at work, too, especially when I run into incompetence.
> *Client B:* I'm awfully touchy. I blow up at the slightest cue. My kids have begun avoiding me because at times I scream at them for no reason. Last night I hung up the phone on one of my best friends when I thought she had said something insulting. Today I realize her remark was probably innocent. I've taken tranquilizers, but they don't seem to quiet me down enough.

Client A thinks that his interpersonal behavior could be improved. His outbreaks are not severe, but they are not creative either. There are better ways of channeling his frustrations and dealing with annoyances. Client B, on the other hand, is not in control. She is even trying to drug herself in order to maintain control. Distressful behavior ("touchiness") has become much more than touchiness because of its uncontrollable quality.

Frequency of distressful or unwanted behavior can be a separate factor in itself or a sign of loss of control.

> *Client A:* When I'm on a vacation, I tend to go on an eating spree. I know I shouldn't do it. Last month I gained twelve pounds while I was in Florida. I hated myself when I came back. There was the awful misery of dieting.
> *Client B:* Whenever I feel almost any degree of stress, I find myself at the refrigerator door a dozen times a day. At work it's the candy machine. In January I gained three pounds. Four last month. And then I don't lose it.

If a person gets drunk or goes on an eating spree once in a while, it is a loss of control and is hardly a sign of effective living, but it need not destroy him or his life. However, frequent heavy eating or drinking is obviously more severe: loss of control is complicated by frequency. Then his overindulgence complicates his life in a geometric fashion.

Obstacles to effective self-exploration

Even when the helper is very skillful in Stage I, the client often finds self-exploration quite difficult, for a number of reasons. Let's list some of these reasons, for, if the helper is to get a feeling for the world of the client, he has to understand some of the sources of the resistance he will often meet. Why might a client balk at revealing himself and exploring his behavior? What can the counselor do to deal with such resistance?

Confidentiality.   Research has shown that role-expertness usually handles the client's fear of being betrayed. He expects the professional to keep whatever he says to him confidential. However, since many clients initially put more stock in role-expertness (the "credentialed" professional) than in behavior-expertness (the "functional" professional, the noncredentialed functional professional must demonstrate clearly by his behavior that he is trustworthy—through behavioral manifestations of genuineness, respect, and accurate empathy.

When counseling or human-relations training is done in a group, however, the question of confidentiality becomes more crucial. Especially if group members or trainees know one another or come from a geographically compact space (for example, they are students in the same program), worries about confidentiality will be more pressing. In this case, the question of confidentiality should be dealt with directly as one of the factors that affect the trust level of the group. More positively, the members should demonstrate high levels of trustworthiness to one another as quickly as possible. That is, they should be genuine, respectful, and understanding in the behavioral ways described in this chapter. These behaviors, in conjunction with a willingness to take reasonable risks in self-disclosure, can raise the trust level of a group dramatically. There is no other way: group members must *work* at creating trust, for fears about confidentiality can cut down drastically on the quality of self-exploration in a group.

Fear of disorganization. Many people fear self-disclosure because they feel that they cannot face what they might find out about themselves. This is a very critical issue. The client feels that the facade he has constructed, no matter how much energy he must expend to keep it propped up, is still less burdensome than exploring the unknown. Such a client often begins well, but, once he begins to be overwhelmed by the data produced in the self-exploration process, he begins to retreat. Digging into one's inadequacies, which is essential to social-influence processes (Mehrabian, 1970; Strong, 1968), does lead to "disequilibrium" (Piaget, 1954), disorganization, and crisis (Carkhuff, 1969). But, as Piaget suggests, disequilibrium is a price a child must pay to assimilate new stimuli into an existing schema: it is the price of growth. In a similar way, Carkhuff suggests that growth takes place at crisis points. The high-level counselor realizes that the self-exploration process will be ineffective if it produces either very high or very low levels of disorganization. High disorganization immobilizes the client, while very low disorganization is often indicative of a failure to get at the real issues in his life.

Let's consider an example. John Doe, as he explores his behavior, begins to see that there is a great deal of sham in his life. He discovers that he does not really act on his supposed values—justice, integrity, and friendship. He begins to feel that his life has been worthless and that there is little he can salvage from it. Such feelings are obviously disorganizing and of crisis proportions. The skillful counselor does not let John get lost in self-recrimination or self-pity; he insists that he see the entire picture, including his successes and his resources, both mobilized and unused. He helps the client weather the storms of frustration, self-doubt, and despair.

Shame.   Shame, a much overlooked experiential variable in human living (Egan, 1970; Lynd, 1958), is an important part of disorganization and crisis. The root meaning of the verb "to shame" is "to uncover, to expose, to wound," and therefore it is obviously related to the process of self-exploration. Shame is not just being painfully exposed to another; it is, *primarily,* an exposure of self to oneself. In shame experiences, particularly sensitive and vulnerable aspects of the self are exposed, especially to one's own eyes. Shame often has the quality of suddenness: in a flash one sees his heretofore unrecognized inadequacies without being ready for such a revelation. Shame is often touched off by external incidents, such as a casual remark someone makes, but it could not be touched off by insignificant incidents unless, deep down, one was already ashamed. A shame experience might be defined as an acute emotional awareness of a failure *to be* in some way.

In a study by Talland and Clark (1954), clients judged the therapeutic value of fifteen topics discussed during counseling. There was general agreement on the relative value of the topics. Ratings showed a high correlation between the perceived helpfulness of a topic and its disturbing qualities. The topic called "shame and guilt" was experienced as extremely upsetting, but the discussion of this area of life was considered most helpful. A group of psychologists also rated the same fifteen topics for their intimacy. There was a high correlation between what the psychologists deemed intimate and what the clients judged to be helpful. Self-exploration must eventually deal with intimate areas that are relevant to the client's problems. If this exploration entails disequilibrium, disorganization, shame, and crisis, these are the price that must be paid for growth.

Fear of change.   Some people are afraid of taking stock of themselves because they know, however subconsciously, that if they do they will have to change—that is, surrender comfortable (but unproductive) patterns of living, work more diligently, suffer the pain of loss, acquire skills needed to live more effectively, and so on. For instance, a husband and wife may realize, at some level of their being, that if they see a counselor they will have to reveal themselves and that, once the cards are on the table, they will have to go through the agony of changing their interactional styles. We all have to pay a price to live more effectively.

I once dealt with a man in his sixties whose presenting complaint was high, even debilitating, anxiety. The self-exploration process indicated that he had been treated brutally by his father. He finally ran away from home, but he had developed a peculiar logic. It went something like this: "No one who grows up with scars like I have can be expected to take charge of his life and live responsibly." He had been using his mistreatment as a youth as an excuse to act irresponsibly at work (he had an extremely poor job record), in his life with himself (he drank excessively), and in his marriage (he had been uncooperative and unfaithful and yet expected his wife to support him). The idea that he could change, that he could take responsibility for himself even at his age, frightened him, and he wanted to run away from the group. But, since his anxiety was so painful, he stayed. He had to learn that a change in his style of living was absolutely necessary if he wanted to break out of the vicious circle in which he was caught.

The manner of self-exploration: "Story" versus "history"

A recent television documentary showed excerpts from a marathon group experience conducted at a rehabilitation center for drug addicts. During the early hours of the marathon, a young addict began talking about himself and his past life. He related many facts about himself, but he did so in a rather cold, analytical way. He clicked off experiences and behaviors, but he did not put *himself* or his feelings into his disclosures. As a result, the other members of the group knew many things about him, but they were still not in touch with him. He was accounted for but unrevealed. I use the term "history" for the kind of self-disclosure that does not really reveal the client or put him in contact with those listening to him. "History" is actuarial and analytic: the client relates many facts about himself, even intimate details, but his self-revelation is detached and devoid of feeling. There is little ego-involvement in such disclosure and therefore little risk. The speaker deals with himself as object rather than subject.

"Story" is a far different mode of self-disclosure. It is an attempt on the part of the client to reveal the person inside, both to the counselor and to himself. The client dealing in the modality of "story" perceives that the transmission of self is as important as the transmission of fact. "Story" does not avoid detail, but it is selective. Concrete detail is chosen to reveal rather than obscure the client. "Story" invites dialogue, while "history" discourages it. In the example mentioned earlier, the young addict rambled on and on and no one responded to him in any way (his manner of self-disclosure did not *invite* response, although, in the developmental model, the group members would not allow him to distance himself in monologue). "Story," since it is filled with the person, is filled with the feelings and emotions of the person. History is dull, dead. History is related to the self-disclosure involved in the "stranger-on-the-train" phenomenon: there is disclosure or ventilation or even exhibitionism, but it is without involvement, without fear of negative consequences.

The counselor, using Stage-I skills, calls for dialogue; he makes demands on the client to meet him as a person. Since most clients have problems with interpersonal relations, he makes the counseling process a laboratory in which the client can recognize interpersonal deficits and learn interpersonal skills.

Training-as-treatment in Stage I

Just as you, as trainee, master the skills of Stage I through practice in a training group, it is possible for you, as helper/trainer, to train a group of clients in the skills of Stage I, especially accurate empathy and concreteness. These two skills serve two functions for the client/trainee: (1) they teach him focus and concreteness in his exploration of his own problems, and (2) they give him skills that are indispensable in human relationships.

The following general training methodology can be used in client-training groups:

1. Explain the skill (for example, accurate empathy, concreteness) cognitively. Answer questions. Be sure the trainees grasp the *concept*.
2. Demonstrate the skill yourself. If possible, use the contrast method:
   a. Show how it should *not* be done.
   b. Show how it should be done.
3. Demonstrate the skill with various members of the group in front of the whole group. Make sure that everyone has an experiential understanding of the skill in question. Have the members of the group give one another feedback. Give feedback yourself.
4. Break the group up into threes (or whatever number is practical for the skill being taught). Have at least two interactants plus one observer in each group. Continue practice in these smaller groups.
5. Supervise: correct, encourage, and reinforce what is being done well. Give the observer a chance to give feedback first. Make sure that feedback is concrete and don't let it become longwinded. Give short feedback and then have the trainees engage in further skills practice.
6. Toward the end of the training session, call the whole group together for processing: find out what learning did or did not take place. Give the trainees a chance to air their feelings about being trainees and going through the work of learning counseling skills.

During these training sessions, the content of the practice sessions should focus on those problems-in-living that are the reason the clients are there, plus the learnings taking place through the training process.

It should be noted that skills training as part of the helping process can take place in one-to-one counseling as well as in groups. The counselor, for instance, can weave into the helping process training in accurate empathy, concreteness, and assertiveness as they are called for. Since self-exploration is an important part of helping, the client can be trained in the skills of self-exploration. This training tends to decrease his resistance to self-exploration. Even in group training sessions, the amount of skills training administered can vary according to the needs of the clients and the style of the helper.

Some concluding notes to Stage I

Intensity. If the counselor uses high levels of attending, accurate empathy, respect, concreteness, and genuineness, and if the client cooperates by exploring the feelings, experiences, and behaviors related to the problematic areas of his life, the helping process will be an intense one. The high-level helper knows that counseling is potentially intense. He is prepared for it and knows how to support a client who is not used to such intensity.

The temptation to stop. A good counselor cannot be effective "to a point." Some counselors seem to have the skills needed to be effective in Stage I of the developmental model, yet they do not seem to help the client move on to Stage II and, especially, Stage III. In these cases, self-exploration achieves a kind of functional autonomy that does not help the client. Unless the helper realizes in his bones that what is happening in Stage I is meaningful only to the degree that it is ultimately related to constructive behavior change, he will fail. He will not even be effective in the skills he thinks he possesses, for, when these skills lose their relational character—they are good not in themselves but insofar as they help—they lose their effectiveness, even in Stage I. These skills are going nowhere because the process is going nowhere. One sign of this kind of failure is what can be called "circular" counseling: the counselor (and often the client, too) begins to realize that they are going over and over the same territory—that things "have been said before."

Rigidity in the application of the developmental model. The high-level counselor, because he has a wide repertory of skills and responses from which he can draw naturally and spontaneously, does whatever is most useful for the client at any given moment of the helping process, whether it is called for by any stage of the model or not. The beginner and the low-level counselor tend to apply the model too rigidly. Sometimes a beginner tries to deal with problems sequentially—take care of problem A entirely, then problem B, then C, and so on—because this way is both logical and less confusing. But, while counseling is presented here as a logical, clear-cut, discrete process in order to give the trainee a cognitive map and demonstrate as clearly as possible the repertory of skills and responses he must develop to become an effective helper, the actual helping process is much more messy. It is true that in some cases the counseling process proceeds more or less according to the model. In other cases it does not. The final criterion for the steps taken during counseling, however, must be what is helpful for the *client.* The model is for the helping process and not its master, and helping is for the client. Perhaps an application of Horace's principle of the golden mean might be useful here: don't underestimate the value of an integrative model in learning how to be an effective helper, but don't overestimate the value of such a model in the helping process itself.

Chapter Five

Stage II: Integrative Understanding/ Dynamic Self- Understanding

1. The goal of Stage II is to help the client achieve the kind of objective understanding of himself, his problems, and his world that leads to effective action.
2. There is a set of skills that enables the helper to help the client achieve this goal. Learning this composite of skills—advanced accurate empathy, self-disclosure, confrontation, and immediacy—constitutes the goal of human-relations-training groups. Mutuality, being able to engage skillfully and meaningfully in direct, mutual talk, is used to communicate these basic skills.
    a. *Advanced accurate empathy* means that the counselor not only understands the world of the client but also sees the implications of what he understands and communicates this further understanding to the client. The helper uses a variety of techniques to communicate this deeper understanding to the client: he expresses what the client only implies, uses focused summaries of what the client has said, connects "islands" of feelings, experiences, and behaviors that the client leaves unconnected, helps him draw conclusions logically from premises, and presents him with alternative frames of reference for understanding his own behavior and that of others.
    b. Helper *self-disclosure* implies that the helper is willing to disclose anything about himself that would help the client, but actually does so only when he sees that it will not frighten or distract the client.
    c. In *confrontation,* the helper invites the client to examine some aspect or dimension of his behavior that is preventing the client from understanding himself fully or from moving toward constructive behavioral change. He confronts discrepancies, distortions, games, tricks, smoke screens, and evasions. Confrontation is a mode of caring and involvement; it is not punishment. Low-level counselors either confront irresponsibly and punitively or are afraid to challenge the client at all.
    d. *Immediacy* is the ability to discuss directly and openly with another person what is happening in the here-and-now of an interpersonal

relationship. The helper can use immediacy to deal directly with differences between him and the client, as well as with trust issues, dependency and counterdependency issues, directionless sessions, and client resistance. Immediacy is a complex of skills involving advanced accurate empathy, helper self-disclosure, and confrontation.

3. Stage-II skills represent "stronger medicine" than Stage-I skills and are to be used cautiously and tentatively.
4. Since Stage-II skills constitute another part of the wider repertory of helping skills, they should be used whenever they are needed, even at the beginning of the helping relationship. But they should always be used carefully.
5. The helper should not become a specialist in any single helping skill or set of skills. The needs of the client should dictate what the helper does.

In Stage II the counselor uses a variety of skills to help the client understand himself more fully in order to see the need to act more effectively. The counselor not only helps him piece together the data produced through the self-exploration process but also helps him probe wider and look deeper in order to find the "missing pieces" he needs to understand himself better. Once the client begins to see himself both as he is and as he wants to be, he will see the necessity for action. As I have already noted, the goal of this stage is not any kind of self-contained insight but dynamic self-understanding—self-understanding that stands, as it were, on the verge of action.

I. DYNAMIC SELF-UNDERSTANDING: CLIENT GOAL FOR STAGE II

Kaul and Parker (1971) suggest that one index of success in counseling is the client's acquisition of a new conceptual scheme for understanding his behavior. Strong (1970) sees this understanding as a basis for control: "To the extent that counseling increases the client's knowledge of how he typically behaves and the effects he typically intends, counseling increases his ability to predict and control his behavior" [p. 390]. The relationship between the client's understanding of himself and his environment and behavioral change is, as Strong's article well points out, complex and not completely understood. However, while it is naïve to suppose that insight in itself "cures," and while it is also true that some behavior-modification techniques do "cure" without any dependence on client insight, still, self-understanding can mediate behavioral change. The purpose of this chapter is to examine the practical relationship between self-understanding and behavioral change and to outline the skills needed by the counselor to help the client achieve such understanding.

Below are a number of statements that indicate some kind of dynamic self-understanding on the part of the client. In each case you can ask yourself whether the client is showing the kind of understanding that leads to action; that is, does the client himself see the need to act?

> *Client A:* I've been sitting around college waiting for someone to come give me an education. Well, I think I begin to see that no one is going to give me anything, no one's going to educate me but myself. These past two years I've alternated between anger over not being taught right and self-pity. I thought college should be like high school. I haven't been flirting with self-pity. I've been wallowing in it. I have to salvage the next two years, but I don't know how to go about it.
>
> *Client B:* I'm losing out on most of life by being so mousy. It's very hard for me to be assertive with others, especially with men. But I've had it, I can't be like this—especially if I am interested in helping others. I just have to find ways to reach out to others.
>
> *Client C:* What a revelation this group experience has been! I had no idea how manipulative I am. As I look back now, I see that I got better grades than I deserved in school by the way I "cultivated" my teachers. I'm still trying to do the same thing in graduate school. I control my whole social life. At one time I actually thought it was altruism—I mean the way *I* would always be the one to seek others out. But this was just my way of controlling the situation. I want to control whom I see and whom I don't see. I even tried to manipulate you into counseling me the way I wanted to be counseled, but you wouldn't play my game.
>
> *Client D:* I've been a clown so long that I'm not sure that there's a solid me left underneath for others to interact with. My blustering, my "wit," my bull-in-the-china-shop relationships with others—all a coverup. I tried to be just me this past week—no stream of jokes, no putting others down —and I was scared. I was actually shaking at times because I didn't know what to do and my friends didn't seem to know how to interact with a serious me.
>
> *Client E:* Just for the hell of it, I tried to make last week altruism week. I did things for others. Without being asked. I went over to my mother's and helped clean out the basement. I took some of my brother's kids to the zoo. I called up some friends and had a party Friday night. I just got out of myself in half a dozen ways—no big deal, just ordinary things. I've been sitting around discussing my self-centeredness to death. I think I found out more about altruism last week than I have in all these sessions up to now. Last week I actually *liked* putting my own needs second. But also, what I did was easy because it was so new—a kind of experiment. I still fear living consistently for others.

In the case of Client E, self-understanding *followed* action instead of preceding it. He had to experience altruistic behavior before being able to discuss it in relation to his own life. His case illustrates concretely the need to be flexible in the application of the stages of the model.

Vague and abstract self-understanding is often equivalent to no understanding because it simply does not lead to action. Ideally, self-exploration yields concrete data; these data, when put together effectively, yield concrete self-understanding, the basis for specific, concrete action programs. Consider the difference between vague and concrete self-understanding.

> *Client A:* I think that I deal with my wife the way I deal with most women. The best word I can think of is "ambivalently." There are contradictory patterns of interaction that are not satisfying or fruitful. It makes me think of the ambivalent ways my mother and sisters related to me, and how I reciprocated. I think we've got something here.

Here the words are vague, the concepts are vague, and the directionality of the whole process is vague. It is impossible to build an action program on such a sandy foundation. It's too shifty.

> *Client B:* I think I can say that I love my wife. I work hard to see to it that she has a comfortable life. I try to spend as much time as I can at home —working around the house, helping with the chores. I even take her places I don't particularly want to go because she wants to go—I mean out to dinner, and even to vacation spots she chooses. Yet, even as I say this, I realize that my heart isn't in what I do. She must get a completely different message from my attitude at times and from some of the other things I do. For instance, even though we are together a lot, I don't talk to her much. I'm around the house a lot, but I'm there and not there. I do things for her, but sometimes so reluctantly that it would be more honest not to do them. Even when we go where she wants to go on vacations, we end up doing what I want to do once we get there. I do very little to understand her, and she does very little to understand me. I think you know me better than she does in some ways. I keep giving her double messages—"I love you" and "I'm indifferent to you"—and she gives them right back to me. We have to do something to get our marriage into shape. We've got to do something about the way we don't communicate with each other honestly. Otherwise what we do have will just die.

This client has not only explored his relationship with his wife but has been able to put the data together into a larger picture. He sees that he and his wife have begun to practice separation or divorce—something neither of them seems to want. He sees the need for action, he is motivated to act, and he has some idea of the direction his actions must take: that is, he and his wife must take the steps necessary to achieve the kind of communication he has experienced in the counseling relationship. Let's take a look at another example.

> *Client A:* All the literature says that drugs don't lead anywhere, and I guess that's right. They are substitutes for better things in life. I guess if there is something better out there you have to go out and look for it.

This client does not sound convinced; he does not *own* what he's saying. He talks objectively about what others say and a general need to search for a better life. His understanding does not seem to be *self*-understanding; neither is it on the verge of action.

> *Client B:* I don't think smoking pot every once in a while will wreck my life. But I've become a heavy smoker and have even tried "speed" a couple of times. That scares me. I really don't know if heavy smoking really causes any physical damage. I'm still in good physical shape, play basketball a lot. But maybe smoking a lot is not the point. It's what I say to myself when I smoke so much: when I'm in never-never land, I don't give a damn about anything. That kind of thinking will do me in eventually if smoking doesn't. It's like practicing suicide. In fact, it's no use giving up pot-smoking if I don't give up pot-thinking. If I stop smoking, I'll be one nervous cookie. I've got to have something strong in my life, like strong action. Smoking all the time has been a cheap way of doing that, but what'll I do now?

This client understands that he has to kick the drug habit, but he also understands that he has little purpose in life. He is tentatively ready to give up his flight from life, but he is not sure what he wants to move toward. His self-understanding is much more concrete than Client A's, but he still needs help in two ways. He needs help in kicking the drug habit and he needs a concrete way to search for meaning in his life. He needs what Hobbs (1962) calls a working "cosmology" or approach to life. The counselor can help him find experiences that will provide directionality for his life. In Client A's case, the counselor has to help him to explore himself much more concretely in terms of feelings, experiences, and behaviors. Client A may understand *ideas,* but he doesn't understand *himself.*

A shift in perspective

In order to help the client reach dynamic self-understanding, the helper shifts the perspective of the counseling process in Stage II. In Stage I the helper concentrates on the client's frame of reference. He tries to see the world from the client's perspective rather than his own. Primary-level accurate empathy is the principal tool used in this process. The helper tries to get a feeling for the experience of the client and then communicate this understanding to him. Generally, throughout the self-exploration process, the helper tries to understand the client's feelings, experiences, and behavior from the client's point of view.

In Stage II, however, there is a shift. The counselor now helps the client see the world from a more *objective* point of view. As Levy (1968) notes, if the counselor sees the world only as the client does, he will have little to offer him. The client's implicit interpretation of the world is in some ways distorted and unproductive, at least in the areas of life in which he is having problems. The helper assumes, however, that the client has the resources eventually to see the world, especially the world of his own behavior, in an undistorted way. He needs a specific set of skills to help the client come to this kind of understanding. He does not ignore the client's feelings, experiences, and behaviors. Indeed, he uses these to help the client see the world more objectively. This change in perspective is necessary if Stage II is to be a bridge between the data of Stage I and the action programs of Stage III. The disturbed, disorganized, problematic person is usually a person in a rut. He keeps blaming others for his problems, refuses to admit that he has any problems, or continues to apply solutions that don't work.

Let's consider the case of the client who comes to some kind of dynamic understanding of his relationship with his wife (Client B, page 130). He did not start with those understandings. His data in Stage I looked quite different.

Stage-I Data

I'm an easygoing person.
I've been depressed lately.
I've become less efficient at work.
My wife is a nagger.
I do not deserve my wife's treatment.
I'm around the house a great deal.
I help with chores.
My present distress is caused by my wife's behavior.
I provide well for my wife's needs and comfort.
I let her have her way.
My faults are insignificant compared with hers.

At this stage we can well ask ourselves: what are some of the ruts this client is in? Some of the possibilities are:

Possible Ruts

I'm right; she's wrong.
I try; she doesn't.
I'm in pain; she is not.
I keep acting maturely; she responds immaturely.

As we have already seen in examining Client B's case, this client comes to a set of self-understandings quite different from the data of Stage I.

Stage-II Understandings

I'm sending many double messages (such as like-dislike) to my wife.
We're practicing separation or divorce.

Some of my behavior is childish.
Our marital distress is not mine or hers, it's *ours.*
There is little open, direct communication between us.
We're in a downward spiral.
We need to learn adult-to-adult communication skills.
My wife and I should be here together.

This client has obviously come to a more objective perspective on his relationship with his wife. How does a counselor help the client get a new perspective on his life and behavior? How does a counselor help a client see the ruts he is in? What are the specific skills the helper needs to be effective at Stage II? These are the questions to be answered in this chapter.

II. HELPER SKILLS IN STAGE II

Mutuality in counseling and human-relations training

It has already been noted that the skills of the counseling process are the skills people need to be effective with one another in all kinds of interpersonal relationships. The skills of Stage I provide a basis of caring and support that people need, not only or primarily in counseling but in everyday life. The same can be said of the skills of Stage II— advanced accurate empathy, self-disclosure, confrontation, and immediacy. They belong to life and not just to the helping process. Indeed, one of the goals of counseling is to help the client develop these skills. Stage-II skills add an intensity to life that can be either challenging and constructive or overwhelming and destructive. Stage-II skills are at the heart of what we have called "mutuality." There is not a high degree of mutuality in one-to-one helping. Since there is a helper and a helpee, there is something one-way about this process. The client is not there to help the counselor, even though it is true that the high-level counselor grows in a variety of ways through helping others. In day-to-day living, however, even though friends help one another greatly, both directly and indirectly, they do not see one another under the titles of "helper" and "helpee." Indeed, most of us would rebel if our friends looked upon themselves as our helpers rather than as our friends. The best friendships, however, are not just safe harbors in which the participants are comfortable and free from challenge. Good friends support and help one another, but they also challenge one another. Good human relationships are defined by mutuality, each person moving out toward the other in understanding, self-sharing, caring, and confrontation. The skills of Stage II are essential for deeper human relationships. Stage-II skills, however, function differently in counseling and in day-to-day living with friends. In counseling, the helper uses these skills to the degree that they help the client achieve self-understanding and move on to constructive behavioral change. As human-relations skills, however, advanced accurate empathy, self-disclosure, confrontation, and immediacy ("you-me" talk) have a kind of value in themselves. Since these interactions put people in deep, growthful contact with one another, they constitute a large part of the relationship and are not merely means to some further end. They are, for those who will risk them, ways of being present to others in more demanding and fulfilling ways.

Training groups (either human-relations or counselor-preparation groups) and counseling groups fall somewhere between one-to-one helping relationships and friendships. Since such groups are by nature temporary, they cannot be called friendship groups, even though strong relationships might form during the life of the group. Furthermore, the purpose of these groups is not to provide a place where people can find friends. On the other hand, they are characterized by much more mutuality than takes place in the ordinary one-to-one helping relationship. What can you, as a trainee, expect from a training group? When you practice skills in subgroupings (as helper, as helpee, and as observer), you will ordinarily adopt the one-to-one helper stance. In this case, you will use Stage-II skills insofar as they help the "client" understand himself and ready himself for action. However, during subgroup feedback sessions and during whole-group interactions, you become *mutual helpers.* This kind of give and take is similar to the give and take that characterizes friendship, except that it is not as extensive, intimate, or permanent. The same can be said of counseling done in groups. Such groups are not substitutes for intimate relationships in everyday life, but they can go far to prepare participants for greater depth and effectiveness in such relationships. However, a training or counseling group is, in some meaningful way, an intimate community of learners. The more solid the relationships formed in such groups, the better the learning.

In the following sections, the Stage-II skills are described and illustrated as they appear in one-to-one helping relationships. However, with little effort, you can apply what is said to transactions in training groups, counseling groups, and friendships.

Advanced accurate empathy

Accurate empathy is central to the entire developmental model, with primary-level accurate empathy predominating in Stage I and advanced accurate empathy in Stage II. Consider the following example.

> *Client:* I don't know what's going on. I study hard, but I just don't get good marks. I think I study as hard as anyone else, but all of my efforts seem to go down the drain. I don't know what else I can do.

> *Counselor A:* You feel frustrated because even when you try hard you fail.
> *Counselor B:* It's depressing to put in as much effort as those who pass and still fail. It gets you down and maybe even makes you feel a little sorry for yourself.

Counselor A tries to understand the client from the client's frame of reference. He deals with the client's feelings and the experience underlying these feelings. Counselor B, however, probes a bit further. From the context, from past interchanges, from the client's manner and tone of voice, he picks up something that the client does not express overtly: that the client is feeling sorry for himself. The client is looking at himself as a victim, as the one who has failed, as one who is depressed. This is *his* frame of reference. But in reality he is also beginning to say "Poor me, I feel sorry for myself." This is a *different* perspective, but one that is also based on the data of the self-exploration process. Advanced accurate empathy, then, goes beyond the expressed to the implied. If the helper is accurate, however, and if his timing is good, this kind of communication helps the client move beyond self-exploration to self-understanding. Let's take a look at the client's response.

> *Client:* Boy, you're not kidding! I get to feeling so sorry for myself that I stop entirely. I mean I not only give up on books but on people, too.

The client begins to see that self-pity is perhaps more problematic and self-defeating than the failures themselves. He now has a chance to explore the unproductive character of his self-pity and do something about it. Primary-level accurate empathy gets at relevant *surface* (not to be confused with *superficial*) feelings and meanings, while advanced accurate empathy gets at feelings and meanings that are somehow buried, hidden, or beyond the immediate reach of the client.

Stage II is the phase in which "piecing together" takes place so that the client can see a bigger picture, and advanced accurate empathy is the principal tool in this process. Even when the helper sees the world from the point of view of the client, he often sees it more clearly, more widely, more deeply, and more cogently. He not only understands the client's perspective but sees the *implications* (for effective or ineffective living) of this perspective. The communication of advanced accurate empathy is the helper's way of sharing his understanding of these implications with the client. Ultimately, however, the client himself must be able to say "Now I'm beginning to see what I'm doing wrong and what I'm failing to do, and I want to remedy it."

Advanced accurate empathy can be communicated in a number of different ways. Let's consider some of them.

Expressing what is only implied.   The most basic form of advanced accurate empathy is to give expression to what the client only implies. In Stage I, the helper, for the reasons we have already discussed, limits himself to stating only what the client states. In Stage II, once rapport has been established and the client is exploring his feelings, experiences, and behavior, the helper can begin to state or point out what the client implies but does not say directly. Take the following client, for instance.

> *Client:* I write a lot of verses—I'm not sure I should call it poetry. My friends tell me they like it, that it's good. But then they're not critics, they're not experts at all. I keep writing and keep sending it off to various magazines and all I get back are rejection slips. This has been going on for two full years. I could paper my bedroom wall with them.
>
> *Counselor A:* It's disheartening to put in that much work with so little success.
> *Counselor B:* It's disheartening to put in that much work with so little success. It maybe even makes you wonder about your talent, and you don't want to kid yourself.

Counselor A's response is fine for Stage I, but in Stage II the counselor wants to help the client dig deeper. Counselor B bases his response not only on the client's immediately preceding remark but on the entire self-exploration context.

> *Client:* Right! If I really don't have top-quality talent for poetry, I don't think I should invest myself as much as I'm doing right now. It just keeps my hopes up—or, rather, it just keeps me on edge. I'll still write, as a kind of hobby, but I won't think of writing as a career.

As with primary-level accurate empathy, the sign of an effective stab at advanced accurate empathy by the counselor is the way in which the client responds. In this example, the client moves forward. He has to ask himself frankly if he has talent for writing, at least the seeds of talent. If he sees that he does not, he will see that he has to invest himself differently.

Let's take a look at another example.

> *Client:* I don't know why she acts the way she does. One day she will be chattering away on the phone in the most engaging way. She's carefree and tells me all that's happening. She's great when she's in that mood. But brother! at other times she's actually rude to me and moody as hell—and it seems so personal. I mean not just that she's in a bad mood generally, but that somehow it is directed at me.

Counselor: It's unsettling not to know where you stand with her. You wonder whether she is just fickle or, perhaps, whether you do anything, in her eyes, to provoke such a reaction.

The implication of being the object of someone's anger is that one has done something (advertently or inadvertently) to provoke that anger. The counselor's response opens up that area for the client to consider. He does not accuse or blame, but he does follow a lead that is implicit in the client's statement.

Let's consider one more example.

Counselor: You keep telling her that you feel so tentative and uncertain about your relationship because you wonder when she'll discover the "real" you and give you the brushoff. But it seems that this message works both ways. I mean, you might also be telling her that, when you discover that she is not the one for you, she can expect to get the brushoff from you.

Client: You mean that I might not appear so altruistic to her. She might think that by leaving the door open for her, I'm also leaving it open for myself. Hmmm . . . that's probably more than possible. I've done that before.

There is a message hidden in the message the client has been relaying to his friend. The counselor discovers it, and it helps the client understand himself and his motivation a bit more clearly. One important demand is to have the client look at feelings he has been trying to sweep under the rug.

Student: I really like my teacher. Everybody in the whole school admits that she's about the best. She makes English and history come alive, not like the others. But still I can't talk to her the way I'd like to.

Counselor: You really like her and are glad that you are in her class; but, Jim, it seems that you are a bit resentful because she doesn't show you much personal attention.

Advanced accurate empathy places demands on the client. The counselor is no longer merely responding to the client, as he did in Stage I; he is demanding that the client take a deeper look at himself. The genuineness, respect, understanding, and rapport of Stage I have created a power base for the helper. He now uses this power to influence the client to see his problems from a more objective frame of reference. These demands are still based on an accurate understanding of the client and are made with genuine care and respect, but they are demands nevertheless. The low-level counselor finds it difficult to make such demands on the person he is helping.

Summarizing core material. Advanced accurate empathy is also communicated when the helper brings together in a summary way relevant core materials that have been presented in a fragmented way by the client. Brammer (1973) lists a number of goals that can be achieved by judicious use of summarizing: "warming up" the client, focusing scattered thoughts and feelings, bringing the discussion of a particular theme to a close, prompting the client to explore a theme more thoroughly. In the following example, the counselor tries to focus the thoughts and feelings of the client in order to help him move closer to a consideration of some action program.

> *Trainer:* Let me see if I can put some of this together. You think that you can be an effective helper, but you see both strengths and weaknesses in yourself at this point. On the one hand, you are enthusiastic to learn. You feel that you care deeply about others and can get in touch with their feelings and experiences—and you communicate this accurately and effectively to your clients. And yet the counseling process tends to bog down. You get to a certain point and can't go further. This has something to do with your being uncomfortable with being assertive. You are especially fearful of saying things that might challenge the client. You feel tied up in yourself and tied down in your interactions with the client.
>
> *Trainee:* Yes, and I want to break free. I respond well but I don't initiate well. I am so hesitant to do the things that insert *me* into the life of the client.

This trainee is beginning to realize that an intellectual understanding of the counseling process, coupled with warmth and primary-level accurate empathy, does not carry the day. The trainer, using a summary, pulls together the data of the self-exploration process and lets them speak for themselves. His summary is effective because (1) he gathers together points that the client himself has brought up in the self-exploration phase and (2) he chooses *relevant* data, data that will help the trainee see his problem more clearly. A summary, then, is not a mechanical pulling together of a number of facts; it is a systematic presentation of relevant data. This particular trainee's problem is quite common. He has learned the skills of Stage I, but the skills of the rest of the model are still intellectual constructs that have not been mastered experientially. The trainee is comfortable with responding to the client, but he is hesitant to initiate (Stages II and III) because he has not practiced the skills of initiating.

It is obvious that summaries can be used both to further the self-exploration process and to help the client reach a degree of dynamic self-understanding. But even when they are used to further the self-exploration process they indicate at least the beginnings of initiative on the helper's part. He is doing more than just responding; he is actively juxtaposing facts in order to stimulate further exploration or laying out the facts in a way that enables the client himself to see the implications.

Let's take a look at another example of a summary that helps the client understand himself more fully.

> *Counselor:* Let's go over what we have seen so far. You're down, depressed—not just in a normal slump: this time it's hanging on. You worry about your health, but this seems to be more a symptom than a cause of your depression. There are some unresolved issues in your life. One is the fact that your recent change in jobs has meant that you don't see much of your old friends anymore. Geography has made a big difference. Another issue—one you find painful and embarrassing—is your investment in trying to stay young. You don't want to face the fact of getting older. A third issue is the way you overinvest yourself in work—so much so that, when you finish a long-term project, suddenly your life is empty.
>
> *Client:* It's painful to hear it all that baldly, but that about sums it up. I really have to look into my values. I feel I need a new lifestyle, one in which there is much more immediate involvement with other people.

This client, in the self-exploratory phase, produced data that point to certain painful conclusions: he is immature (for example, in his overvaluing of youth), he is "out of community" (his interpersonal life is at a low ebb), and he is trying ineffective solutions to his problems (for example, flight into work). The counselor's summary, which is an effective assembling of the salient points produced in the self-exploration process, hits home—somewhat painfully. The client begins to see the rut he is in. He seems ready to consider the possibility of change.

A summary can be used effectively at various times during the interview. First, a summary can help add directionality and coherence to a self-exploratory process that seems to be going nowhere. Let's assume that a young ghetto resident, who has had several run-ins with the police, is talking to a counselor associated with the probation office. He has been jumping from topic to topic and the counselor is having a hard time pulling it all together.

> *Counselor:* I'm not sure what you're trying to tell me, Jeff. You're angry because the probation officer made you come here. You feel it's a waste of time to talk to me because I'm white. And also you feel you're not going anyplace because the whole system has you boxed in.
>
> *Client:* That's right! How you going to fight a whole system by just sitting around and talking here? You get in a gang and you fight back.

Since the client's self-exploration has been confused and rambling, the counselor, in a summary, digs out what he thinks is important up to this point. The client responds by choosing the one question that bothers him most—how can a counseling interview make him feel less crushed by his neighborhood, the school he is in, and the political and economic forces that make him feel helpless? The summary helps him identify the issue that is uppermost in his mind. Incidentally, this example illustrates another aspect of the counseling process. Since the counselor comes from a very different socioeconomic, educational, and cultural background, he has to fight harder to understand and stay with the client. His difficulty points up the necessity of training indigenous counselors and helpers.

Second, a summary can be used at the beginning of a new session. But care should be taken to let the client move where he thinks it is important to move. Something important might have taken place since the last meeting, and he should be given ample opportunity to explore it. In a word, don't use a summary at the beginning of a new interview to *sidetrack* the client.

> *Counselor:* Any reflections on the last session, or has anything come up since then that we should discuss?

This question gives the client a chance to take the initiative himself. For instance, the client might say something like this:

> *Client:* I thought a lot about what we discussed last time. You know, I'm like a little kid. I have to get my way all the time. I *do* get it most of the time, and it's making me miserable.

This client has mulled over the data of the self-exploration process and has achieved some self-understanding on his own. If the counselor had launched into a summary immediately, he might have distracted the client. Techniques and strategies are for the client, not goals in themselves. On the other hand, if the client has nothing to say to begin a new session, a summary can be quite useful. It shows the client the helper's interest and prevents the client from merely retracing old ground.

Third, a summary can be used when the client seems to have exhausted everything he has to say on a certain topic. A summary of what the client *has* said can help him see the whole picture and move closer to self-understanding. Suppose that a client gets "stuck" and has nothing more to say about a given topic.

> *Counselor A:* It's hard to go on. You feel you really don't have much more to say about your relationship with your father.
> *Client:* Yeah. That's about where it stands.

> *Counselor B:* Your father never had a good word for you when you were young, just criticism when you did something wrong. He even seemed to resent it when you went to college—getting more education than he had. He ridiculed the idea. Then his divorcing your mother was the last straw. Since you saw him as pretty much in the wrong, you were angry and hurt, so you cut off all communication with him. That was over three years ago.

Now you have begun to talk to each other again, but you're still not satisfied with the way things stand.

Client: No, I still would like to get all of this off my chest to him. I don't know whether he even understands why I stopped talking to him. But this thing is like a rock on my chest.

Counselor A makes the wrong choice here: he uses a statement of primary-level accurate empathy and leads the client (and himself) up a blind alley. Counselor B, on the other hand, sees that this is a good time for a summary of the salient facts in the client's experience with his father. The summary helps the client achieve some degree of self-understanding (he will have to *do* something to get the "rock" off his chest). Later in the counseling session (this is an actual case), the counselor role-played the client's father and had the client say directly what he wanted to say. This "rehearsal" was part of an action program that culminated in the client's actually speaking directly to his father. In general, summaries are often good ways to lead into a consideration of action programs.

Finally, from time to time the counselor can ask the *client* to summarize. After modeling this kind of behavior a few times himself, it is not unseemly for him to ask the client to do the same. If he has trouble summarizing, the helper can teach him how to summarize. This is a small way of making training a part of the treatment process; it helps to make the client an agent in the helping process. Brammer (1973; see p. 94 for his guidelines for using summaries) says that the main purpose of summarizing is to give the client a feeling of movement, both in exploring content and feelings and in reviewing action programs (in Stage III). Once he learns how to do his own summarizing, he will be more in touch with movement or lack of it in the counseling process.

The use of newsprint in the counseling process. I would like to offer a practical suggestion related both to the topic of the use of summaries in counseling and to the whole question of counselor initiative. The suggestion is simple, but it can make the counseling process much more concrete and fill it with a greater sense of direction. In the room where I counsel, I keep a very large pad of newsprint on an easel and a generous supply of broad-tipped felt pens. From time to time throughout the counseling process, I use the newsprint to summarize graphically the most important points that arise in the interaction with the client. For instance, halfway through a counseling period, I might summarize the principal data on the pad. This summary helps both the client and me in two ways: (1) it helps us focus as concretely as possible on the most salient issues, and (2) it helps prevent time-consuming "circular" counseling—going over the same issues in the same way. When both counselor ànd client see before their eyes where they have already been, they are mildly pressured to move forward. Graphic representations dramatize progress (or lack of it). The pad can be used at each stage of the counseling process. In Stage I, it can be used to list the principal data produced in the exploratory process. In Stage II, it can be used to list the client's understandings of himself. In Stage III, it can be used to plot strategies and action programs. The use of the pad emphasizes that the counseling sessions are work periods and not just friendly chats.

Obviously, such a technique can be overused and abused. The counselor who cannot get involved with the client will get involved with the pad, and the client will become secondary. This technique, like all others, should complement the counseling relationship, not substitute for it. It goes without saying that the helper should not be constantly running up to the easel to illustrate his latest finding. One counselor, who had only a couple of hours to spend with a client, summarized the problems or "baggage" the client was carrying around *and* the resources he possessed to handle this baggage. The two sheets of newsprint side by side looked something like this:

Baggage	*Resources*
being depressed	interest and talent enough to make music a career
failure to make a go of first marriage	genuineness and sincerity
looking upon self as failure	a caring and supportive wife
poor relationship with father, extending over years; doing nothing to improve it	a demanding but good relationship with stepson
failure to be a good disciplinarian as a high school teacher	ego-strength: has not cracked in face of a number of crises
having a part-time menial job with income far less than wife's	genuine care and respect for others
	good motivation: coming to counseling in order to face up to job, emotional, and other real-life issues
	simplicity in lifestyle: being an uncomplicated, open person
	friends to help him get better part-time job for money for further training in music
	integrity: sticking to values, commitments; honesty (even with hostile ex-wife and her relatives)

This client had never taken an inventory of his resources before. Seeing them graphically was a peak experience for him. This was the first time anyone had actively suggested that he had the resources necessary to seize life rather than be its victim.

Newsprint summaries, then, are reality checks. They can be used to list the client's salient feelings, experiences, and behaviors, his newly acquired understandings of himself and their concomitant demand for action, and the working out of the action programs themselves in terms of both planning and execution, successes and failures. The helper can let the client know that he, too, may use the newsprint, or he can teach him how to do so. This is another way the helpee can become more of an agent in the helping process.

Identifying themes. Advanced accurate empathy includes the identification of behavioral and emotional *themes* in the data presented by the client during the course of his self-exploration and the communication of these themes to the client. For instance, without stating it explicitly, the client might intimate through what he reveals about his feelings, experiences, and behaviors that he is a very dependent person.

> *Counselor:* I've been thinking about what you've said to me. I see something that may be a pattern in your life, and I'd like to check it out with you. It's hard for you to act on your own. Letting others make decisions for you has proved less complicated, because you seem to get hurt when you decide for yourself, but because of this you don't feel like a fully functioning human being.

The client may hint that he is operating from a poor self-image.

> *Counselor:* As I've listened, this thought has struck me; in growing up you have learned one lesson well, and that is, "I am not a worthwhile human being." You seem to say this to yourself at work, in your relationships to your friends, and even when you're alone with yourself. It's a huge weight on your shoulders.

He may intimate that he acts as a parent toward his wife almost constantly.

> *Counselor:* I wonder if your wife experiences something that I have begun to feel here. It seems that your taking over the household finances, your controlling social involvements for both of you, making unilateral decisions about your job location—I wonder if you see these as ways of saying to your wife: "I am parent, you are child." And now she seems to be rebelling. Maybe she doesn't want to be child any longer.

Or the client may indicate that he retreats from social involvement whenever there is any threat of intimacy.

Counselor: Let's see if this makes any sense to you. On the one hand, you feel quite lonely; but on the other hand, you are reluctant to get close to others. You mentioned, for instance, that your friend talked more intimately with your brother when you visited him than you ever have. It's as if intimacy demands a price that you're not sure you're ready to pay.

In each of these cases, the counselor goes beyond what the client has said explicitly. The thematic material might refer to feelings (such as themes of failed enthusiasm, of depression, of anxiety), to behavior (such as themes of controlling others, of avoiding intimacy, of blaming others, of overwork), to experiences (themes of being a victim, of being seduced, of being feared, of being loved, of failing), or to combinations of these. Once the helper recognizes these themes, his task is to communicate those that are relevant to the client in a way that enables the client to see them too. This task demands a high degree of accurate empathy, tact, and initiative. If the helper tries to force thematic material down the throat of the client prematurely, the client will balk and the counselor will have to retrace his steps. On the other hand, if the helper is accurate in his identification of themes and tactful in his communication of his understanding to the client, he can help the client greatly to see himself in a new light. To some, the counselor's remarks in the examples above might sound too direct or premature. These remarks, however, are taken out of context—both the context of the Stage-I behaviors (which establish rapport) that have preceded them and the communication context itself (which includes important paralinguistic and nonverbal behaviors). It is obvious that themes should not be just invented, or borrowed from the abstract personality dynamics of some school:

Counselor: Your inferiority complex contaminates much of what you do. Your will to fail runs much deeper than your will to community.

Such a statement is obviously a caricature, but the point is clear: themes must be based solidly on an accurate understanding of the client's feelings, experiences, and behaviors and must be communicated as concretely as possible through the client's experience. Finally, a very important theme, but one that is often overlooked, is the theme of client resources, especially unused or underused resources.

Connecting islands. This metaphor suggests another approach to advanced accurate empathy. The helper attempts to build "bridges" between the "islands" (Ivey, 1971) of feelings, experiences, and behaviors revealed in the self-exploration stage. For instance, the client talks about being progressively more anxious and tired in recent weeks. Later he talks about getting ready for his marriage in a few months and about deadlines for turning in papers for current courses. Still later, he talks about his need to succeed, to compete, and to meet the expectations of his parents and grandparents.

> *Counselor:* John, it could be that your growing fatigue and anxiety have relatively simple explanations. One, you are really working very hard. Two, competing as hard as you do and striving for excellence have to take their physical and emotional toll. Maybe it would be more useful to look at these factors before digging around for more esoteric causes.

John talked about these three "islands" as if they were unrelated to one another. Once he was willing to explore their interrelatedness, he could also explore his values. For instance, did he want achievement and competition to rank as high in his priorities as they actually did?

Advanced accurate empathy means helping the client fill in the missing links in the data produced in the self-exploration process. For instance, if the client presents two separate "islands" of behavior—(1) his disagreements with his wife about sex, training the children, and budget and (2) his progressively heavier drinking—the missing link might be that the client is using his drinking behavior as a way of punishing his wife.

> *Counselor:* I wonder what the relationship is between your drinking and your disagreements with your wife, Bill. It sounds like an effective way of punishing her. Especially since you present it to the family as a separate problem, medical in nature.

The client has presented these two problems as separate. The counselor, in listening to the client, no longer sees them as separate, and he suggests the concept of punishment as a possible bridge between the two.

Of course, the counselor must be accurate in the connections or relationships he proposes. The counselor who works from a controlling rather than from a collaborative model of social influence might well be able to force the client to accept interpretations of his behavior that are not valid. But interpretations that are not based solidly on the experience and behavior of the client simply do not help. They lead the client into blind alleys and, in general, do more harm than good. For instance, a counselor may convince a client that he is the sole cause of the trouble in his marriage. If he would stop drinking, communication between him and his wife would get better. On the supposition that the man's wife is adding her share of irresponsibility to the marriage, such an interpretation simply would not help. When the client realizes he is going nowhere in counseling and quits, the low-level counselor attributes his quitting to a lack of motivation, an unwillingness to work at change, a refusal to face the truth about himself, and the like. A helper's power base is a source of great potential harm when used without behavior-expertness.

Helping a client draw conclusions from premises.   Still another way of conceptualizing advanced accurate empathy is to help the client draw his own conclusions from premises. Very often, in the data produced in the self-exploration process, there are certain implied premises from which certain logical conclusions can be drawn.

> *Client:* I really don't think that I can take my boss's abuse any longer. I don't think she really knows what she's doing. She thinks she is doing me a favor by pointing out what I do wrong all the time. She has no idea that she comes on patronizing and even abusive. I like the work and I'd like to stay, but, well, I just don't know.
>
> *Counselor A:* What makes this really frustrating is that your boss might not even realize what she's doing to you.
> *Counselor B:* The alternatives, then, are limited. One is to stay on the job and just "take it." But you feel that this has become too painful. Another is to talk with your boss directly about this whole destructive relationship. A third is to start thinking about changing jobs, even though you like the work there. We really haven't talked about the second or third possibility.

Counselor A's primary-level accurate empathy might help the client probe more deeply into her feelings, but the assumption here is that she has already done that. It is a question of moving forward. Counselor B combs through what has been said in their interaction up to this point and draws some conclusions from the premises laid down by the client. Perhaps the client is avoiding the subject of a direct confrontation with her boss. At some level of her being she might realize that she, too, has some responsibility with respect to this unproductive relationship. This possibility would have to be investigated.

In certain cases, the counselor may draw a tongue-in-cheek conclusion from the client's premises in order to show the client that the argument he is constructing is leading nowhere. Beier (1966) calls this response an "asocial" response, for it is not the kind of response expected by the client. For instance, suppose that a married man has been describing his wife's faults at great length. After a while, the counselor responds:

> *Counselor:* It was a mistake to marry such a woman, and maybe it's time to let her go.

Although this is not at all what the client has in mind, since it *is* a logical conclusion to the case the client has been constructing against his wife, it pulls the client up short. He realizes, perhaps, that he has gone too far, that he is making things sound worse than they really are.

> *Client:* Well, I don't think things are that bad. She does have her good points.

Beier claims that such "asocial" responses make the client stop and think. They provide what Beier calls "beneficial uncertainty" for the client. Asocial responses, obviously, can be overused, can be too facetious, and—in the hands of an inept counselor—can sound actually sarcastic (in expression if not in intent). The counselor who is uncomfortable with this kind of communication can get the same result by using a "social" rather than an "asocial" response. For instance, the counselor in the last example might have said:

> *Counselor:* I'm not sure whether you are trying to say that your wife has no redeeming qualities.
> *Client:* Oh. Well, I didn't mean to be too hard on her.

Some clients, in a relationship that is not working out, have to make the other person the scapegoat in order to reduce their own culpability, at least initially. In this example the counselor realizes that the client is engaging in hyperbole, and he helps the client understand what he is doing. The goal of Stage II should always be kept in mind. The "asocial" response and the state of "beneficial uncertainty" it causes are useful only to the degree that they help the client understand himself more adequately.

From the less to the more. One way to look at advanced accurate empathy in summary is to see it helping the client move from the less to the more. If the client is not clear about some issue, or if he speaks guardedly, then the helper speaks directly, clearly, and openly. For instance, a client might ramble, touching on sexual issues lightly as he moves along. The counselor helps him face these issues more squarely.

> *Counselor:* George, you have alluded to sexual concerns a few times. My guess is that sex is a pretty touchy issue for you to deal with. But it also seems to be a pretty important one.

Through advanced accurate empathy, what is said confusedly by the client is stated clearly by the helper; what is said half-heartedly is stated cogently; what is said vaguely is stated specifically and concretely; and what the client presents at a superficial level is re-presented by the helper at a deeper level. In a sense, the helper *interprets* the behavior of the client, but his interpretations are based on what the client reveals about his own feelings, experiences, and behavior and how the client acts during the counseling sessions themselves—*not* on abstract psychodynamics. Neither does the high-level helper lay his interpretations on his client like so many laws; he suggests them and invites the client's response so that they can collaborate in trying to understand the world as it really is.

Alternative frames of reference.   As Levy (1963, 1968) points out, the same set of facts and data are open to a variety of interpretations. Sometimes a client does not change because he is locked into an unproductive interpretation of certain facts. For instance, Fred has had strong affectional feelings for some of his classmates at a boys' school. On a couple of occasions he has engaged in sexual play with other boys. He has begun to be haunted by the idea that he is "a homosexual" (that is, a person who defines himself by his sexuality, especially atypical sexuality). The counselor, as a form of advanced accurate empathy, can offer Fred some alternative frames of reference.

> *Counselor:* I realize you've had these feelings and experiences, Fred. I'm not so sure that the only conclusion is that you are homosexual. You are very needy of love and affection—you don't get much of that at home. It could be that you get it when and how you can. And you have also told me that you are shy generally, but especially with girls. It's hard for you to go up and talk to a girl.

Suggesting alternative interpretations or frames of reference gives Fred room to move. He is not locked into a single and (for him) self-defeating view of his sexuality.

While this form of helper behavior is a kind of social influence, it is not the same as trying to talk someone out of something.

> *Counselor:* The way you describe your teacher's behavior, he sounds pretty insecure—maybe afraid of the class and especially you.
> *Student:* You mean he doesn't have it in for us? He just panics? I never thought that I could scare anyone.

This alternative view gives the student a chance to experiment with his own behavior rather than merely complain about another's. The purpose of suggesting alternative interpretations is to help the client control his behavior more effectively: "To sum up, psychological interpretation, viewed as a behavior ... consists of bringing an alternate frame of reference or language system to bear upon a set of observations or behaviors, with the end in view of making them more amenable to manipulation" (Levy, 1963, p. 7).

The categories of advanced accurate empathy described here are not meant to be completely distinct categories. There is obviously a great deal of overlap. They are cited to give the trainee a feeling for the concept of advanced accurate empathy and the way the communication of such empathy places a demand on the client to move forward toward self-understanding and action.

The manner of communicating advanced accurate empathy

Advanced accurate empathy is strong medicine: it gets at more critical, deeper, and more delicate issues and therefore puts the client under added stress. The supportive relationship that has been established between helper and client helps the client bear up under this added stress; still, the object of Stage II is not to overwhelm the client but to help him move forward toward self-understanding and action. As a sign of his care and respect, then, the counselor should move *tentatively* and *cautiously* to expressions of advanced accurate empathy. Indeed, he should be initially tentative and cautious in *all* the interactions that typify Stage II: advanced accurate empathy, helper self-disclosure, immediacy, confrontation, and the suggesting of alternative frames of reference.

Expressions of advanced accurate empathy should first be suggested in a tentative way and not just dumped on the client.

> *Counselor A:* You're not trying to help your wife see her mistakes. You're just punishing her.
> *Counselor B: From what you have said,* it *may be* that your wife sees your behavior as punishing rather than helpful.

> *Counselor A:* You are not trustworthy, for you keep letting your friends down.
> *Counselor B:* You *seem* to be saying that your friends *might well interpret* your behavior as letting them down. Then *it would follow* that they see you as untrustworthy.

> *Counselor A:* You just have to stop feeling so sorry for yourself. It's getting you nowhere.
> *Counselor B:* School is not going well and you are depressed, but *do you think* that this whole picture is made worse by a *tendency* on your part to feel a bit sorry for yourself?

In each of these cases, Counselor A bluntly confronts the client, while Counselor B tentatively and cautiously suggests something that the client might consider painful to hear. The italicized words and the question mark in the examples above show verbal ways of presenting advanced accurate empathy tentatively. However, tentativeness is also shown in nonverbal ways—by facial expression, tone of voice, and so forth. There are a whole host of verbal ways of indicating tentativeness (see Gazda, 1973, pp. 161–162, for a complete list):

> "Let's see if this makes sense to you. . . ."
> "If I hear you correctly, you seem to be saying that . . ."
> "Tell me if this sounds too strong to you. . . ."
> "Could it be that . . ."
> "I have been wondering whether . . ."

In the examples used so far to illustrate various kinds of advanced accurate empathy, some verbal indication of tentativeness has been included.

Another way of striking a tentative note is to respond *first* with primary-level accurate empathy and then to move on to advanced accurate empathy (or self-disclosure or confrontation or immediacy). Some might object to such caution and tentativeness, seeing in it a lack of genuineness. "Say what you mean, and say it directly, without any frills" would be the motto of this group. However, both respect for the client and concern for the overriding goal of Stage II (dynamic *self-understanding*) suggest a more tentative approach. One of the behavioral manifestations of respect is that the counselor helps the client use his own resources in the helping process as much as possible. If the helper *suggests,* at that point the client can actively *respond* to the suggestion and work it out in his own terms.

> *Counselor:* Could it be that the whole picture is made worse by a tendency on your part to feel sorry for yourself?
> *Client:* I'm beginning to see that I wallow in self-pity. Sometimes I daydream that I have been hurt by my friends just to be able to feel sorry for myself. I'm much more of a self-centered person than I've ever realized.

In this example, tentativeness on the part of the counselor helps the client understand himself a bit better. He does not have to defend himself against an accusation. The communication of advanced accurate empathy is not an abstract exercise in truth; it is the counselor's way of being with a person who has come for help. The effective helper neither retreats from dealing with important and painful issues directly, openly, and honestly, nor does he see any value in overwhelming the client needlessly. The goals of the helping process should define its techniques, not vice versa. In Stage III, as the relationship between helper and client grows stronger, the helper need not be as tentative and cautious as he might have been at the beginning of Stage II. He simply tries to do whatever he sees to be most helpful at any given moment. In certain cases, this can even mean talking less tentatively than has been indicated here, even in Stage II.

Counselor self-disclosure

If a counselor reveals something about his own personal life to his client, does this help the client? The answer to this question, worded that generally, is that it depends. As we have already noted, social science researchers have become quite interested in self-disclosure as a form of human interaction, encompassing at least three areas: mutual self-disclosure in human-relations-training programs, self-disclosure in everyday life, and both client and helper self-disclosure in counseling and psychotherapy.

When it comes to helper self-disclosure in counseling, however, the evidence is not all in yet and the evidence that we have is not completely clear. There are two somewhat contradictory sets of evidence: one set urges helper self-disclosure, while the other cautions against it.

The foremost proponents of helper self-disclosure are Mowrer (1973) and Jourard (1968, 1971a, 1971b), but their approaches are quite different. Mowrer's position on helper self-disclosure grows out of his whole philosophy of helping, to which self-disclosure is central. The client, if he wants to be helped, must reveal himself completely to the members of a peer self-help group, especially in those areas of his life in which he has lived or is living irresponsibly and dishonestly. The leader of the group also discloses himself completely. When someone wants to enter the group, the leader (or a member designated by the leader or by the group itself) meets with him before entry and models the kind of self-disclosure that will be demanded of him once he enters the group. In this case, self-disclosure of both past and present irrespon-sibilities takes place all at once. Before he enters the group, the prospective member must contract to engage in the same kind of self-disclosure. This kind of immediate and total self-disclosure (at least with respect to the areas of life in which the client is not living effectively) is charac-teristic of many peer self-help groups, such as Alcoholics Anonymous (see Hurvitz, 1970).

Jourard's approach to self-disclosure is much less moralistic and perhaps more pragmatic. He sees self-disclosure as an essential part of the process of self-actualization. His approach to helper self-disclosure is more restricted than Mowrer's but more extensive than Carkhuff's (1969). Jourard, too, urges the helper to disclose himself to his client in the early stages of the helping process because, according to his research, such self-disclosure increases the quantity and heightens the quality of the client's self-disclosure. Like Mowrer, he sees the average person in psychological trouble as an underdiscloser who must, in the safety of the helping process, learn how to disclose himself more effectively. The troubled person invests too much time and energy in constructing facades and trying to keep them from crumbling. The counselor helps the client by modeling self-disclosure himself. In social-influence terms, this modeling adds to the helper's power base, for it increases his attractiveness to the client (through "positive similarity" self-disclosure), enhances his trustworthiness (for he first trusts the client enough to reveal himself), and adds credence to his statements of accurate empathy ("I know your world because, at least in some analogous way, I've been there, too"). A disclosing counselor also decreases the *role* distance between himself and the client. Hopefully, then, the heightened mutuality that ensues increases the probability of collaboration between client and counselor. All in all, a helper's self-disclosure increases his ability to *work with* the client (Murphy & Strong, 1972) early in the helping process in order to encourage the client to engage in self-exploration. In a sense, such modeling is an act of social influence: it places a demand on the client to reveal himself. Bundza and Simonson (1973) and Combs (1969) also offer evidence for the usefulness of helper self-disclosure.

On the other hand, Weigel and his associates (1972) have found evidence suggesting that helper self-disclosure can frighten the client or make the helper seem less effective.

Many of the studies urging self-disclosure have used so-called "normals" (for example, college students) as subjects in analogue studies. Such subjects constitute relatively high-level "clients." It may well be that interviewer self-disclosure does help such clients to disclose themselves. However, the more disorganized the subject (such as a real client with relatively severe problems) is, the more he is affected adversely by helper self-disclosure. He sees it not as a help but as a threat.

What principles can be stated, then, to govern the use of counselor self-disclosure? First of all, a high-level helper should be willing to do whatever he ethically can to help his client. Therefore, he should be willing to disclose himself to the client if and when he believes it will be helpful. He should also hold responsible and appropriate self-disclosure as a value in his own life. Practically speaking, this means that there should be people with whom he shares himself intimately. Since a helper expects his clients to reveal themselves to him intimately in the counseling interviews, it would be worse than anomalous if the helper did not know what it meant—in terms of both cost and benefit—to reveal himself deeply to another person.

Next, since self-disclosure in human relationships is not an end in itself, counselor self-disclosure should be related to some counseling goal. In Stage I, as has been noted, the goal is to improve the quality of client self-exploration, while in Stage II it is to help the client come to a better understanding of himself. Counselor self-disclosure can achieve neither of these goals, however, unless it is responsible and appropriate. What does "appropriate" mean in this context?

First, counselor self-disclosure should not add another burden to an already overburdened client. Many years ago, a friend of mine came to me to talk over a problem that was bothering him. I thought it was only right to let him know that he was not alone in having this problem, so I began to let him know something about myself. But he cut me off quickly, saying "Hey, don't tell me your problems. I'm having a hard enough time dealing with my own. I don't want to carry yours around, too." Our interchange illustrates two points. First, the helper cannot help unless he is living more effectively than the client, at least in the areas in which he is trying to help. Second, the helper should not add another burden to those of the client by his self-disclosure. Therefore, even though a counselor should be *willing* to disclose himself, he should first determine whether his disclosure is likely to *help* the client explore himself further or understand himself better. Both the quality and the timing of his disclosure are critical.

Second, counselor self-disclosure is inappropriate if it distracts the client from his problems. More positively, helper self-disclosure should help the client focus more clearly, concretely, and accurately on his areas of ineffective living and the resources he can draw upon to live more effectively.

> *Client:* I seem to be most anxious when I wake up in the morning. I just don't want to face the day. It's too scary.
> *Counselor A:* I experienced this kind of morning anxiety at one period of my life. It was when I was in graduate school and wasn't sure that I was good enough. I didn't know what I wanted out of life. But it all passed away.
> *Client:* Do you think that yours was related to the aimlessness of school life?

> *Client:* I seem to be most anxious when I wake up in the morning. I just don't want to face the day. It's too scary.

> *Counselor B:* It becomes a painful struggle just to get out of bed. I think that I went through some of that in the army. It made the world seem pretty grim.
> *Client:* It's just that it's such a painful struggle. But I think that the world would be even more grim if I were to give up the struggle.

Counselor A distracts the client and shifts attention to himself, while Counselor B blends self-disclosure with accurate empathy and wins a much more growthful response from the client.

Third, helper self-disclosure is inappropriate if it is too frequent. This, too, distracts the client and shifts attention to the counselor. Research (Murphy & Strong, 1972) has shown that if an interviewer discloses himself too frequently, the client may see him as a phony or suspect that he has ulterior motives.

Some suggest that there is a curvilinear relationship between counselor self-disclosure and effective helping. They hypothesize that the low-disclosing counselor is ineffective because he is seen as aloof, weak, and role conscious ("I am the helper; you are the helpee"). On the other hand, the high-disclosing counselor may be ineffective because he is seen as too powerful and/or lacking in discretion (and therefore untrustworthy). The moderately disclosing counselor is effective, so the theory goes, because he provides a competent model of self-disclosure, encourages mutuality, and proves himself trustworthy (by saying to the client, in effect, "I trust *you*"). ·

I suggest that the high-level counselor knows when to disclose himself and that he can safely do so either in Stage I or in Stage II. It is better for the beginner to wait until Stage II, for he does not yet have enough experience to judge the impact of his interactions. As he learns how to handle self-disclosure in the counseling interview, he can use it whenever it seems appropriate. Some research (Tuckman, 1966; Vondracek, 1969) suggests that the helper can get the client to reveal more by using probing techniques (such as open-ended questions) than by "reflecting" (as Rogers and Carkhuff suggest) or "revealing" (as Jourard suggests). But, first of all, client self-revelation is not a goal in itself. While it can be cathartic and healing in itself, it is usually subsidiary to other goals—that is, dynamic self-understanding and action. Second, accurate empathy is far more than mere "reflecting"; it is in itself a kind of probing. Third, since much of the research on self-disclosure takes place in the laboratory over very restricted periods of time (such as one session) with clients who are not particularly disturbed ("normals"), one should keep in mind that both client and counselor self-disclosure take on a different meaning in longer-term helping relationships. Therefore, at least at this stage of theory, research, and model elaboration, it seems unwise to overemphasize *or* to minimize any particular helping skill. The effective counselor has a wide repertory of skills and responses, including "probing," "reflecting," and "revealing." He draws easily on these and on any other skill to help him achieve the goals of counseling.

In summary, then, counselor self-disclosure is a skill or response that should certainly be part of the helper's repertory. He should use self-disclosure whenever it seems appropriate—in Stage I to encourage client self-exploration, in Stage II to further client self-understanding—but he should be careful not to burden, overwhelm, or distract the client.

Self-disclosure in training groups

In any experiential approach to learning helping skills, the trainees take turns being helper, helpee, and observer. I have already suggested that the trainee, in the role of helpee, deal with some of the real problematic in his life. Role-playing, of course, is another possibility: trainees take turns playing a variety of "problem people." However, the trainee not only should learn a set of helping skills in the training process but should also use training as an opportunity to consider how effectively he himself is living, especially in those areas of life that have the greatest impact on his ability to help (such as his interpersonal style, his ability to face crises, the discipline in his life, or his ability to make legitimate demands of others). Therefore, even though trainees begin by role-playing "problem people" until they become more comfortable with one another and develop a degree of trust in the training group, eventually they should become real clients; that is, they should deal with whatever constitutes an obstacle to their effective helping. If the trainees are serious about becoming a "learning community," this kind of self-disclosure will not be inappropriate at all. I do not suggest that the trainees engage in secret-dropping or self-disclosure for its own sake. But, since they are eventually going to place demands on others to live more effectively, I believe that they should begin by placing these kinds of demands on one another.

Let's consider a simple example. During a general group session or a subgroup practice session, John, a helper/trainee, reveals the following about himself:

John: Whenever I'm uncertain about myself in interpersonal situations —like here—I compensate by becoming cocky, "witty," or even cynical. I could almost say that I use my own kind of "theater" to defend myself from being put down by others. I've been doing a certain amount of that here, and I don't like it. I doubt if you like it. It just doesn't fit in with what we're trying to do here.

This is hardly dramatic secret-dropping, but it is disclosure of a problem that might well interfere with John's ability to help. If the trainees can work out problems like this during the course of their training, they are double winners: they develop skills and they deal with some of the problematic areas of their lives. One trainee said, at the end of a semester, "I'm still unsure of my ability to be a helper, but I've received more help here on a variety of problems than I have anywhere else."

How far, then, should the members of a training group go in self-disclosure? Where do fellow members fit on the privacy ladder, or in what Simon and his associates (Simon, Howe, & Kirschenbaum, 1972) call "the privacy circles" (self, special intimates, intimates, friends, acquaintances, strangers)? It is easy to see that in some respects a helper becomes for a client a kind of *ad hoc* intimate or special intimate for a certain period of time. But where do fellow helper/trainees fit? Perhaps the ideal runs something like this: just as a counselor should be willing to reveal anything that might help his client but does so only if he sees that it is appropriate, so the members of training groups should be willing to deal with those issues that are related to achieving the goals of the group. The level of trust in a group depends on two interrelated factors: the willingness of the members to share themselves and the quality of the response they receive once they do share themselves. Stage-I skills, then, are critical to the life of any helping community.

A number of authors have addressed themselves to the question of the criteria for judging the appropriateness of self-disclosure, both in everyday life and in human-relations-training and helper-preparation groups (Culbert, 1967; Egan, 1970, 1971, 1973a; Luft, 1969). Whatever a training group's approach to self-disclosure might be, the ground rules should be clear from the start.

Confrontation

Interpersonal confrontation is a fact of everyday life. It is also a fact that confrontation is used fairly widely in helping relationships—both in one-to-one relationships and in groups. For instance, confrontation plays an important part in many kinds of peer self-help groups (Hurvitz, 1970; Maslow, 1967; Mowrer, 1968a; Yablonsky, 1965) and encounter groups (Egan, 1970). Both confrontation and self-criticism have characterized a wide variety of successful utopian communities (Kanter, 1972, pp. 14ff, 37ff). Whether confrontation is used wisely in all of these situations is another matter. At any rate, confrontation is certainly a controversial issue, and both helpers and trainers in human-relations groups continue to argue its pros and cons, its effectiveness and its risks. Confrontation has been the topic of a certain minimal amount of research: some researchers have found it useful (for example, Berenson, Mitchell, & Laney, 1968; Berenson, Mitchell, & Moravec, 1968), while others have found it relatively ineffective (for example, Kaul, Kaul, & Bednar, 1973). To add to the confusion, there is no standard definition of confrontation and no agreement in the literature on what results it is supposed to have. What *is* the function of confrontation? In the Kaul, Kaul, and Bednar study it is seen as related (ineffectively) to client self-exploration (a Stage-I function), while Carkhuff (1969a,b) sees it as related to client self-understanding and action (a Stage-II function). Berenson and Mitchell (1974) have written the most comprehensive study available on confrontation. They warn against its abuse and take issue with the helper who makes confrontation his specialty.

Given all this confusion, the beginning helper is faced with the question: should I confront or not? The answer is that it depends. No more definitive answer can be given without a more concrete explanation of confrontation—of both its nature and its goals. The purpose of this section on confrontation, then, is to help the counselor understand the nature of confrontation so that he may decide what place this particular skill should have in his helping repertory. This section will consider the nature and goals of confrontation, what areas in the client's life should be confronted, how to confront, the impact of confrontation on the client, and some cautions in the use of confrontation.

Toward an understanding of the nature and functions of confrontation

Some see confrontation—and I hope this is a caricature—as an attack, often a vicious attack, on another person, generally for this person's "own good." As such, it is highly negative and highly punitive —designed, it seems to me, to help the confronter get a load off his chest rather than to help the confrontee live more effectively. It would seem that such confrontation, almost by definition, is useless in helping relationships. Nevertheless, there are those who see such "attack therapy" as growthful if it takes place in a structured way in the context of a supportive community (Maslow, 1967). But whatever the value of this kind of punitive confrontation, this is not the meaning of confrontation here.

Confrontation as an extension of advanced accurate empathy.   Confrontation at its best is an extension of advanced accurate empathy; that is, it is a response to the client, based on a deep understanding of the client's feelings, experiences, and behavior, that involves some unmasking of distortions in the client's understanding of himself and some (at least implied) challenge to action.

> *Counselor:* You would like your daughter to respect you and think of you as honest. You especially would like her to be honest with you, now that she is about to go out with boys. On the other hand, you feel that there are some things she shouldn't know about you "for her own good," especially in the area of your relationships with men. You have to put her off when she asks you questions in this area. And at times you even have to tell her "white lies" so that she won't be hurt by the truth. But all of this makes you uneasy—more than uneasy; you feel pulled apart by it.

Here the counselor helps the client put together some of the facts that have emerged in the process of self-exploration. His response is based on facts the client herself revealed, but the counselor puts these facts together in a way in which the client has so far failed to do. This involves a certain unmasking and an implied challenge to action. Let's suppose that the client replies something like this:

> *Client:* I've never thought of it that way before, but this *is* what I'm doing—and it's not a very pretty picture. It seems that I have two standards: one for myself and one for my daughter. And I rationalize my behavior by thinking of what is "best for her." If I think that my relationships with the men in my life are right, moral, and good for me, then I should be able to share this part of my life in some responsible way with my daughter. But if I think what I'm doing is wrong—and I'm not sure I'm ready to do that —then I should start thinking of changing my behavior. Anyway, something has to be done.

She finds this kind of self-exploration and understanding painful but real. The client often has to make painful decisions, but the counselor is there both to understand his pain and to help him through it.

Confrontation, as it is described in the following pages, means a responsible unmasking of the discrepancies, distortions, games, and smoke screens the client uses to hide both from self-understanding and from constructive behavioral change. It also involves challenging the undeveloped, the underdeveloped, the unused, and the misused potentialities, skills, and resources of the client, with a view to examining and understanding these resources and putting them to use in action programs. Confrontation is an invitation by the helper to the client to explore his defenses—those that keep him from understanding and those that keep him from action.

The goals of confrontation are to help the client explore areas of feelings, experiences, and behavior that he has so far been reluctant to explore.

> *Counselor:* We keep digging into the deficits of your marriage, almost as if there were nothing good about it. It might be helpful to try to put it into perspective by examining what is good in it.

They help the client understand modes of self-destructive behavior and unused resources.

> *Counselor:* It seems that one thing you've learned is that punishing your son over and over again hasn't worked. It has not changed his behavior appreciably. Could it be that your persistent use of punishment even when it proves ineffective says something about you?

> *Counselor:* Jim, you really don't like your teacher. You can admit that to yourself. You also see that you're not going to change her style. You're enough of a realist to see that. So, disrupting her class, while it does help you vent your anger, doesn't really change her. You end up the loser. There are two months of class left this year. How can you be honest about your feelings and still not keep hurting yourself?

They help him learn how to confront himself.

> *Counselor:* Mary, we've written down on the newsprint all the things you see your husband doing wrong. I wonder if you could come up with another list: a list of things you do or don't do that you think might bother *him.*

In Stage II, the first two goals (exploring, understanding) are of primary importance, while the second two (acting, learning) are more important in Stage III. The logic of counseling applies also to confrontation: if the counselor confronts responsibly, the client will learn how to confront himself and, eventually, how to confront others—not destructively, but with respect and care. Indeed, one of the behavioral manifestations of respect is that the person who respects another uses negatively valanced responses such as confrontation in a way that promotes the growth of the other.

What should be confronted?

Discrepancies.   In all of us there are various discrepancies: between what we think and feel and what we say, what we say and what we do, our views of ourselves and others' views of us, what we are and what we wish to be, what we really are and what we experience ourselves to be, and our verbal and nonverbal expressions of ourselves. These categories, obviously, have to be translated into specific instances:

> I'm confused and angry, but I say that I feel fine.
> I hold that it's important to be physically fit, but I allow myself to become overweight, and I don't exercise.
> I see myself as witty, while others see me as biting.
> I would like to be a skillful helper, but I'm awkward and inept in a number of necessary helping skills, yet I do not practice.
> I experience myself as ugly, when in reality my looks are somewhat above average.
> I say "yes" with my words, but my body says "no."
> I say that I'm interested in others, but I don't attend to them or try to understand them.

The skilled counselor can help the client understand himself better by helping him see the variety of discrepancies that exist in his life.

> *Counselor:* Jim, you've talked about a need for discipline in your study habits. I was wondering whether you think that there might be a more general need for discipline in your life. For instance, do you think it might be important to get yourself in better physical shape?
> *Client:* I know I need a great deal of discipline, but I'd never thought of my body. In fact, until this moment I thought the fact that I didn't care what my body looked like was a good sign. My body is pretty sloppy, and it might be just one sign of my sloppy approach to life.

The integrated person cannot say to his body, "I have no need of thee." In this example the counselor confronts this discrepancy in the form of a question, for asking is one way of expressing tentativeness. His confrontation, then, is not an attack but an invitation to the client to explore, understand, and act.

> *Distortions.*   People who cannot face things as they really are tend to distort them. The way we see the world is often an indication of our needs rather than a true picture of what the world is like. For instance:

> I'm afraid of you and therefore I see you as aloof, although in reality you are a caring person.
> I see a teacher in some kind of divine role, and therefore I make unwarranted demands on him.
> I see my wife's getting a job as a sign of alienation from me rather than her way of exercising her own creativity and independence.
> I see my stubbornness as commitment.

One way the counselor can help the client who is caught up in his own distortions of life is to suggest alternative frames of reference for viewing self, others, or life itself. For instance, he might suggest:

Life can be seen as challenge rather than as just pain.

You're indulging in self-pity rather than engaging in heroic forbearance.

You should think of learning as more than formal education and things such as grades and degrees.

You seem really sarcastic, not just witty.

You are somewhat of a seducer rather than just a victim.

Helping others is a privilege rather than a burden.

You are afraid to act rather than unable to act.

Your care for your daughter is smothering rather than nurturing.

Intimacy is rewarding rather than just demanding.

Counselor: Jim, you have described getting close to people as a pretty burdensome thing. It cuts into your study time, people let you down, people make unreasonable demands of you. I wonder whether you have experienced any rewards in your closer relationships.

Counselor: Sarah, you say that your boy friends tend to take advantage of you—so much that now you are beginning to fear for your reputation. On the other hand, your dress is sexy, you agree to go parties where being "taken advantage of" is part of the scene, and one of your goals is to be popular. I wonder whether you see any contradictions here?

Suggesting alternative frames of reference helps the client break out of self-defeating views of self, others, and the world. One of the functions of Stage II is to help the client see himself and the world from a less personal and more objective point of view. Alternative frames of reference serve this function, provided that they are accurate and that they are presented in a way that helps rather than merely punishes the client.

Games, tricks, and smoke screens. If I am comfortable with my delusions and profit by them in some way, I will obviously try to keep them. If I'm rewarded for playing games—that is, if I get others to meet my needs by playing games—then I will continue a game approach to life. For instance, I'll play "Yes, but . . ."—that is, I will present myself as one in need of help or counsel and then proceed to show my helper how ineffective the advice given to me is, how such a solution will not work, and so on. Or I make myself appear helpless and needy to my friends, and then when they come to my aid, I get angry at them for treating me like a child. Or I seduce others in one way or another and then become indignant when they accept my covert invitations. The number of games people can play in order to avoid intimacy and other forms of effective living is seemingly endless. Clients who are fearful of changing will often attempt to lay down smoke screens in order to hide from the counselor the ways in which they fail to seize life. Such clients use communication in order *not* to communicate (Beier, 1966).

If the counselor is effective in Stage I, he creates an atmosphere in which it is almost impossible for the client to play games during the counseling interviews themselves. The good helper does not get "hooked" into client games. For instance, since he doesn't start out by giving the client advice, this prevents him from playing the "Yes, but . . ." game with the client. However, if the client does attempt to play games or to lay down diversionary smoke screens during the counseling interviews, the helper should challenge the client in a caring and responsible way.

> *Client:* I really like you. And I like the way we've been going about these sessions. You're so strong, and it feels good to be with such a strong person.
> *Counselor:* In a way I appreciate your liking me, but in a way it bothers me a bit. If I had to choose, I think I would prefer your respecting me to your liking me. This is a painful process you're going through, in which I place demands on you. I'm not sure that you always like my demands. But that's all right if what we do here is helpful. Does this make any sense to you?

This interchange is taken out of context, but let's suppose that the client is, at least subconsciously, trying to "engage" (Beier, 1966) the helper in order to slow him down or lead him away from delicate issues. The counselor says, in effect, "We have work to do here and the quality of our relationship should help us get this work done rather than stand in the way of it." His confrontation can lead to their exploring what is happening in their relationship to each other (direct, mutual communication: "you-me" talk).

The counselor should also challenge games the client is playing with others outside the counseling relationship.

> *Counselor:* You've spent a lot of time letting your friends know that you are incapable of certain tasks or not available, and now it seems that it's backfired. A number of your friends have stopped making demands on you, and your social life has become quite hollow.
> *Client:* Yes, in subtle ways I kept saying "You can't expect me to do this or be available to do that." I kept representing myself as a fairly helpless person so that I wouldn't get caught in things I didn't want to do. Now I'm paying for it. There's a great distance between me and many of my friends.

This client got caught in his own game. The counselor's statement is one of accurate empathy, but it also helps unmask the game the client had been playing in his social life. The client reacts by making this understanding his own. His question now is: "How do I reverse this process?" He is ready for an action program. And this is one of the functions of confrontation: to prepare the client for action.

> *Counselor:* You're not really this weak, incapable person you've made yourself out to be. In fact, you have a number of solid interpersonal strengths: you can be direct, open, and honest. You're capable of caring for

others, even though you may have avoided this in the past. You have a desire for community, even though you've allowed this to be thwarted in the past. You know how to admit your mistakes, to face them, and you want to do something about them. I think we've seen all of this in these interviews.

The counselor goes on to enumerate some of the strengths that the client possesses but has not used effectively in his interpersonal life. The client has to decide how intensively he wants to live, for he does have the capability to live intensively—at least more intensively than he is living now. Listing his resources in itself challenges him to act.

Evasions.   Clients have a way of avoiding real issues because real issues are, of course, painful. One way of doing this is to blame others for everything that is going wrong in one's own life.

> *Counselor:* I have a pretty good feeling for what your teacher does wrong. What do you think you do to annoy *her?*
> *Student:* I don't do anything. I mind my own business.
> *Counselor:* Let me put it another way. What do you think *she* thinks you do wrong? What would she say about you if she were complaining about you to someone else?
> *Student:* Well, she'd say that I'm lazy, that I don't pay any attention in class, that my work is sloppy.

The counselor is not trying to take sides, but he is trying to see both sides of the picture. He now has a few more leads to examine.

Some clients try to claim, directly or indirectly, that they don't have the resources for a particular action program.

> *Client:* I've tried to stop drinking, but I just can't.
> *Counselor:* Can you tell me some of the things you've tried?

Making a client be more concrete about his generalizations (and therefore less evasive) is a kind of confrontation. There are many ways in which a client can be defensive (Gazda, 1973, pp. 42ff). Confrontation should help the client move from a defensive posture, but it should not make him feel defenseless.

Behavior versus values.   Should the helper confront the client's behavior or the source of his behavior—that is, his values? Let's take a look at a confrontation of nonproductive *behavior.*

> *Counselor:* John, when you speak, there is almost always an edge of hostility in your voice. And yet I see in you a person who is fundamentally "for" others—but maybe also afraid of tenderness or closeness.

This is a confrontation of the client's behavior, but it also includes a reference to the client's resources. The message is, "You have the potential to be more effective in interpersonal relationships. Let's see what we can do to pursue that goal."

It is much more difficult to challenge the client's values (unless a given value is patently inhuman—for instance, sadistic pleasure derived from punishing others). Let's consider a case in which the counselor confronts a value the client holds.

> *Counselor:* Bill, you invest too much of yourself in work. Work doesn't really enhance your life; it imprisons you. You don't own your work; it owns you.
> *Client:* It's my life and it's what I like to do. Do I have to be like everyone else?

Work is a legitimate value, and, if the counselor attacks it directly, he can expect the client to react defensively. However, the counselor should challenge the client to probe his values and get a clear picture of what his value priorities are so that the client can see what value *conflicts* exist in his life. If the client is pursuing self-destructive or other-destructive values, these can be challenged directly. If, on the other hand, he is pursuing values so divergent that they are pulling him apart, he should be challenged to establish value priorities.

> *Counselor:* Tom, you like your work, it's satisfying in itself, and the pay is good. But it keeps you away from your family a great deal. You've complained of the lack of communication between you and your wife and between you and your children. Work and family life are not mixing well. It might be time to take a more serious look at this.
> *Client:* I'm so into my work that I don't think I want to even think about changing jobs. But you're right, the home situation keeps deteriorating and the only way I've handled that is by spending more time at work.

It is not the function of the counselor to try to get the client to adopt his set of values or the value priorities he espouses. But he should help the client face the value conflicts that are causing turmoil in his life.

The manner of confronting

The question is not whether the counselor should confront the client or not but *how* he should go about it *if* he sees that confrontation might help. His manner of confronting should increase the probability of achieving his goals: the client's increased self-understanding and action. How, then, should confrontation take place?

In the spirit of accurate empathy. We have already seen that advanced accurate empathy is often confrontational in itself. As Carkhuff notes, "The deepest level of empathy will tell the helper that the helpee wants not so much to be reinforced by a communicated understanding of his expressed ... existence as he wants to be enabled to *break free* from life's confusing and suffocating processes" (Carkhuff, 1969a, p. 210). Even if a given expression of confrontation is not seen as identical with advanced accurate empathy, it should still take place in the *spirit* of such empathy. All interactions with the client should be based on an accurate understanding of the client.

> *Counselor:* If I can put together what you are saying, Mary, there are two themes. You love your husband and show your love by being available to him, by caring for him, by the way you work around the home and with the children, and by expressing your happiness when things are going well for him. But there is also a theme of distrust, alienation, and perhaps dislike. For instance, you have not really forgiven him his past infidelity; you're no longer willing to share what is deepest in you with him; and by your cynicism you might be destroying him in little ways. How do you see this?

If this assessment is accurate, it is likely to be constructively confrontational.

Tentatively. As in the case of all Stage-II interventions, confrontation should take place tentatively, especially in the early part of this stage.

> *Counselor:* Could it be that the anger you "swallow" at faculty meetings doesn't "stay down"? From what you've said, it seems to dribble out somewhat in cynical remarks, aloofness, and uncooperative behavior. Does this make any sense to you? I'm wondering if I have the correct picture.

The fact that this counselor's statement is filled with qualifications enables the client to accept the picture more easily, to add to it, and to qualify it without feeling accused by the helper. If the counselor dumps a load of bricks on the client by his confrontation, the client will have to pour his energy into recovering from the blow rather than try to assimilate and work with the confrontation. See how different the following example of intervention sounds from the preceding ones.

> *Counselor:* You don't really "swallow" your anger. It's dribbling out unproductively all the time. I don't think you're fooling anyone but yourself.

This is confrontation, but the counselor's manner is accusatory. The counseling session should not be a courtroom scene in which the counselor is trying to prove his case against the client. Still, many counselors fall into this trap, for their actions indicate that their being right is more important. They forget the fundamental rule: helping is for the client.

With care.   Basic respect demands that the counselor confront with care. Let's try to operationalize the expression "with care."

Involvement.   Confrontation should be a way in which the counselor involves himself with the client. If, through confrontation, the helper finds himself standing off from the client, he is probably not confronting with care.

Motivation.   The motive of the counselor should be to help the client, not to be right, to punish, to get back at the client, or to put him in his place. Some counselors tend to vent their frustrations through confrontation, not realizing that their lack of skill is often the real source of their frustration. A counselor who appears to be working from a motive other than helping is seen as untrustworthy by the client and loses his base of influence.

Relationship between client and counselor.   Confrontation should be proportioned to the relationship between the counselor and the client. We all know that we are more willing to hear strong words from some than from others. If the helper has done little to establish rapport with the client, there probably should be no confrontation. Caring confrontation presupposes some kind of intimacy between confronter and confrontee. This intimacy should be real and not merely some kind of role-intimacy presumed to exist because of the counseling relationship itself.

The state of the client.   The counselor should judge the *present* ability of the client to assimilate what he is saying. If the client is disorganized and confused at the moment, it does little good to add to his disorganization by challenging him further.

> *Client:* Boy, I had no idea things were as bad as I see them now. It's like being groggy—I don't even want to look at myself for a while.

> *Counselor A:* Even now, you're running away from what I'm saying. It's the same thing you do with your wife, your friends, anyone who gets close to you or challenges you.
> *Counselor B:* What you're learning about yourself here is painful and confusing. You need time to let all this sink in, to settle down, to get your bearings.

Counselor B recognizes the client's disorganization and tries to help and support him by understanding what is going on (primary-level accurate empathy). Counselor A, on the other hand, moves in for the kill, for he wants to hear a response (a confession of guilt) *right now* that will satisfy *him.*

The method of successive approximation.   In many cases, confrontation will be more effective if it is gradual. The client has to assimilate what is being said to him; he has to make it his own, or it will not last. Good behavior-modification technique does not demand everything from the client all at once. Behavioral demands are spaced, and successes are rewarded. This movement in small steps, each of which is reinforced, toward a behavioral goal is called the method of "successive approxima-tion." To use this method, the helper has to break down the client's undesirable behavior into simpler components or units. He will be more likely to succeed if he starts with *concrete* units that are not so crucial as others and that are relatively easy to change. Let's take a look at an example of what *not* to do.

> *Counselor:* If you want to get rid of these feelings of loneliness, you have to get out there *today* and start interacting effectively with other people.

This counselor is not concrete, and he asks for everything at once. If he asks for everything at once, he will most likely get nothing. Let's take another example, in which the helper is much more aware of the method of successive approximation. The client is worried over the fact that he makes a poor impression on others. We pick up the interview some-where in Stage II.

> *Counselor:* You've said that you make a poor impression on people—that you seem, almost invariably, to start off on the wrong foot. One thing that might help is to try to be more attentive to others right from the start. When we are together here, for instance, your posture frequently seems to say that you are someplace else. I think that others might see you as being interested in them if you simply attended to them more carefully.

This counselor realizes that there might be many things wrong with his client's approach to others, but his approach is systematic: he starts with a behavior that is relatively easy to change, and he challenges the client to change his behavior here and now, in the counseling session itself.

Let's consider another example. In this case the client is too passive and ends up being ignored by others.

> *Counselor A:* You're too passive, Ted. You have to go out and seize life if you expect others to pay any attention to you.

The concept "passive" is too general, and the solution offered is too vague for Ted to seize. "Being passive" should be broken down into concrete behaviors that can be learned gradually.

> *Counselor B:* Ted, it could be that one reason people overlook or ignore you is that you don't assert yourself very much. Since you hang back, soon no one is noticing you. For instance, your voice is so soft and quiet that sometimes it's hard to hear you. It might help to begin by speaking up more.

Counselor B realizes that Ted needs some degree of assertiveness training. He confronts the client with a general view of his behavior, but he gets explicit immediately. He also uses the counseling situation itself as a place to start; it is a safe situation and can be controlled. The examples given deal with both self-understanding and action. The method of successive approximation will be taken up again in the discussion of Stage III, in which action programs are treated specifically.

The response of the client who is confronted

Even when confrontation is a response to a client's plea to be helped to live more effectively, it usually precipitates some degree of disorganization in the client. As we have seen, different writers refer to this experience under different terms: "crisis" (Carkhuff), "disorganization" (Douds), "a sense of inadequacy" (Mehrabian), "disequilibrium" (Piaget), and "beneficial uncertainty" (Beier). All of these authors suggest that counseling-precipitated crises *can* be beneficial for the client. Whether they are or not depends, to a great extent, on the skill of the helper.

Social-influence theory says that a person who feels inadequate is open (for better or for worse) to social-influence processes to a greater degree than others. Confrontation, since it usually does induce some sense of inadequacy in the client, can render him more open to influence. One way of looking at confrontation is from the point of view of cognitive-dissonance theory. Confrontation induces dissonance. For instance, if the client is playing a game with the helper, confrontation robs him of the security of the game. Or, if the helper points out to the client that he is punishing others under the guise of helping them, the client, thus "found out" or challenged, experiences confusion or dissonance. Since dissonance is an uncomfortable state, the client will try to get rid of it. Let's examine the typical ways in which a person experiencing dissonance attempts to rid himself of this discomfort.

Discredit the confronter.   Attack the confronter; discredit him; show him that he is no better than anyone else.

> *Client:* It's easy for you to sit there and suggest that I be more "responsi-ble" in my marriage. You've never had to experience the misery in which we live. You've never experienced his brutality. You probably live in one of those "nice" middle-class marriages.

This is one of the most prevalent strategies for coping with confrontation: counterattack. The counselor who elicits this kind of response from his client knows that he is doing something wrong. He is not being experienced as being "with" the client and, therefore, his help is seen as attack. Counterattack is hardly a creative response to confrontation, so the helper should not elicit it.

Persuade the confronter to change his views.   Reason with him; show him that you're not really that bad or that he is misinterpreting what you do. Here the client rationalizes his behavior:

> *Client:* I'm not so sure that my anger at home isn't called for. I think that it's part of my identity, at least in the sense that if I were to lie down and die, I would become a doormat at home. I think you see me as a fairly reasonable person. I don't get angry here because it isn't called for.

Sometimes a client like this will lead the unwary counselor into an argument about his behavior. A client who is highly committed to rationalization is difficult to deal with, but argument is not an effective instrument.

Devaluate the importance of the topic being discussed.   This is another form of rationalization. For instance, if the client is being confronted about his sarcasm, he points out that he is rarely sarcastic, that "poking fun at others" is a minor part of his life and not worth spending time on. The fact that clients sometimes run from topics that are too painful emphasizes the necessity of an accurate understanding of the client's feelings, experiences, and behavior. The client has a right to devaluate a topic if it really isn't important. The counselor has to be sensitive enough to discover which issues are important and which are not.

Seek support for one's own views elsewhere.   Some clients change coun-selors because they "aren't being understood." This can be one way of seeking support of one's own views elsewhere. But a client can remain with a counselor and still find such support elsewhere.

> *Client:* I asked my wife about my sarcasm. She says she doesn't mind it at all. And she said she thinks that my friends see it as humor and as part of my style.

This is an indirect way of telling the counselor he is wrong. The counselor might well be wrong, but if the client's sarcasm is really dysfunctional in his interpersonal life, the counselor should find some way of pressing the issue. If counseling takes place in a group, it is much more difficult for a client to find and present nonexistent support for his own views.

> *Jane:* Does anyone else here see me as biting and sarcastic?
> *Susan:* I think you do get sarcastic from time to time. The only reason I've said nothing about it so far is that you haven't been sarcastic with me.

Jane can get direct feedback on her behavior from the group. It is much harder for her to play rationalization games with her fellow participants.

> *Change cognition to correspond to that of the confronter.*   The client can agree with the counselor, see his point. This, too, can be a game.

> *Client:* I think you're right. I'm much too blunt and forward when I speak: I should try to think what impact I'm going to have before I open my mouth.

A client can agree with the confrontations of the counselor in order to get the counselor "off his back." If such confessions do not lead to behavioral change, however, the sincerity of the client is open to suspicion. The goal of the counselor in confrontation is not to have the client agree with him but to have the client re-examine his behavior in order to understand himself better and act more effectively.

> *Examine his behavior with the help of the counselor.*   The ideal client response to confrontation would include the client's indication that he understands what the counselor is saying. Let's consider an example.

> *Counselor:* Whenever your son explains how he feels about his relationship to you, you tend to explain what he'd said in a way that agrees with your own views of the relationship. I'm not sure that you listen to him intently, since what you're saying sounds so different from what he's saying.
> *Client:* It sounds like I'm trying to pour his words into my mold so that I can say "See, we're really saying the same thing!"

This client does what few people do when they are confronted in any situation: he first checks to see whether he has an accurate understanding of the nature of the confrontation. This reaction is extremely important, for it it an indication of the client's openness to a more objective view of his behavior, and it lets the confronter know that his words are not being twisted by the client. This willingness both to understand and to reflect on a confrontation is a skill that the counselor should try to help his client develop. Once a client begins to develop such a skill, then he is ready for the next step: learning how to confront himself.

> *Client:* In the last half hour I've begun to do what I'm always doing outside: I've become the obedient mouse. I've been trying to talk with you in a way that will please you rather than help me. I'm constantly looking for cues in your behavior that tell me whether I'm doing the "right thing" or not.

This client catches himself in unproductive behavior and confronts himself. Once he recognizes unproductive behavior, he can explore it with the helper and try to come up with measures to prevent its recurrence.

Cautions and conclusion

Context. Talking about confrontation separately confers a kind of importance on it that it does not have in the helping process. Prospective counselors begin to think that it can be separated from other skills, especially Stage-I skills. The counselor who lacks a wide repertory of helping skills, especially the skills of accurate empathy and the skills needed to help launch the client on effective action programs, will often try to mask his lack of skills in overly reactive and negatively confronting responses. Helping is an organic process, and confrontation must grow organically out of it. The confrontation specialist is often a very destructive person, a person who is not even good at his own specialty.

The discussion of confrontation in the last few pages includes a number of cautions. Very often the beginner ignores these cautions. It would be far better for the beginner to pour his energy into learning the art of advanced accurate empathy than into devising new approaches to confrontation. In a word, confrontation is meaningful only in the *context* of counseling as it has been described up to this point.

Confrontation and the effective helper. Research shows that the effective helper does confront more than the low-level helper, but the quality of his confrontation is high, and he does not set out to be confrontational. Let's put it frankly: *the entire helping process is confrontational.* When carried out skillfully, it places many demands on the client. The high-level helper is the agent of this confrontational process, but he does not focus on confrontation as a separate technique. A low-level helper confronts weakness, while a high-level helper tends to confront the unused strengths, capabilities, and resources of the client. When it comes to direct confrontation, a low-level helper persists in his confrontations even when they are doing no good. The high-level helper, on the other hand, is a good discriminator: he knows when to unmask, when to challenge.

Confrontation and the "MUM" effect. The "MUM" effect refers to people's tendency to withhold bad news from others (Rosen & Tesser, 1970, 1971; Tesser & Rosen, 1972; Tesser, Rosen, & Batchelor, 1972; Tesser, Rosen, & Tesser, 1971). In ancient times the bearer of bad news was often killed. In modern times he might not fear death, but he does fear something. Research has shown that, even when the bearer of bad news was assured that the one receiving the news would take it with equanimity, he was still as reluctant to bear such news as the bearer who knew that the receiver would take it hard. Bad news arouses negative feelings in the sender no matter what the perceived reaction on the part of the receiver.

Some counselors seem to fall victim to the MUM effect; that is, they are hesitant to respond in any negative way to the client. They are uncomfortable with counseling as a confrontational process; they are uncomfortable with counseling as a social-influence process. As a result, their communication with the client is frequently watered down. Counseling is a process in which the client is confronted with those areas of life in which he is living less than effectively. It is strong medicine. It is not the function of the counselor to force this medicine down the throat of an unwilling client, but it is his job to help the client "take the medicine." If the communications of MUM counselors are examined, it is soon discovered that their reluctance and hesitancy cloud all their communications and not just confrontation as such. There is a built-in dynamism in high-level counseling: if Stage I is carried out effectively, it gravitates toward Stage II; if Stage II is carried out effectively, it gravitates toward Stage III. If this dynamic process does not take place, the counselor should step back and see if, possibly, he has fallen victim to the MUM effect. Confrontation involves interpersonal risks, but if they are reasonable and carried out in a spirit of caring and involvement, they should be taken.

Direct, mutual talk (immediacy)

Clients seeking counseling and psychotherapy usually present a wide variety of complaints—depression, anxiety, sleeplessness, boredom, a variety of physical symptoms, failure experiences, and so on—but, no matter what the presenting complaint, it takes little exploration to uncover the fact that they are also having trouble with interpersonal relationships. For instance, an office worker might complain that he doesn't like his work, feels depressed because it is so hard to change jobs because of the tight job market, and sees no immediate solution to his problem. Exploration, however, shows that he has changed jobs three times, each time because of "the people there." He has never learned how to relate effectively to others and more often than not he ends up alienating his fellow workers. Or consider the client who is highly successful but who is also highly anxious. Exploration reveals a series of negative relationships with significant adults during his formative years. During those years, he learned to dislike himself: it was the only lesson available. Ever since, he has been trying to prove his worth to himself by being successful. But, since his present business success has not solved his problem of self-worth, he has become a highly anxious individual. Business concerns, of course, leave little time for contact with people on a social-emotional basis: he is "out of community." Yet only in a community of people who genuinely care for him will he learn that he is worthwhile in himself and not just for what he can accomplish.

A good starting place to explore any client's ability to relate interpersonally is the client-counselor relationship itself. If counseling takes place in a group, the members have a splendid opportunity not only to form relationships with one another but also to explore directly successes and failures in relating. One skill they need in order to explore interpersonal relationships is called "direct, mutual communication" (Higgins, Ivey, & Uhlemann, 1970; Ivey, 1971) or "immediacy" (Carkhuff, 1969a,b): it is the ability to discuss directly and openly with another person what is happening in the here-and-now of an interpersonal relationship. I sometimes refer to it as "you-me" talk. Let's take a look at an example of this kind of communication.

Trainee A: This is the first time you and I have been together to practice skills. I must admit that I feel very uncomfortable with you right now. I see you as a very strong person, a person with a lot of interpersonal initiative. Maybe I've built up a mythology about you, which I think I have to clear up before I can interact with you freely.

Trainee B: The "strength" thing strikes me as almost funny because I'm just as nervous as you are. My palms are sweating and I'm trying to appear my "normal" comfortable self. I've watched you interact with others in the training exercises and I like what I see. Initially, I'm very uncomfortable with people I like but don't know.

These trainees are dealing with what is going on between them in the immediacy of the here-and-now. Another example, this time from a counseling relationship:

Client: I'm still not convinced of the value of counseling. You sit around and talk about yourself a lot, but things don't seem to get much better. And it isn't even easy to keep talking about yourself.
Counselor A: This whole thing doesn't seem to be going anyplace, so it's frustrating and hard to stick to.
Client: It certainly is!

Client: I'm still not convinced of the value of counseling. You sit around and talk about yourself a lot, but things don't seem to get much better. And it isn't even easy to keep talking about yourself.
Counselor B: Bill, from a number of things you've said so far, I have the feeling that you're not sure whether you can trust me or not. You're still not convinced that I'm on your side.

In this example, Counselor A responds with primary-level accurate empathy, but, as the client's response shows, it goes nowhere. It may be that Counselor A is stuck in Stage I. Counselor B, on the other hand, has picked up some cues indicating that one reason the counseling process is bogged down is that the client is still not convinced that he can trust the counselor. The client may respond something like this:

Client: Well, I'm not sure you like me. I know you're busy, and I don't know why you should give me the time of day. I'm just another punk kid that's got himself messed up.

Here the counselor knows he has hit the mark, for the client, too, has responded with immediacy. The communication is now direct and mutual.

The function of immediacy responses

The purpose of immediacy responses on the part of the counselor is to help the client understand himself more clearly, especially what he is doing and how he is relating in the here-and-now of the counseling interview or the group-counseling experience. The counselor models a kind of behavior that will help the client become more effective in all of his relationships. The logic of counseling in this instance is that the counselor initiates immediacy so that the client may learn to be immediate in this counselor-client relationship so that, in turn, he may ultimately become more immediate in his relationships outside the counseling sessions.

Direct, mutual communication, however great its potential for stimulating interpersonal growth, is nevertheless quite rare in everyday life. It is a way of processing what is happening in the here-and-now of any relationship—in a classroom, for instance.

> *Teacher:* What's going on in this classroom—I mean besides the fact that learning doesn't seem to be taking place today?
> *Student A:* I think we're in a kind of power struggle. You're trying to get us to do something that most of us don't want to do.
> *Teacher:* And I'm just getting more and more angry with you, which only ties me in knots. You've become the "enemy."
> *Student B:* I think I made a silent promise to myself this morning during class. I said "We're going to win this one no matter what the cost." I get very stubborn inside when I see you getting stubborn.

This kind of dialogue not only clears the air, but it is a valuable learning experience in itself. Both teacher and students see themselves engaged in a game called "classroom learning as war." As they come to understand the roles they are playing in the struggle, both parties gain a new freedom. Once they understand what they are doing (immediacy should lead to self-understanding), they can decide to move beyond games to more creative forms of learning; that is, self-understanding leads to action. Perhaps education would be a much more interesting experience if the air in classrooms were cleared in this way.

Being cautious in immediacy responses

One function of Stage II is to help the client understand himself and the world from a more objective point of view. Immediacy contributes to this goal. The client, in the safety of the helping relationship, learns to do what many people are afraid to do in everyday life: he learns to "process" a relationship, he learns that it can be growthful both to be told how he is being experienced in a relationship and to tell another how he is experiencing him in a relationship. Since this mutuality does not happen often in everyday life, it is usually a new and quite demanding experience for the client. The counselor should realize this and, as with all Stage-II techniques, proceed tentatively and cautiously. His goal is to help the client understand himself better, not to frighten him.

Counselor A: You don't trust me. That's why we're bogged down here.
Client: I don't know what we're trying to do.

Counselor B: I get the feeling that it's still hard for you to talk to me—as if you're still not sure whether I'm on your side.
Client: Well, I think I'm beginning to believe that you are, but I'm not used to *anyone* being on my side. It makes me a bit wary and scared. I'm not used to it yet.

Counselor A's basic instinct is good; that is, he knows that immediacy is appropriate when the relationship between him and the client seems to be going nowhere; but his execution is poor. His direct communication sounds like an accusation, and it elicits a defensive response from the client. Counselor B is much more tentative and avoids seeming to blame the client, who in turn responds with much greater candor.

If the counselor is skillful, the client first learns to accept direct communication from the helper and then learns to address the helper in the same way. But if the helper does not know how to accept immediacy himself, he can hardly expect the client to learn the skill.

Client: At times you push me too hard. Like right now. And it scares me. You *are* helping me, but slow down.

Counselor A: Pushing is part of helping. You have to expect some of that.
Counselor B: I'm not really pushing. It seems like that to you because you are beginning to change, and that's painful.
Counselor C: You feel you'd do just as well—or maybe even better—if I held off a bit. That makes sense. You've been working hard.

Counselors A and B respond defensively: A engages in a kind of counterattack, while B defends himself. Counselor C, on the other hand, both understands the client (accurate empathy) and reinforces him by recognizing the good work the client has been doing. He also models nondefensive responsiveness to direct communication. His response says, in effect, "It's all right to speak directly and openly to me about what is going on between you and me in this relationship." Nondefensive response allays the fears and the embarrassment of the client in addressing the helper directly. This is important, for, if the client is successful in the initiative he takes in this relationship, the probability increases that he will become more creative in all of his relationships.

Systematic training in direct, mutual communication

Kagan (1971, 1973) trains prospective counselors systematically to use the here-and-now of the relationship to further the goals of counseling. The average counselor, he finds, fails to use the awareness he has of both his own behavior and that of the client during the counseling relationship. It is not that the counselor doesn't know what is happening between him and the client but rather that he fails to *act* upon what he sees happening in the interview. Part of Kagan's training process is to have the trainee recall as much as he can from a short training interview with a client.

> *Supervisor:* What did you experience during the interview?
> *Trainee:* I noticed that the client kept looking away from me. I began to get a little irritated because I thought he was avoiding the real issues in his life. When he asked me what I thought about finishing one's education before getting married, I thought he was trying to move the discussion to an intellectual plane. I think also that I let him talk too long without interrupting him. I felt that he didn't give me enough chance to respond. Maybe I should have cut in more often. We weren't really engaged in a dialogue.

The trainee recalls many things about the interview that he *did not act upon* during the interview itself. His reason for not dealing directly with these issues in the interview itself was not that he was unaware of them. If this were the case, he wouldn't be able to recall them after the interview in the conference with his supervisor. The purpose of these recall sessions is to make the trainee aware, in a reflective way, of the issues he fails to use in the here-and-now of the counseling interview. Once he sees the richness of this unused material, he can learn to step back from the interview during the interview itself, see what the client is doing, see what he himself is feeling and doing (or not doing), and use what he notices immediately, if it is appropriate. This is immediacy.

> *Client:* Last year I spent a lot of time reading. And I even took a couple of psychology courses on my own—just because I wanted to.
> *Trainee:* John, I've been watching my reactions to you, and I notice that I'm beginning to squirm a bit in my chair. I'd like to check something out with you. It seems that, when we begin to talk about your social life, we often get sidetracked by some other topic—an important topic, like what you're doing to keep up intellectually. I think that maybe that is what just happened now. My feelings say that you more or less instinctively run from discussing your relationships with people and that I've been your accomplice. I've been helping you run.
> *Client:* Maybe you've guessed it by now: my interpersonal life is very messy. I do run from it. I'm afraid of closeness. I'm even afraid of closeness with you here.

This time, instead of filing cues away in his mind for future reference, the trainee uses his feelings about the client to help him face an important issue, one he has been avoiding. Since the client replies in kind, the dialogue ends up as direct, mutual communication.

Later on in practice sessions, Kagan has a supervisor sit down with *both* the helper/trainee and the "client" and process what took place between them. Not only do they learn what they failed to verbalize during the counseling session itself, but they are now given an opportunity to discuss these issues openly.

It is evident that attending is a prerequisite for immediacy. The counselor must constantly be monitoring the verbal and nonverbal cues emitted by the client and his own reactions to the client. This ability to stand back psychologically from the give and take of the relationship and to observe and process what is happening is a skill that does not come easily.

Some occasions for the use of immediacy

Immediacy is called for when the counselor sees that either he or the client has *unverbalized* thoughts and feelings about what is taking place in the helping session that are getting in the way. Immediacy is, in a sense, a higher-level response than either self-disclosure or confrontation, for it combines both of these. The helper both reveals his own feelings and in some way confronts or challenges the client. Indeed, some feel that immediacy should provide the primary vehicle for counselor self-disclosure. Counselor disclosure should be "existential"—dealing with feelings about the relationship here and now—rather than revelation of past or present secrets.

The following might be fruitful areas for "you-me" talk. A word of caution: the following counselor statements are taken out of context, and therefore it is difficult to judge their appropriateness.

Different styles.

Counselor: Through our sessions, I've learned that you and I have different approaches to life. Yours seems to be free and easy, while mine is more goal-oriented and ordered. In these sessions, we seem to go in different directions at times. You're comfortable with a more rambling style and pace. I'm eager to move on to action, so I end up a bit frustrated.

Trust issues.

Counselor: I'm beginning to feel that you don't trust me. It makes me feel as if my hands were tied. I'm not sure whether it's hard for you to trust anyone or whether you have a special problem with me.

Dependency.

Counselor: As I review what we've been doing here, I see that *I* have chosen most of the topics we've discussed. And sometimes I get the feeling that you see feedback from me as more important than how you see yourself. Does this strike you the same way?

Counterdependency.

Counselor: I hope that what I'm going to say sounds more like an observation than an accusation. Anyway, I'm a bit nervous saying it. I feel that it's hard for you to admit to yourself that you might be able to use a little help at this point in your life. I feel you are fighting me—or maybe just fighting being helped—and this makes us go around in circles.

Directionless sessions.

Counselor: We seem to be missing each other today. Maybe we should talk about what's going on between us. I feel it might help.

Attraction.

Counselor: I think we've instinctively liked each other from the start. In some ways, this seems to help what we are doing here. We relate quite easily and nondefensively. In other ways, it may be an obstacle. Maybe we're too comfortable with each other. I'm not sure, for instance, that we've been dealing with the problems that bother you most. It's almost as if there were a conspiracy between us to avoid them. Is this just my perception, or do you see any of this happening, too?

This is hardly an exhaustive list. Carkhuff (1969a,b) suggests that the counselor ask himself, during the course of the interview, "What is the client trying to tell me that he can't tell me directly?" The answer lies buried in the verbal and nonverbal behavior of the client. The skilled helper can dig it out and make it an "immediacy" topic.

Confrontation and immediacy in training groups

Confrontation and immediacy are skills that can be taught experientially to the members of training groups. Then the participants can use them in their interactions with one another. In my experience with training groups (both helper-training and human-relations groups), the members tend to misuse confrontation (by dumping their frustrations and hostility on one another) and to avoid immediacy (which means putting themselves on the line). The members of a learning community should challenge one another, but they should do so responsibly; they should deal with the here-and-now issues that are obstacles to their learning. In the training-as-treatment model of helping, clients should be taught these skills directly. In human-relations-training groups, the kind of direct, mutual talk urged here is one of the most important training goals. Indeed, immediacy is at the core of mutuality.

Some cautions

In the initial phases of Stage II, the counselor should be careful in initiating "you-me" talk. As the relationship between himself and the client grows stronger, however, immediacy responses can also become stronger; but immediacy is still not an end in itself. Just as it is useful for friends to "process" their relationship from time to time—especially at times of stress or when the relationship seems empty or directionless —so the counselor and client should engage in direct, mutual communication whenever it is useful, especially in times of stress and when the relationship seems aimless. Both underuse and overuse of immediacy in interpersonal relationships, including counseling, are stultifying. Constant "you-me" talk is a sign of mutual fear, distrust, or dependency rather than a cure for it. Finally, just as with empathy, immediacy responses are helpful to the degree that they are *accurate.* If the counselor sees fear or distrust or dependency that in fact does not exist, he should examine himself and what needs *he* might be fulfilling in his relationship with this particular client.

Some concluding notes on Stage II

A few things should be said to put Stage II in perspective, for it is just one phase of the developmental model.

The helper should not be too literal with respect to the *timing* of Stage-II interactions. The model exists for the helper and the helpee, not vice versa. If, on occasion, Stage-II interactions seem called for earlier than is indicated by the model as presented here, they should be used. Ultimately, the high-level helper depends on himself and his judgment rather than on a paper model. He does whatever is necessary at the moment to help the client, even if it involves some rearranging of the stages of the model. For instance, immediacy responses might be called for rather early in Stage I.

Counselor: It may be my imagination, but I get the feeling that it's really hard for you to talk to me.

This gives the client an opportunity to clear the air with the helper early in the counseling sessions. Such an interaction might prevent or break up counseling "log jams."

Stage-II interactions, as they have been explained here, involve overlap. Take the following counselor statement, for instance:

> *Counselor:* I think that right now you might be saying to yourself, "I'm not sure I can trust this guy." And maybe there's some truth to that, for I might have been too heavy-handed with you up until now.

In this one response, the counselor involves himself in immediacy (self-sharing), and—to a degree—confrontation. It can also be seen as an instance of advanced accurate empathy. The issue is not whether or not his response can be assigned to a clear and distinct category but whether it helps the client move forward.

The counselor should not try to become an expert in any given kind of interaction or intervention, especially the interventions of Stage II. Stage-II interventions stand on the shoulders of Stage-I skills: they must be suffused by the spirit of Stage I, just as Stage I interventions must have within them a dynamism that moves the counseling process toward Stage II. Even though the counselor should be expert in Stage-II responses, he should not think in terms of these responses but in terms of the client's goal: self-understanding that prepares the client for action. If the dictum "helping is for the client" is in his bones, the helper will be able to choose the appropriate response at the appropriate time.

Stage-II interventions are strong medicine. They might well at times induce some degree of crisis in the client. Crises, if faced, are growth points in the life of the client; but, if the helper's interventions induce some kind of crisis in the life of the client (heightened anxiety, disorganization, tears, depression, anger, confusion), the helper should help the client to weather the crisis and grow through it.

Chapter Six

Stage III: Action Programs

1. The goal of the entire helping process is action: constructive behavioral change.
2. Therefore, the helper should learn thoroughly and experientially the basic principles that underlie the maintenance and change of behavior:
   a. Reinforcement: people tend to initiate and repeat behaviors for which they are rewarded. Lack of reinforcement results in extinguished behavior. Undesirable behavior is also maintained by reinforcement; to eliminate it, it is necessary to eliminate what reinforces it. Ideally, constructive human behavior becomes rewarding in itself.
   b. Punishment: punishment reduces the probability that a person will repeat a certain behavior. But punishment does not, of itself, teach or substitute more creative behaviors; punishment creates a negative emotional climate; and punishment sometimes satisfies the emotional needs of the punisher rather than the growth needs of the person being punished.
   c. Avoidance: avoiding a painful situation is reinforcing in itself. Avoidance behavior is extremely common and often extremely difficult to detect. It limits the possibility of new learning; and avoidance learning is highly resistant to extinction.
   d. Shaping: shaping uses reinforcement systematically in a gradual process in order to institute, increase, and strengthen desirable behaviors. The counselor should avoid action steps that are too large. Lack of client motivation or willpower often means just poor shaping.
3. Stages I and II of the developmental helping process can of themselves in certain cases constitute action programs. They help relatively high-level clients to free blocked resources. Once these resources are freed, the clients act on their own.
4. The force-field analysis approach to problem-solving is one systematic, common-sense technique that can be used to help the client act in more constructive ways:
   a. Identify and clarify the problem. This is done in Stages I and II.

    b. If there are a number of problems, establish working priorities related to the client's distress and value system.

    c. Establish concrete, workable goals.

    d. Take a census of the means available to achieve these goals. List means that help reduce restraining forces; list means that help increase facilitating forces. Underline the most workable means in each list.

    e. Choose the most effective means available: the means that are in keeping with the client's value system and that have the highest probability for success.

    f. Establish concrete behavioral criteria by which success and failure of the action program can be gauged.

    g. Implement the action program. During the action program the helper should use Stage-I and Stage-II skills to sustain, reinforce, and challenge the client.

5. Training-as-treatment: just as the client can be trained in Stage-I and Stage-II skills himself so that he can become his own helper, so he can be trained directly in problem-solving methodologies.

6. Low-level counselors either never get to Stage III or try to start Stage III prematurely, without any preparation.

7. The ultimate criterion for judging any helping process is whether or not it actually does help the client change.

Once the client sees the need to act, he often needs to be helped to act. However, while the counselor will use the skills of Stages I and II in Stage III, he now also needs action-program skills. This chapter deals with some of these skills.

Sherman (1973) asks a number of pointed questions about the helping process that have particular relevance for programs of behavioral change:

Identifying Behavioral Objectives

1. *Maladaptive behavior.* What is the nature of the maladaptive behavior, and what are its component features?

2. *Severity of components.* What is the relative severity of the components?

3. *Objectives and priorities.* What are to be the behavioral objectives of therapy, and what is their order of priority?

4. *Basis of objectives.* Are the objectives a function of the client's complaints, the therapist's theories, or some combination of the two?

5. *Agreement on objectives.* To what extent are the objectives stated and agreed upon at the outset of treatment?

Specifying Treatment Procedures

1. *Procedures and basis.* What procedures will the therapist use, and what is the basis for their selection?

2. *Relationship between procedures and maladaptive behaviors.* Do the procedures vary for the several components of the maladaptive behavior?
3. *Order of procedures.* What will be the order of application of the procedures?
4. *Changing procedures.* Might there be changes in the procedures as
therapy progresses, and what will be the criteria for introducing such
changes?
5. *Therapist characteristics.* What personal characteristics of the therapist
may make him more or less suited or inclined to use particular procedures with particular clients?
6. *Client characteristics.* What personal characteristics of the client may
make him more or less inclined to seek a therapist noted for using
particular procedures?

Assessing Behavior Changes

1. *Measures of change.* What measuring instruments and rating scales will
be used to express the extent of therapeutic change for each component
of the maladaptive behavior?
2. *Weights for different sources of judgment.* What are the relative weights
to be given to the judgments of the therapist, the client, the client's
family and friends, and independent observers?
3. *Success and termination criteria.* What criteria are to be used for deciding
whether the behavioral objectives have been achieved and/or for deciding that treatment ought to be terminated?
4. *Daily life influences.* How can the changes due to specific treatment
procedures be isolated from those due to variable factors in the client's
daily life—his work situation, marital harmony, and physical health?
5. *Interdependence with client characteristics.* To what extent are the therapeutic changes (or lack thereof) which appear to be due to specific
treatment procedures partially due to an interdependence with certain
client characteristics such as age, sex, and social class?
6. *Stability and durability of changes.* How might the stability and durability of the therapeutic changes be assessed after the treatment is completed, and how might such information be incorporated in the overall
evaluation of the treatment?
7. *Treatment side effects.* Might there be positive or negative changes
which result from the treatment procedures but to which the procedures
were not directed, and how might such side effects be incorporated into
the overall evaluation of the efficacy of the treatment procedures [pp.
9–10]?*

The developmental model itself, since it is a *procedure* and not merely
a theory, clearly helps to answer some of the questions Sherman poses.
The work of Stages I and II, for example, helps to identify problem areas
and resources concretely and behaviorally and to begin to set behavioral
objectives. However, the action programs of Stage III must be designed

*From *Behavior Modification: Theory and Practice,* by A. R. Sherman. Copyright ©
1973 by Wadsworth Publishing Company, Inc. Reprinted by permission of the publisher,
Brooks/Cole Publishing Company, Monterey, California.

to give concrete answers to those questions that deal with change processes as such. This chapter suggests procedures that can answer a number of Sherman's questions, and references are made to other resources that can help the student/trainee acquire a comprehensive overview of problem-solving methodology.

Client action goals

As we did in Stage II, let's begin with the end; that is, let's take a look at some examples of client action goals first and then consider the skills needed by the counselor to help the client achieve these goals.

The presenting problem.   Tom is above average in intelligence, but he is depressed and doing failing work.

Exploration of the problem.   Tom is on drugs. He has become a part-time pusher in order to afford the drug habit. He is both anxious and depressed because he is operating against personal values and because he is afraid of getting caught. He found his school curriculum fatuous even before he started to experiment with drugs. He is not sure that he wants to pursue a college degree.

Goals.   To break the drug habit. To find sources of income other than pushing. To find a challenging and profitable academic program or to quit school and find suitable work. To get "into community" with some friends at school.

The presenting problem.   Karen is so highly anxious at work that the quality of her work is suffering. She is making the kinds of mistakes that could cost her her job.

Exploration of the problem.   Karen is very much afraid of her employer, but the kind of work she is doing demands daily contact with him. She withdraws from him emotionally, and he reacts by becoming more demanding. She also has poor telephone presence.

Goals.   To help Karen improve the interpersonal skills she needs in order to be more effective with people. To desensitize her to her employer's presence. To provide her with assertiveness training that will enable her to present herself more forcefully so that her employer's presence does not overwhelm her. To allow her to rehearse telephone skills in a nonthreatening atmosphere. To help her acquire greater self-esteem.

The presenting problem.   Jim and Mary have a deteriorating marriage. They communicate poorly, engaging in games of "uproar" and periods of silent withdrawal. Neither lives up to the demands of the marriage contract; there is infidelity, irresponsibility in household management, and neglect of the children.

Exploration of the problem.   Jim and Mary "had" to get married; they both entered into the marriage resenting each other and the child to come. Neither was ready for marriage: there was little discipline in their lives, they identified intimacy with sex, and they were both very self-centered. The same kind of irresponsibility has characterized their married years. Because of religious convictions, they feel they must stay married. Both are still quite adolescent. They do have several friends who are happily married.

Goals.   To improve communication skills ("decency" skills). Gradually to introduce discipline into their lives, first in easy areas, then in more difficult areas. To stop mutual recriminations. To obtain parent-effectiveness training. To try long-term membership in a peer self-help group that deals with lifestyle (composed perhaps of some couples who are living married life more effectively than Jim and Mary).

These are obviously sketchy overviews of much more detailed processes. But the objective of Stage III is to help the client establish concrete, viable goals and concrete, viable means to attain these goals, and to provide support and direction for him as he pursues these goals. It is impossible to achieve Stage-III concreteness without concreteness in Stages I and II: if the problem is clear, the goal will be clear. As John Dewey noted in 1910, a question well put is half answered.

The purpose of Stage III is not just to help the client meet present crises. The counselor can teach the client how to avoid crisis living, how to take counsel with himself and with his friends in order to avoid unnecessary crises, and how to plan and program his life so as to enrich and enjoy life as a process of being as well as becoming.

The developmental character of the process of behavioral change

What seems to me to be an unfortunate and unproductive dichotomy exists among some current helper-training programs. On the one hand, some programs are still quite "nondirective"; that is, they emphasize the skills of Stage I (and, perhaps, advanced accurate empathy from Stage II) but generally ignore the action-preparation skills of Stage II and the action programs of Stage III. The proponents of such programs have traditionally seen the counselor as one who helps the client sort out the problematic issues of his life rather than one who both prepares the client directly for behavioral change and assists him throughout the change process itself. Proponents of such programs are also very wary of the social-influence process. They are afraid that such a process necessarily entails the counselor's becoming a problem-solver *for* (rather than *with*) the client. On the other hand, there are programs that emphasize learning-theory and behavior-modification techniques but do not adequately teach the skills of Stages I and II. Hence the dichotomy. However, the developmental model suggests that the best helper is the one who has the widest repertory of helping skills and who can readily call upon any of these skills to meet the different needs of any client. The helper who restricts himself to any set of stage-specific skills is doing a disservice to his clients.

Helping, as defined here, is about behavior and behavior change—whether that behavior be internal or external, self-oriented or interpersonal, public or private, individual or social. The helper who limits himself to a consideration of only certain classes of behavior (such as intrapsychic or interpersonal) limits his ability to help. For instance, the behaviorist who is overly preoccupied with strictly overt or external behavior overlooks recent *behavioral* research into the importance of "covert behaviors" (that is, thoughts, images, feelings, physiological events) on both internal and external behavior (see Thoresen & Mahoney, 1974, pp. 108–128, for a summary of this research). The helper who exercises the skills of Stages I and II (that is, the skills ignored or inadequately taught by some behavioral programs) is very effective in helping the client uncover and deal with his "covert behavior" and its impact on his lifestyle.

The developmental model does not begin to deal with behavior just in Stage III; it deals with behavior and behavioral change in Stages I and II also—the behavior of the helper as he listens to, responds to, and initiates with the client, and the behavior of the client as he responds to the respect, challenge, and influence of the helper. Furthermore, it has already been suggested that skills training can be incorporated into the entire helping process (for example, teaching married couples how to communicate decently with each other from the beginning of counseling). In this case, Stage III becomes incorporated into Stages I and II. Stage III deals with the "action" dimension of the helping process, whether this action is part and parcel of the counseling encounter itself or whether it takes place in the "back home" world of the client.

The rest of this chapter is divided into three major sections: the first dealing with the principles that underlie behavioral change, the second dealing with Stages I and II as action programs, and the third dealing with a systematic problem-solving methodology.

Principles involved in the maintenance and change of behavior

This section does not attempt a complete review of the principles underlying the maintenance and change of behavior (much less the behavior-modification technologies derived from these principles). However, since these principles are critical to the helping process, I will briefly review and illustrate a few of them. I would urge the student/trainee to learn these principles (see Bandura, 1969; Ferster & Perrott, 1968; Sherman, 1973), to begin to become skilled in helping technologies that directly or indirectly flow from these principles (see Rimm & Masters, 1974), and to use them to help others develop more constructive approaches to living. The wider the repertory of approaches to behavioral change the helper possesses, the higher the probability that he can collaborate with his client in behavioral-change programs and the higher the probability that he can teach the client the kinds of problem-solving and behavioral-change methodologies that will enable him to exercise greater control over his own behavior. The skilled helper, although, hopefully, immune to fads, is always open to new action programs, problem-solving methodologies, and behavioral-change technologies, for these increase his ability to serve the needs of his client.

The basic principles of learning as applied to human behavior, some of which are illustrated in the following pages, help the counselor answer certain key questions: How is a desirable but presently inoperative behavior stimulated or promoted? How is an undesirable behavior eliminated? How is a behavior that is presently part of a person's behavioral repertory maintained and strengthened? I will review a few of the principles that help us answer questions like these and illustrate how they relate both to helper and client behaviors of Stages I and II and to the problem-solving methodology outlined later in this chapter.

Reinforcement

The principle of reinforcement states that a person tends to initiate and repeat behaviors for which he is in some way rewarded. The reward is called a reinforcement. The reinforcement can be intrinsic to the behavior performed (eating a banana, having a serious conversation with a friend) or extrinsic (receiving money for cleaning out a sewer, winning the approval of parents and friends for excelling in a difficult course of studies). Of course, a person may receive both intrinsic and extrinsic reinforcement for the same behavior (a nurse finds cooperating in the healing profession rewarding in itself but is further reinforced by the gratitude of the patients and the praise she receives from the hospital staff for work well done).

While reinforcement is often something positive that is gained (then termed *positive* reinforcement), as in the examples just cited, it may also be the *removal* of something unpleasant (payment of a parking ticket removes the threat of further and more costly legal action; cleaning one's room removes the threat of a parent's disapproval). Something is called a *negative* reinforcer, then, if its removal has the power to initiate, maintain, or strengthen behavior. The whole issue of positive and negative reinforcement can be quite complex; but for our purposes, some relatively simple principles are quite useful.

A person tends to repeat behaviors he finds rewarding (Peggy gets a great deal of satisfaction in smoking a cigarette or two after a meal; smoking after meals becomes part of her mealtime ritual).

The "reward" has to be experienced as a reward by the person whose behavior is in question (a prize of a trip to Alaska might be seen by some as a reward but by others as something indifferent).

The strength of a given reward also depends on how it is experienced by the individual (food as a reinforcer is not very appealing to someone who has just eaten).

Reinforcers can be positive or negative.

Even undesirable behaviors that are unwittingly reinforced will tend to be repeated (a teacher meets Jack's announcement that he will be late in turning in a paper with acceptance and understanding but without any challenge, and then wonders why Jack's tardiness behavior increases).

Lack of reinforcement makes even constructive and desirable behaviors extinguish—that is, disappear (Jean does her homework carefully; the teacher collects the papers and never refers to the task again; Jean drifts into doing her homework haphazardly).

One of the best rewards is the satisfaction that comes from the actual doing of a desirable behavior (reading a good book becomes a reward in itself).

Rewards usually work best when they are not delayed but are given as soon as the behavior is performed (hence the ideal nature of desirable behaviors that are rewarding in themselves). Delayed rewards tend to work better if the person receives some symbol or token indicating concretely and immediately that the reward will be conferred (patients in mental hospitals receive tokens for cooperative behavior that can later be redeemed at the commissary).

These principles of reinforcement apply to Stages I and II of the helping process and to the problem-solving methodologies and action programs of Stage III. Let's consider a few examples.

The helper who communicates accurate empathic understanding and respect reinforces the client's self-exploratory behavior.

The helper who trains clients in the skills of Stages I and II uses social reinforcement (such as praise) to reward effort expended in learning the skills, and the clients find newly won skills (such as listening and responding caringly and accurately) rewarding in themselves. When clients use these skills and see that they work in "back home" situations, they are further reinforced.

A helper who merely listens carefully and empathically to a client's description of his chaotic family life without probing further and challenging him to do something about it may unwittingly be conspiring with the client to maintain an undesirable situation. For instance, Peter, after a game of "uproar" with his wife, is "rewarded" by the friendly caring of the counselor. In general, the counselor should consider carefully his own influence as a provider of social reinforcement. Otherwise he may unknowingly reward undesirable behavior or fail to reinforce behavior leading to more constructive living.

In helping a person get rid of a self-destructive drinking problem, the counselor soon sees that the client's drinking is negatively reinforced: it keeps him from the risks, threats, challenges, and punishments of the real world. His drinking blots out the unacceptable realities of a boring job, unused talent, and a lifeless marriage. It therefore gains great negative reinforcement value. A skilled counselor might use a multiple approach in helping this person get out of the drinking rut: he helps the client reinterpret his environment and thus see it as less lifeless and threatening (Stage II); he helps the client initiate behaviors that have greater reinforcement value (changing jobs, learning new communication patterns); he tries to make drinking itself lose its reinforcing quality, by having the client take a drug that produces nausea if the client drinks or by pairing drinking with electric shocks so that the client comes to associate drinking with pain rather than with relief; he gets the client to join Alcoholics Anonymous, where he will receive a great deal of social reinforcement for not drinking and for helping others to stay sober.

When a counselor tries to help a client change, either by initiating desirable behaviors or by getting rid of undesirable ones, he himself has to be aware, and help the client to be aware, of the reinforcement characteristics and demands of each behavioral situation. Each of us is constantly being bombarded by a wide variety of internal and external stimuli. Since individuals differ in what they experience as reinforcing ("One man's meat is another man's poison"), it is very difficult to determine just what combination of reinforcers sustains an undesirable behavior or what combination of reinforcers is needed to institute or strengthen a desirable behavior. Still—within certain useful limits—the counselor, by means of Stage-I and Stage-II skills, can often help a client determine the principal sources of reinforcement sustaining or needed to sustain a particular behavior. Indeed, since behaviors are usually partially sustained by the client's own covert behavior (his thoughts, feelings, images, and physiological reactions), the kind of directed self-exploration that takes place in Stages I and II is extremely important in determining actual and potential reinforcement.

Punishment

Punishment, as defined here, refers to the addition of some unpleasant stimulus following a behavior (getting a ticket for speeding; being ignored after revealing oneself intimately to another person). Even if one does not intend to punish another, his behavior might be experienced by the other as punitive. Punishment is a tricky, even dangerous, form of behavior control. Many people fail to appreciate the complexities of intended or unintended punishment; it backfires on them, producing the opposite of the effect desired. Let's review a few of the principles related to punishment.

Punishment ordinarily reduces the probability or frequency of the behavior it follows; that is, punished behavior will tend to occur less often (a child will tend to stay away from the stove after touching it and being burned; a person will tend to talk less in a group if what he says is ignored or laughed at).

While punishment tends to suppress behaviors, it does not, of itself, teach new behaviors. In a sense, it leaves a vacuum, which should be filled by reinforced alternative behaviors (a knife is taken away from a child but a harmless toy is offered in its place; a group member is challenged to stop monopolizing the group's time by engaging in long monologues, but he is socially rewarded when he engages in dialogue).

Punishment generally creates a negative emotional climate, which can easily generalize to behaviors that are not necessarily desirable (the teacher yells at John for speaking out of turn, but the punishment generalizes to his speaking as such, and John tends to remain silent in class).

Punishment too easily satisfies the needs of the punisher to vent anger and frustration rather than the needs of the person being punished to grow.

Punishment can become a factor in all stages of the helping process. Let's consider a few examples.

Kathy terminates her sessions with the counselor because the latter has ignored her feelings and has tended to give a great deal of advice. She feels ignored and misunderstood; she feels that the counselor has been treating her as a child. Obviously the counselor did not intend to punish her, but his help was experienced as punishment.

The counselor confronts Patricia for engaging in self-pity. He tells her that her constant "poor-me" talk stands in the way of constructive action by keeping her eyes focused on her problems rather than on her resources. However, he confronts her without taking enough time to establish a relationship that will support such confrontation. While the content of his confrontation is accurate, his timing is poor and his mode is punitive. Patricia reacts as a punished person might: she defends herself, attacks the counselor for his lack of understanding, and leaves the session confused and upset.

The counselor helps Ted see that much of his classroom behavior, even though it is not Ted's intention, is most likely perceived as punitive by the teacher. Ted is bright, and he publicly challenges much of what the teacher has to say. When he is bored, he ignores what is happening in class or diverts the attention of some of his classmates. The teacher responds by ignoring Ted or by punishing him in a variety of traditional ways. While it may be that the teacher could use some help, Ted is the only one seeing the counselor. The counselor helps Ted see that his classroom behavior has many of the unproductive effects of punishment on the teacher. He helps Ted modify his behavior without sacrificing his integrity or individuality. The ensuing peace may not be ideal, but it is more productive than the warfare that preceded it.

Bill and Mary have been married for over twenty years. They communicate relatively little except at those times when they disagree about something. Then they break out into yelling matches, using words like clubs, venting stored-up resentment, and saying things they don't mean. The counselor helps them see that their mutual yelling is, in part, a form of reinforcement, since it is about the only time they give each other any kind of intense attention; that their mutually punitive behavior is unproductively self-indulgent (each feels "better" after he/she screams at the other); and that their punitive tactics constitute a cheap and unproductive way of trying to suppress undesirable behavior in each other. In this case, the counselor trains the couple in basic communication skills; that is, he helps them substitute more productive behavior for their mutually punitive communication.

Avoidance

Avoidance behavior is closely connected with the issue of punishment, for punishment ordinarily leads to escape or avoidance behavior. Avoiding the situation that results in punishment is certainly a "cure" for punishment. The problem is that avoidance behavior is quite often very unproductive. The following issues are involved in punishment/avoidance situations:

Avoiding a painful situation is a form of negative reinforcement; that is, avoiders always reap the reward of avoiding the painful situation, no matter what else they might lose (a student has a punitive encounter when he tries to talk to a teacher outside the classroom; he then avoids ever trying to do that again with any teacher).

Avoidance limits the possibility of new learning, since the once-painful situation is never revisited or re-examined (the student never learns that many teachers are open to frank give-and-take discussions outside of class).

Because of the intensity of the negative emotions in punishment/avoidance situations, avoidance learning often generalizes to similar situations. For example, the boy who finds encounters with his father punishing might tend to avoid direct encounters with a wide variety of authority figures.

Avoidance learning is highly resistant to extinction, since it is always rewarding (the punishment is always avoided).

People learn cues that signal "Danger: a situation in which you could be punished is at hand; avoid it." Whenever Sarah experiences cues, such as rising anxiety and discomfort, that she and those she is with are about to disagree or conflict in some way, she changes the subject, pours oil on the waters, or leaves; she thus never learns how to make productive use of conflict.

Avoidance learning can help explain some behaviors that persist even though they are not positively reinforced. Peter, even though he is a rather gregarious person, spends a great deal of time in his room alone at home; the reinforcement for such behavior lies in his avoiding the subtly destructive communication taking place among the other members of his family.

Avoidance behavior can be found in the helping process itself. It is also one of the more difficult problems to identify and deal with in trying to help a client with "back home" problems.

Theresa will not see a counselor even though she is experiencing a great deal of emotional pain. She has been yelled at on two occasions by a priest in the confessional and is now deeply fearful of revealing her "shadow" side to anyone. She has learned to avoid all situations in which any kind of intimate self-disclosure plays a part.

The counselor has a great deal of difficulty in getting Paul's parents even to consider the possibility that their behavior contributes to his uncontrolled behavior in school. They have schooled themselves to view the problem as entirely Paul's. Their reward has been to keep at bay their fear, guilt, shame, and the work of their own behavioral change.

Angela comes to the counselor because she is depressed and lonely. She has some acquaintances but no friends. She supports herself and lives alone in a large city geographically removed from her home town. The counselor discovers that a chaotic home life and a few traumatic failures in interpersonal situations have caused her to withdraw from any serious attempt at establishing relationships of any closeness. Since she has had little interpersonal experience, her social skills are minimal. The counselor does what he can to help her reduce her fears of relating to others. He realizes that his relationship to her in the helping situation is an important part of her emotional re-education. He uses desensitization techniques (see Carkhuff, 1969a, pp. 271–290; Sherman, 1973, pp. 49–89, for an introduction to these techniques) to prepare her for entry into a small, supportive group in which communication-skills training can take place. In the context of this training group, she begins to explore ways of gradually expanding her social life.

Avoidance behaviors are among the most difficult to treat because they are often difficult to identify and, once identified, difficult to deal with because of their resistance to extinction. The helper who is not familiar with the workings of avoidance mechanisms is at a great disadvantage and often ends up blaming the client for "lack of motivation" instead of himself for lack of skill.

Shaping

The last issue to be treated here is a procedure rather than a principle. Shaping means using reinforcement systematically in a gradual, step-by-step process in order to institute, increase, and strengthen desirable behaviors. Conversely, it refers to the gradual but systematic elimination of undesirable behaviors (for example, the ability to actively eliminate tension in one's body, a behavior that is incompatible with anxiety). If effective shaping procedures are followed, the client is never asked to bear an intolerable burden during the behavioral-change process. Let's look at some of the principles involved in shaping.

Take the client where he is. Never put demands on a client for which he is not sufficiently prepared. Ordinarily, one can never begin too low in any hierarchy of behaviors (for example, start by teaching the client the skills of attending in a human-relations-training program; these skills are easily learned and constitute an immediate reinforcement for the client.)

The steps in the change program can never be too small (teach the client to discriminate feelings before trying to teach him to respond with accurate empathy, a skill that includes both feeling and content).

Failure in client "motivation" and "willpower" are often due to ineffective shaping procedures. The client is asked to take too big a step or one for which he does not have the skills or resources (the counselor asks the student to "talk things out" with his teacher, even though the student does not have the skills and the self-confidence even to talk things out with his peers).

Shaping procedures also apply to the elimination of undesirable behaviors. In general, to eliminate an undesirable behavior, find an alternative desirable behavior that is incompatible with the undesirable behavior and initiate and strengthen this alternative through appropriate reinforcement procedures (train married couples in listening and responding skills that are incompatible with recrimination and "uproar" behavior).

The problem-solving methodology outlined later in this chapter is based heavily on shaping procedures.

I have presented a mere outline and some illustrations of a few of the principles and procedures involved in the maintenance and change of human behavior. The helper who is unaware of these principles tends to be ground up by them, for the principles are still operative even when they are unknown. The helper who learns these principles and incorporates them into his own life is ready both to help the client use them (instead of becoming their victim) and to develop and use the technology (behavior-modification techniques) based on these principles. The humanistic use of behavior-modification techniques is one of the ways in which the social-influence dimension of helping is extended into Stage III. And, since the principles of behavior change have been demonstrated to be effective even though they are openly communicated to the client, collaboration, rather than control and manipulation, can characterize the counselor's helping the client to translate dynamic understanding into action.

Stages I and II as action program

As I have already suggested, some client problems can be handled or solved by the kinds of interaction that constitute Stages I and II of the helping model.

Problem. Jonathan is a minister in his forties. For some time now he has been feeling anxious and depressed. More recently, he has allowed himself to feel sorry for himself. There are no great crises in his life, but his ministerial work is drab and lifeless. He fulfills his tasks responsibly, but he feels that he is going nowhere. He goes to a counselor for some guidance.

Exploratory and understanding stages.   In the counseling sessions, Jonathan comes to the following realizations:

While he is responsible in his work, his earlier enthusiasm has slipped away. He reviews his resources for creativity in the ministry and finds them intact but unused.

His conception of the ministry entails "going it alone." "Who ministers to the minister?" is a question he must ask himself. Paradoxically, though he finds himself in the role of encourager to his community, he is "out of community" in some sense of the term. He comes to realize that he is as much in need of human nourishment as the other members of the congregation.

He realizes that he is facing, at least to a mild degree, the "crisis of the limits." Life is no longer the unlimited thing it seems to be for the young. He now sees time as precious—to be harvested and used creatively. He also realizes that life is not over, that some of the most challenging years lie ahead.

With the help of the counselor, Jonathan takes a rather complete inventory of his talents and resources. This is the first time in his life that he has considered all of his resources together.

Through these dialogues with the counselor, Jonathan regains some of his lost zest for life and for the ministry. His anxiety is allayed, his depression lifts, and he finds that he has much more energy for his work. The counseling dialogues stop at this point, for the presenting symptoms have cleared up; and Jonathan, using his own inner resources and those of his environment, goes on to elaborate action programs for himself. For instance, he opens his home to a wider circle of friends, joins a local ministerial peer self-help group, and so forth. The counseling sessions have pumped new energy into his life and Jonathan moves on, seizing life instead of merely submitting himself to it. Stages I and II have had a liberating effect on him.

Problem.   Jean is a single woman about thirty years old. The way she dresses and her bland interpersonal manner make her appear much less attractive than she is. She works in the office of a large company, supports herself, and lives alone. She contacts the counselor because she fears she's going to become an "old maid."

Exploratory and understanding stages. Exploration reveals that when Jean was a girl her family moved very frequently because of her father's work. She was never in one place long enough to sink roots or establish lasting friendships. Her parents were benign but distant and bland. After high school she began to work and finally moved from her parents' home in a small town to an apartment of her own in a large city. She became lost in the anonymity of city life. She had no social contact with her fellow workers or with her neighbors in the apartment complex. She began to realize that she never did have friends and that, the way things were going, she was not going to have any. She felt worthless. Actually, the counselor was the first person to carry on an extended conversation with her. This session was the first time she experienced direct caring and active interest. As she experienced the helper's care, she began to learn a number of things about herself—that she was intelligent and attractive, for instance, qualities that had remained hidden under her bland manner. Her manner brightened both within the counseling sessions and outside, for, being prized, she learned to prize herself. People began to notice her once she emerged from behind her bland facade, not just because she was attractive but because she was more "there," more present to her world. At this point the counseling sessions were terminated.

Again, in this case there was no formal Stage III. The counselor's understanding, respect, genuineness, self-sharing, immediacy, and confrontation had a liberating effect on the client.

Problem. Tony comes to the college counselor because he is anxious and depressed and is experiencing stomach pains and frequent headaches. He says that he thinks he is trying too hard in school. He says he is just an average student who has been trying to get better-than-average grades.

Exploratory and understanding stages. Exploration reveals that Tony's scholastic problem is one he pushes out in front in order to determine whether he can trust the counselor or not. Since the helper is skillful and caring, Tony decides to risk revealing himself more fully. He has been stealing money from the rooms of other students in the dormitory complex. He has used the money, along with some of his own, to buy a small motorcycle. His symptoms refer not to his scholastic efforts but to the guilt he feels. The cycle itself has become a symbol of the way in which he has violated his own standards. He feels no compulsion to turn himself in to the authorities of the school, but he feels that he should in some way try to return the money. After a few sessions, his symptoms vanish almost entirely. The counseling sessions are terminated.

For Tony, counseling has had a cathartic effect. Once he is free of the physical and psychological symptoms of guilt, he is free to invest himself in life once more.

In all three of these examples, the client has been a relatively high-level client. Stages I and II have a liberating effect on the client, who then takes charge of his own life. Stages I and II, if skillfully executed, provide a great deal of emotional re-education for the client. For instance, the client who experienced himself as worthless now experiences himself as respected and prized by the helper. Through contact with a person who genuinely prizes him, he learns to prize himself. In Stages I and II, clients come to see themselves more realistically and get a better picture of their resources, both personal and environmental. For a certain number of clients, this emotional re-education and inventory of resources suffice. It is not our purpose here to determine the kinds of cases in which the effective execution of Stages I and II suffices but to point out that behavioral changes can take place because of Stage-I and Stage-II interactions. Whether such interactions suffice in a given case is something that must be determined.

A comprehensive problem-solving methodology

It is not realistic to expect that the catharsis and emotional re-education effected by successful execution of Stages I and II will offer a complete solution to every client's problems. In most cases clients are in trouble because they are acting ineffectively (for example, a man is trying to solve his problems by drinking excessively; his wife is trying to reform him by nagging at him constantly) or because they are failing to act at all (for example, the lonely person sits in his apartment feeling sorry for himself; the person with a low energy level does not exercise). Let's listen to a client or two who have achieved some degree of symptom relief by effective participation in Stages I and II.

> *Client A:* I feel much better about myself now. I don't look upon myself as empty or worthless or rotten. I don't want to quit school anymore, but I have to decide which programs are best for me, including extracurricular programs. And on vacations, since I'll be living at home, I still have to try to find some way of living in peace with my parents.

> *Client B:* I'm not nearly so anxious anymore—when alone with myself or at work. I have more energy than I ever realized I had. It's amazing how much of my energy was tied up in alternate bouts with anxiety and depression. But now I have a new problem. Now that I have all this energy, I'm

no longer content with the job I have or the very restricted interpersonal life I lead. What do I do now?

In both of these cases, emotional re-education and other forms of liberation have helped the client rid himself of psychological burdens, but now each feels in need of help to elaborate more constructive approaches to living.

Dynamic understanding, however valuable, does not contain in itself the key to more constructive living.

> *Client A:* I see now that my "wit" often takes the form of sarcasm and cynicism—and these turn people off. It's almost as if I *wanted* to alienate people, keep them at a distance. It's hard for me to say it, but intimacy is just very difficult for me. But I'm in such a rut. This week I more or less watched myself as I dealt with others. I'm cynical and sarcastic almost automatically. I've got two things to do: break that habit and find out how to interact with others more sincerely and intimately.

> *Client B:* I guess I'm ready to admit that I try to do too many things. I'm so overinvested that I don't have time for myself and my family, and I don't even do a good job for my clients at work. Making money has been such a primary goal that it has swallowed up everything else with it. Boy, that's really painful to admit! I've got to find some way to retrench at work and start building a more human life.

Both of these clients have achieved significant levels of self-understanding. They are now ready to act, but they are not quite sure *how* to act. They need help in decision making and problem solving.

Gelatt, Varenhorst, and Carey (1972) distinguish decision making from problem solving. The latter, in their definition, is geared to finding the one best or right solution for everyone, while decision making is more personal and takes into account an assessment of personal values in determining courses of action. In the following pages, however, no such distinction is made: the term "problem solving" is used comprehensively and, as we shall see, includes the consideration of personal values in making decisions and adopting courses of action.

The purpose of a problem-solving program is to help the client act. Like the rest of the helping process, problem-solving methodologies are not ends in themselves. Here we will spell out a problem-solving methodology in some detail. However, it may not always be necessary to apply all the mechanics of the following methodology to every client problem. Basically, this methodology is a way of ordering one's thoughts and resources *systematically* in searching out viable courses of action. The methodology presented should be abridged, adapted, or expanded as the need arises. It should even be replaced by any other methodology that may be more effective. The point here is that problems are ordinarily solved more effectively if they are approached systematically. Any effective methodology must be systematic and based on common sense. Too many clients (often under the guidance of a counselor) try merely random approaches to the solution of problems. Using random approaches to problem solving is a problem in itself. On the other hand, the low-level helper is usually a slave to methodology: he cannot adapt, invent, or improvise because he is imprisoned by his own lack of skills. Therefore, use the following methodology, but don't abuse it by chaining yourself to it. Furthermore, constantly search out other methodologies that will enable you to serve your clients more effectively.

A force-field analysis approach to problem solving

Force-field analysis is a sophisticated term for a process that is, conceptually at least, relatively simple. Basically it means this: John has a problem. The solution to that problem is his goal. Once he sees what his goal is, he sees what forces keep him from his goal (restraining forces) and what forces help move him toward his goal (facilitating forces). He then determines what courses of action will help him decrease the strength of the restraining forces and increase the strength of the facilitating forces. He chooses those means that are most ,practical and that are in tune with his personal values. Finally, he implements these means and evaluates his progress. If the means he chooses are inadequate, he chooses other means by the same process until he reaches his goal or sees that it is impossible.

The "field" in which the client works is illustrated in Figure 1. The field is a kind of battleground on which the client struggles to live more effectively.

Since this methodology is systematic, it involves well-defined, concrete steps. First I will give a summary of the steps and then explain each step in greater detail.

1. Identify and clarify the problems in the client's life.
2. Establish priorities; that is, determine which problem is to receive immediate attention. Don't help the client defeat himself by having him work on too many problems at the same time.
3. Establish concrete, workable goals, to which the client is committed.
4. Take as complete a census as possible of the means available for achieving each concrete goal. List concrete ways of instituting and strengthening facilitating forces and of weakening or eliminating restraining forces.

5. Choose the means that are in keeping with the client's value system and that will most effectively help him achieve established goals.
6. Establish criteria by which the effectiveness of action programs can be evaluated.
7. Implement: use chosen means to achieve established goals.
8. Review and evaluate the client's progress.

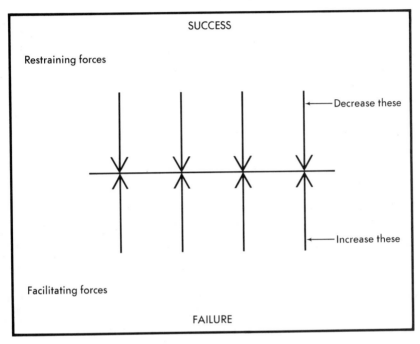

Figure 1

Let's now consider each of these steps in greater detail.

1. Identify and clarify the problem

The client comes to the counselor and says: "My life is really messed up. I don't know what I'm doing or where I'm going." Two things are evident: the client is in pain and his problems must be identified and clarified if he is to be helped. Stages I and II of the developmental model serve precisely this function: the client, with the help of the counselor, identifies and clarifies his problems. The client also goes on to the point of understanding the need to act.

In addition to what has already been said in Stages I and II, "identify and clarify" can be further described.

State the problem in such a way that it appears solvable. The client must ultimately define his problems in such a way that some solution seems possible. One of the games clients play (with ineffective helpers) is to state problems in a way that makes them seem insoluble. This game often elicits the pity and the sympathy of the counselor, the payoff the client is looking for.

> *Insoluble Problem:* In sum, my life is miserable now because of my past. My parents were indifferent to me and at times even unjustly hostile toward me. If they had only been more loving, I wouldn't be in this present mess. I am the unhappy product of an unhappy environment.

The client's past cannot be changed. Therefore, since he defines his problem in terms of the past, his problem cannot be solved. "You certainly have it rough" might be the kind of response he is looking for.

> *Soluble Problem:* Over the years I've been blaming my parents for my misery. I still spend a great deal of time feeling sorry for myself. As a result, I sit around and do nothing—I don't make friends, I don't involve myself in the community, I don't take any constructive steps to make something of myself.

The problem, stated in this way, can be solved, for the client can stop blaming his parents since he cannot change them, increase his self-esteem and therefore stop feeling sorry for himself, and acquire the interpersonal skills he needs to enter more effectively into community.

A problem cannot be solved if it is stated in vague terms or is anchored to the past or is defined as forces beyond the control of the client.

> *Insoluble Problem:* The world is going to seed. No matter what the politicians say, there's always the possibility of nuclear warfare. It's frightening . . . you almost wonder why you keep going on.

The client cannot change the complexity of the world or the possibility of atomic war. Since an atomic holocaust *is* a possibility, some concern and fear are realistic. But if the client believes that his present anxiety and passivity are due to the possibility of nuclear warfare, there is no solution.

> *Soluble Problem:* I'm overly anxious and tend to blame my anxiety on things that happen to me—like the mess the world is in. I think I should blame myself much more—the ways I act and the ways I fail to act. I'm too passive; I say that I'm overwhelmed because I can't change the world, but I don't lift a finger to change what I can change. For instance, I gripe about

politicians, but I haven't even voted in the last three elections. I don't work in any community projects. I just watch the TV news and gripe.

Because of the way in which the client states his problems, the counselor can help him begin to take charge of his life in a more active way. For instance, when the client begins to *do* things (such as involve himself in community projects), he will find himself less anxious, for he won't have time for worry.

In sum, before trying to elaborate any action steps, ask yourself whether the client has defined his problem in a way that allows the problem to be solved.

Make sure the client owns the problem.   The client should admit that the problem is *his.* He should not state it in terms of what others fail to do. His problem should be seen as his problem and not the property of others or of systems or of undefined forces.

> *Not owned:* I live in a racist society. It even rubs off on me.
> *Owned:* I am a racist. I live in a neighborhood that excludes minority groups, especially blacks. And I begin to see that this is only one of my prejudices.

> *Not owned:* My friends don't seem to care for me, really. They keep me on the margin of their social life.
> *Owned:* I'm biting and cynical when I'm with my friends. I think sometimes they just say "Ugh" quietly and wish I weren't there. I alienate them. I don't listen well to others. I can hardly blame people for not inviting me to their parties and on vacations.

> *Not owned:* My husband is a drunk and I can't do much to change him, though I try. He has ruined the home, and our children suffer a great deal. He should get out of the house, out of our lives.
> *Owned:* I haven't learned how to cope with my husband's excessive drinking. I know that I've done things that merit having a drunk for a husband. I've always nagged, even before he started drinking. When the children were born, I showed them much more interest than I showed him. I've put the entire blame for our misery on his drinking, but I share the blame.

When two human beings find themselves in conflict, it is rare for one of them to be blameless. A wife cannot directly change her husband, but she can change her own behavior. Even when a client has to face a situation that is patently unjust or unfair—such as parents who are unreasonably punitive—he can (if he is old enough and has sufficient resources) decide how to act toward them so that he may live as effectively as possible, even though they choose not to.

In sum, make sure that the client admits that *he* has a problem, even when others are acting irresponsibly toward him. He has to determine how *he* is going to act in the face of adversity.

Have the client state the problem concretely.   We have already discussed concreteness. Concreteness is especially crucial in Stage III: the more concretely the problem is stated, the more easily it can be translated into a concrete, workable goal.

> *Too General:* The quality of my ministry to my congregation has slipped.
> *Concrete:* I'm bored with what I do in the parish. It's so much routine. I'm overworked. It is physically impossible for me to do as much home visitation as the congregation wants. I haven't enlisted the aid of members of the congregation to fulfill the pastoral needs of the community. I fail to visit the hospital as often as I should.

In the first statement, the minister owns the problem, but he does not state it concretely enough. If in Stages I and II the helper has allowed the client to remain vague and general, then, in order to help the client embark upon the problem-solving stage, he will have to start by going back and helping the client become more concrete. If a problem is stated concretely enough, it is possible to begin to glimpse the solution. For instance, the minister has failed to train other members of the congregation to help him minister. Therefore, he is involved in a logistic absurdity: it is impossible for him to meet all the pastoral needs of the members of his congregation himself. A possible goal, then, is to train some of the members of the congregation in the skills essential to ministry. He can train them, for instance, in the skills needed to visit the sick and shut-ins. He also has to teach the members of the congregation that ministry is a function of the entire community and not just of the appointed minister. He cannot even begin to glimpse the solution to his problem if he merely says that the quality of his ministry to his congregation has deteriorated.

The client should state his problem, if possible, in terms of his behavior—what he does to perpetuate a destructive situation ("I nag my wife") or what he fails to do ("I don't keep the house clean"). Then the goal or objective will be clear: to stop doing what he is doing poorly and to start doing what he should do.

Break the problem down into workable units.   It is impossible to attack a problem if it is too general or if it involves too many subunits.

> *General Problem:* My family life is deteriorating.
> *Breakdown of Problem:*

I spend too much time traveling in the job I have now.

My wife and I don't talk about our relationship or the more intimate values we possess, such as religion.

My two children don't get along. They never cooperate, and I do nothing to facilitate their coming together in understanding.

My wife and I have different views concerning discipline for the children, and I'm inconsistent in the way I administer discipline.

We have a "closed" home. Very few friends visit us.

We have no family involvement in the neighborhood.

I'm tired when I come home, and I spend a great deal of time in front of the TV.

General Problem: I am very depressed and I withdraw both from work and from social commitments.
Breakdown of Problem:

I'm grieving over the death of a very close friend.

A very intimate frind of mine married another person, and I feel left out.

I've always kept my emotions under strict control. Others never know what I'm feeling.

I have pretended to live totally for others without paying any attention to my social-emotional needs.

I feel cheated in life.

I have allowed myself to wallow in self-pity lately; I'm living on regrets.

I don't call my friends anymore.

I don't visit my friends, and I make excuses so that they don't visit me.

I've been calling into work sick about four to six times a month, whereas I never missed before.

I'm a very proud person. I've always prided myself on being self-reliant.

A problem that is stated too generally is like a huge tangle of string: it seems impossible to untangle. While it is always possible to break a larger problem down into smaller units, this process can be carried to absurdity. The subunits should not be so small as to be meaningless. The goal is action, the goal is change—and problem solving is a means. It's possible to work on several problems at once, especially if they cluster around a theme, as do the problems described above. But notice that these subproblems are all still problems. They are not goals.

2. Establish priorities in choosing problems for attention

In order to establish priorities ("Which problems or subproblems should I work on immediately?"), it is necessary for the client to have a preliminary overview of both his problems and some of his resources. If in Stages I and II the counselor helps the client see only his problems and not some of his significant resources as well, he is doing the client a disservice. Let's consider the case of John Doe from the point of view of force-field analysis.

Major problems (destructive forces)
heavy drinking
passive lifestyle
poor interpersonal relations with fellow workers
deteriorating family situation

Major resources (constructive forces)
sound intelligence, both academic and social
caring friends
good work record
high motivation to change
basic ability to care for others

Each major problem can, of course, be broken down into subunits, but the same can be said for the client's resources. For instance, John Doe's intelligence means a number of things: he is a good problem solver, he can see the "wider picture" easily, he can get good jobs, his verbal skills are good, he is a reflective person—he sees details with clarity, and so forth. Once a client has a vision of both his general problems and their subunits and his general resources and some of their subunits, he must ask himself: "Which problems or subproblems do I expend my energy on first?" Let's look at some criteria for choosing.

Choose problems that are under your control.   The person who sets out to change another person in order to solve his own problems is indeed in trouble.

> *Client:* My boss is a very egotistical and punitive person. I react to him by being totally submissive. This keeps the peace, but I am very dissatisfied with myself.

This client has two options: change his boss or change his own behavior. The client must work first on his own behavior. Being egotistical and punitive is his boss's problem, and his boss must deal with that. Being a peace-at-any-price person is this client's problem, and *he* can deal with that. If married couples were to follow this pattern, marriage counseling would be less messy. In my marriage counseling, part of the counseling "contract" I enjoin states that each partner may talk only about ways in which he or she contributes to the misery of the relationship. Each must first work on the mess in his or her own backyard. It is amazing how less tense a relationship can become when each partner is working on his own areas of deficit.

Some clients explain their problems almost totally in terms of the "dirt" others are doing to them, whether the others are individuals or organizations or society itself. And it may well be that they are, to one degree or another, victims of forces over which they have no control.

However, if they cannot control these forces, it is senseless for them to state their problems in terms of these forces. In Stages I and II the counselor helps the client sort out what he can control and what he cannot control. In the problem-solving phase, problems and subproblems should be stated in terms of forces within the control of the client.

Give some priority to pressing problems, crisis situations. It is essential to help a client meet his most pressing or overwhelming problems immediately. These problems should be at least "defused" so that the client is not overwhelmed by anxiety. For instance, if the client is falling apart because his wife has just told him that she is suing him for divorce, attention should be paid to this crisis—that is, to his reaction to his wife's legal actions. Actually, the understanding, respect, and support provided by Stage-I interactions help greatly to defuse such crises. Indeed, the ability to face such crises with the client is one important factor that distinguishes high-level helpers from low-level ones. Stage II then gets at the behavioral roots of the problem and sets the stage for problem-solving programs.

Let's return for a moment to the major problems of John Doe, introduced a few pages back. John is drinking so heavily that he is on the verge of both a physical and a psychological collapse. In his case, excessive drinking is a pressing problem that needs immediate attention. The helper uses whatever combination of Stage-I and Stage-II interactions (for example, accurate empathy *and* confrontation) are needed to help the client stop drinking. Let's say that John, upon withdrawing from alcohol, goes into a deep depression. Again, this depression is a pressing problem, and the helper uses whatever means he needs—both physical and psychological—to help the client weather this crisis. The term "pressing" is obviously a relative one. Some problems are so pressing that Stages I, II, and III must be compacted in a very short time. Others allow for a more leisurely progression through Stages I and II. Perhaps it is misleading to dwell on the time factor. The high-level helper deals with the client's problems as the client's needs require. He doesn't try to fit the client rigidly into a counseling model.

It should also be obvious that not every crisis or pressing problem can be dealt with as easily as is intimated here. Rather, the point is that problems that can potentially do great harm to or actually destroy the client should get top priority. But there should also be some kind of ordering among problems that can be dealt with in a more leisurely fashion.

Choose some problem or subproblem that can be handled relatively easily. A relatively easy problem or subproblem should be dealt with early in the problem-solving stage of the counseling process. The reason is simple: if the client experiences even a small degree of success in handling *any* problem (even a relatively easy one), he finds reinforcement, which helps him trust his resources and gives him added energy to attack more difficult problems. For instance, let's say that drugs (marijuana and some experimentation with the amphetamines) are problematic in Mary's life, but they do not constitute the core of Mary's problems. A larger problem is the fact that she doesn't want to face the responsibilities of adult life (for whatever reason) and used drugs as a means of running away from life. Exploration shows that she is not highly emotionally invested in the use of drugs, so this is one facet of a wider problem that might be handled relatively easily. With the help of the counselor, Mary stops her amphetamine experimentation and tapers off the use of marijuana until she has stopped. On doing this, she feels a sense of accomplishment and almost enjoys the discipline needed to stop. Her success provides her with added energy and motivation to attack the more serious and resistant facets of her problem. Sometimes low-level helpers take such relative success for absolute success and at that point abandon clients to their own means, realizing instinctively that they do not have the resources to work with clients on less tractable problems.

Choose a problem or subproblem that, if treated, will bring about general improvement. Some problems or facets of problems, when treated, yield results beyond what might be expected: improvement in one area often generalizes to other areas. A helper, through his experiences with clients, learns how to spot action programs that have this tendency to generalize. He then gives these areas top priority. For instance, he might focus on improvement in the client's physical well-being while continuing to explore problems in the social-emotional area—the more resistant problems. He helps Tim, who is overweight and suffering from "lack of pep," subscribe to a sensible program of physical fitness. The discipline of a sensible diet and daily exercise helps Tim put more discipline into more strictly social-emotional areas of living: he controls his temper more easily, he is not as impulsive in his "witty" remarks, and he is more patient in listening to his wife and children. The discipline he exercises in the physical area generalizes to more emotionally charged areas.

Let's consider another example. Sue and Bill's marriage is falling apart. The counselor gets a commitment from Sue to keep the house clean and, from Bill, a commitment to arrive home on time for meals and to spend a certain minimum amount of time per week at home. In the meantime they both continue to explore the other facets of their problems. Their keeping to their "contracts" (housework, time at home) has both a practical and a symbolic value: each sees the other as willing to invest himself in the marriage. Their fulfilled contracts are signs of caring and good will that, up to this point, have been missing in their marriage. This heartens both of them. Again, a bit of discipline has wider impact than might be expected.

Move from less severe problems to the more severe.   Aside from dealing immediately with crises and critical problems ("defusing"), a general principle is to proceed from less severe problems to the more severe. That is, effective shaping processes should be used. It is most helpful to get a backlog of success with easier problems before tackling harder ones. Also, the counselor should take as much advantage as possible of the "generalized improvement" effect just discussed. "Less severe" and "more severe" are relative terms: a problem that is quite serious for Andy might be only a moderately serious problem for Jean. Personality makeup, background, learning experiences, socioeconomic status, personal values, and other factors enter into determining what problem is more serious in a given case. If Stages I and II are carried out effectively, the relative seriousness of problems can be accurately determined.

Let's consider an example. Andy and Jean are both dissatisfied with their work because the work in itself is not rewarding, there is little opportunity for social contact with their fellow workers, and both have supervisors who are rigid and self-centered. Both Andy and Jean are also dissatisfied with the ineffective way they move into "community" with their friends. For Andy, the work problem is the more serious. His whole background has taught him that a great deal of his identity depends on the kind and quality of work he does. Work, for him, is a primary value, and to be locked into an unrewarding job is imprisonment indeed. Jean, on the other hand, looks upon work as a necessary evil. She is willing to put up with forty hours of relatively meaningless drudgery as long as she gets satisfaction from the rest of the hours of the week. She does her work conscientiously but is not interested in investing time and effort in improving her work situation. For her, the more serious problem revolves around her community of friends, for this is where she finds her nourishment.

As we have already seen, one way of ranking problems from the least to the most severe is to use Mehrabian's (1970) formula:

$$\text{Severity} = \text{Distress} \times \text{Frequency} \times \text{Uncontrollability}$$

In the example just cited, Andy finds a great deal of distress in his work situation: it causes him a great deal of anxiety and disrupts his life. Jean, on the other hand, suffers relatively little distress in her job, even though she doesn't particularly like it. Extremely distressing days at work are relatively infrequent for Jean, while for Andy they are quite frequent. If Jean finds fulfillment in her social-emotional world, she can control her adverse emotional reactions at work quite easily, while almost any kind of problem sets Andy on edge at work.

Up to this point we have considered problems and subproblems. The next step is to turn the problem or subproblem inside out in order to establish behavioral goals.

3. Establish workable goals

A problem describes a situation as it is now, whereas a goal describes a situation as the client would like it to be. The goal, then, is the opposite of the problem.

> *Problem:* The factory has just closed down and I've lost my job.
> *Goal:* I want another job.

> *Problem:* My relationship with my wife is poor. We fight. We don't listen to each other. Each of us is out for his own comfort.
> *Goal:* I want to improve my relationship with my wife. I want to listen to her and communicate to her the fact that I understand what she is saying. I want to become more aware of her needs and help her fulfill them. And I hope she would do the same for me.

> *Problem:* I'm an undisciplined eater and I'm overweight.
> *Goal:* I want to eat sensibly and lose weight.

> *Problem:* I often feel extremely depressed and feel like committing suicide.
> *Goal:* I want to get rid of both my depression and these urges to take my own life.

It is obvious that, if problems are stated vaguely or too generally, then the statement of goals will also suffer.

Just as there are general problems and subproblems, so there are general goals and subgoals. General goals are the opposite of general problems and subgoals are the opposite of subproblems.

> *General problem:* My interpersonal life is filled with boredom and anxiety.
> *General goal:* I want to improve the quality of my relationships to others and to get rid of both my boredom and my anxiety.

> *Subproblem:* I'm selfish and self-centered. I don't go out of my way to do anything for others.
> *Subgoal:* I want to go out of my way to help my friends, but I want to do so genuinely and not just to put on a show.

Subproblem: I don't take time to listen to and understand others.
Subgoal: I want to learn how to listen more effectively and to communicate understanding to others, especially to my friends.

Subproblem: I'm afraid to reveal any of my deeper feelings or thoughts to my friends. My conversation is always on a superficial level.
Subgoal: I want to learn how to share my deeper thoughts and feelings with my friends. I want to learn how to take the risk of reasonable openness so that my interactions with my friends will be less superficial.

In terms of the force-field analysis diagram, problems and goals stand opposite to each other (see Figure 2).

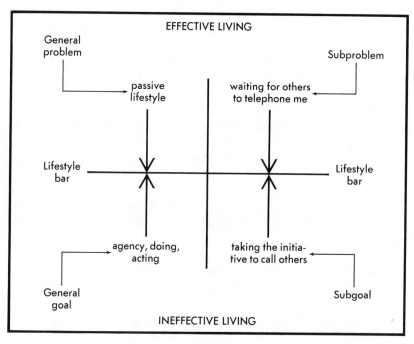

Figure 2

Problems are the "restraining forces" and the goals are the "facilitating forces." The objective is to find means to weaken the restraining forces and to strengthen the facilitating forces.

Just as problems and subproblems should be stated in certain ways, so should goals and subgoals. What are the essential characteristics of goals?

State the goal in a way that makes it workable, possible.   The goals and subgoals should be proportioned to the resources and abilities of the client. Therefore, a goal must be stated in a way that is workable for *this* client. In the following examples, it is assumed that the client has the resources he needs to achieve the "workable" goal.

Unworkable: I want to change the world.
Workable: I want to work to get more effective rubbish collection in the 50th ward.

Unworkable: I've never studied German, but this summer I want to learn to speak it fluently.
Workable: I want to learn as much German as possible this summer— at least enough to be somewhat comfortable on my three-week trip to Germany this fall.

The client will only sabotage his own efforts if he assigns himself goals that are beyond his reach. "Possibility" means that the necessary resources are available. He should not spend time deciding whether to go to a private school if the funds are not available. He can't decide between walking and driving if he doesn't have access to a car. Sometimes it is impossible to judge beforehand whether the personal and environmental resources are available, but he should start with goals for which the resources are certainly available and then proceed to those that are not so sure. Patently impossible goals should be eliminated from the start.

Make sure the client owns the goal.   Just as the client must own the problem ("the lack of understanding in my home"), so he must also own the goal.

Unowned Problem: There is racism in my community.
Owned Problem: I am racist, since I own a home in a community that excludes minority groups and I say nothing about that situation.

Unowned Goal: This problem should be brought up in our community meeting.
Owned Goal: I will bring up the problem of the exclusion of minority groups from this community at the next community meeting. I'll work for change in community policy. If necessary, I'll move out of this community to protest this policy.

If the client's goal is to change someone else's behavior ("My goal is to have my wife stop her nagging"), the goal is not owned.

Have the client state his goals concretely.   The art of problem solving entails becoming progressively more concrete.

Poor: I want to improve conditions.
Still poor: I want to improve myself.

Better: I want to improve my physical condition.
Still better: I want to lose weight, improve my muscle tone, and increase my energy level.

Poor: I want to achieve success.
Better: I want to improve the quality of my interpersonal relationships.
Still better: I want to learn the skill of accurate empathy and make it a part of my everyday interpersonal transactions.

Poor: I want to work for the cause of sobriety.
Good: I want to stop drinking myself. Further, I want to learn the skills needed to help others who have drinking problems.

If the goal is stated concretely, the client can begin to see what means he needs to achieve his goals.

Break each goal down into workable units.   Not only must goals be possible; they must be "work-size." There are examples of workable units (subgoals) above. The client is more likely to work for a goal if he can perceive that he is making progress toward that goal. The goal, then, should be measurable in some way. If a client says that his goal is to become a better husband, his progress toward that goal—stated so broadly—cannot be measured. However, if he says that he wants to spend more time at home talking with his wife, the time can be measured, and he can tell whether he is making progress or not. The word "measurable" refers to both quantity and quality. The client wants more than just to spend more time talking with his wife; he wants their talks to be meaningful. Another way of stating his goal is that he wants to become more available to his wife, both physically and psychologically. The quality of their interactions can also be measured. Merely spending more time with his wife is useless unless he improves the quality of his presence.

4. Take a census of the means available for achieving established goals

Consider the following list of objectives:

1. to live better,
2. to develop a more effective interpersonal life,
3. to learn the interpersonal skills of accurate empathy, respect, genuineness, concreteness, self-sharing, immediacy, and confrontation,
4. to learn interpersonal skills by reading books and articles about them, and
5. to learn interpersonal skills by joining a training group conducted by a high-level trainer.

Though it is obviously *too* general, (1) is a general or master goal. The next objective, (2), is a more concrete expression of (1); it is one of the principal dimensions of "living better." Therefore, (2) is not simply a means of achieving (1) but an end in itself. But (2) also suffers some of (1)'s vagueness. People don't just go out and live more effectively on an interpersonal level; rather, they do specific things. Goal (3), then, is a *means* to achieve goal (2). The assumption is that one doesn't learn skills just for the sake of the skills but in order to involve oneself more effectively with others. Just the ability to communicate accurate empathy is meaningless unless this skill is used to improve the quality of one's interpersonal functioning. Objective (4) is also a *means* used to achieve objective (3), which is itself a higher-order means. Objective (5) is also a means for achieving the objective stated in (3). Coupled with (4), it is an excellent means for achieving objective (3).

Some subgoals, therefore, define a more general goal but are really goals or ends in themselves. Other subgoals, however, are not ends in themselves but *means* to achieve desirable ends. In this section, we are interested in the *means* necessary for achieving established goals. *Force-field analysis is a way of discovering the means that will enable the client to fulfill subgoals.* Up to this point, we have seen force-field analysis as a way of picturing problems and goals more clearly. We will now use it as a process by which to discover the means needed to achieve subgoals. It deals with the question: "How many different means do I have at hand to achieve my goals?" The client, even though he is committed to change and has established some clear goals, is not always aware of what resources he has to achieve these goals. Neither does he have a clear idea of the factors that stand in his way. Force-field analysis at this stage, then, is a tool for analyzing a situation you would like to change, a way of gathering the kind of information essential for change, especially the kind of *practical* information needed, a way of reviewing both the obstacles standing in your way and the resources available for achieving change, and a way of developing alternative courses of action.

There are several steps in the process of searching out means to achieve goals. Let's consider a brief example and then describe the steps in terms of this example. John Smith has the problem, among other problems, of leading a colorless interpersonal life. He is lonely and miserable enough to want to do something about it. He realizes that he is a very passive person, especially when it comes to interpersonal concerns. Unless he can achieve a degree of agency here, his life will remain dull and colorless. His goal, then, is to forge for himself a more active interpersonal life. He engages in the following steps to discover practical means to help him achieve his goals.

List all the restraining forces keeping you from your goal.   In this case, it means all those factors that prevent John from being more creative and active interpersonally. He identifies as many restraining forces as possible but makes no attempt to rank them in order of importance. John's list might include:

> I'm afraid to meet new people. I feel shy and inadequate, and I end up by running away or making myself as unobtrusive as possible.
> I feel that I'm physically unattractive. I fear that I alienate people just by my looks.
> I keep thinking of my past interpersonal failures—the friends I have alienated—and I don't want to try anymore.
> I don't have anything interesting to say to others. My conversation is dull.
> I'm gauche in my manner of presenting myself to others. For instance, because of my shyness and self-consciousness, I end up not listening to what they're saying. Then I can't respond to them, and I feel stupid.
> When I'm with people, in my anxiety I talk too much about myself. So others see me as self-centered.
> I want others to love me, but few even like me. My needs for attention are great and I'm looking for too much.

And John continues to list any further restraining forces, in whatever order they come tumbling from his mind. When he has finished, he sets this list aside and proceeds to the next step.

List all the facilitating forces at work helping you to reach your goal. John asks himself, "What do I have going for me?" He lists everything he can think of that might help him achieve the goal of creating a more viable interpersonal life. His list might include:

> I'm a caring person. I care about others and would like to be helpful when I can.
> I'm an intelligent human being. I can usually discriminate the needs of a social situation, even though I'm gauche in meeting these needs.
> Tom, at work, and Beatrice, who lives down the street from me, have shown interest in me, although I've been afraid to encourage them.
> I'm so lonely right now that my motivation to change is very high.
> I live in a large city where there must be all sorts of resources for human nourishment.

And John continues to list any other facilitating forces that come to mind. The more complete these lists are, the better. Still, there has to be a cutoff point. The objective is to *act,* not merely to gather data needed for reasonable action.

The client might take the construction of these lists as a homework assignment and then finish filling them out with the help of the counselor. He can even put them on newsprint so that they can be taped up on the wall during the next counseling session. Once these lists are reasonably complete, the client is ready for the next step.

Underline the forces in each list (facilitating and restraining) that seem most important right now. If the work of Stages I and II has been successful, this will be a relatively easy task. Still, the client might be seeing some of the forces being considered for the first time. These might need further exploration. John should ask himself, "Which restraining forces are most critical in my life right now? Which facilitating forces are most important to me?" The client should work on those forces that promise the greatest payoff. In our example, John might underline (among others) this one:

> *I'm gauche in my manner of presenting myself to others. For instance, because of my shyness and self-consciousness, I end up not listening to what they're saying. Then I can't respond to them, and I feel stupid.*

When he looks at his list of facilitating forces, he underlines (among others):

> *I live in a large city where there must be all sorts of resources for human nourishment.*

Once John has underlined both the facilitating and restraining forces that he, in consultation with the helper, considers most important to work on, he is ready for the next step.

List all possible action steps for each underlined restraining force that could reduce or eliminate that force. Here the client should "brainstorm"; that is, he should list as many action programs as he can think of, even if some of them seem "far out," without criticizing these programs at this point. With the help of the counselor, John Smith begins to list all action programs (means) that will enable him to eliminate or reduce each restraining force he has underlined. In our example, he is looking for means to eliminate his gaucheness in presenting himself to others. He then lists possible action steps:

> Take a course called "How to Win Friends and Influence People" at a downtown institute.
> Read books on interpersonal communication.
> Go into psychoanalysis in order to discover why I don't develop interpersonally.
> Take a course in speech communication at a local junior college.

Join a competently led group in which a variety of interpersonal skills are taught systematically through group process.

Force myself to spend time in bars just trying to talk to others.

Join a local encounter group, which is a kind of goalless experience in which people try to grow together.

Continue to explore my shyness with the counselor.

Attend a potpourri of experiences at a local growth center.

Take a YMCA course in communication skills.

And John goes on listing all possible action programs he can think of that will reduce the impact of this particular restraining force. At this point, he does not choose the action programs in which he will invest himself.

List all possible action steps for each underlined facilitating force that could enhance that force. John Smith repeats the "brainstorming" process to obtain the facilitating forces he has chosen to work with. As you recall, one of the facilitating forces indicated that he lives in a large city in which there must be all sorts of resources for human nourishment. He lists action programs that will enable him to tap the resources of the city. He lists the following possibilities:

Get some dates through a computer system that brings people together who have like interests.

Advertise for companions in the *New York Review of Books.*

Join the Elks.

Take a vacation tour that is for singles only.

Explore the possibility of contacts with people through the church groups in the congregation to which I belong.

Get involved with some local social-action groups and reap the side benefit of making new friends.

Have occasional dinner parties; invite people from work, from the church, neighbors, and so on.

Work in some volunteer programs dealing with the disenfranchised and the outcasts of society—the elderly, shut-ins, the poor. Try to help others sincerely, but also let them help me by putting me in a wider context.

And John adds as many action programs to this list as he can think of. Again, at this point he doesn't choose which action programs (means) he is going to adopt to try to enhance the facilitating forces in his "field." He should not include means that are just outlandish; even though he should search out a wide variety of means, they should be possible and workable. The search for viable means is not a mere exercise in fantasy.

Up to this point, the client, with the help of the counselor, has been engaged in what may be broadly termed "information gathering." Gelatt and his associates (1972) stress the importance of information gathering in the decision-making/problem-solving process: "A person's choices are increased if he can create new alternatives based on informa- tion" (p. 7). Many people engaged in problem solving overlook viable alternatives and available resources, either because they don't have information-seeking skills or because they simply don't take the time to make an inventory of possible resources. For instance, a clergyman who is leaving the ministry and looking for some secular occupation might fail to make an inventory of the jobs in which his human-rela- tions skills and experience would be invaluable. Or he fails to see his former parishioners as rich sources for job contacts.

Obviously, however, there comes a time when further seeking for relevant information and resources is no longer helpful. Inquiry must be cut short and the client must actually choose specific means, from among those he has investigated, as those that will enable him to achieve his goal most effectively. Of course, time invested in the search for means will vary. For instance, if the problem is pressing (for exam- ple, accompanied by practically immobilizing anxiety), the need for action is great and the time spent in searching out alternative action programs must be curtailed. However, if pressures are not great, and if the decision-making or problem-solving process will involve long-term effects (for example, accepting a job in another city), the client would do well to explore the ramifications of his decision as thoroughly as possible. This brings us to the next step.

5. Choose the means that will most effectively achieve established goals

When further searching for information and resources becomes counterproductive, the client must choose the means (action programs) he will use to achieve the goals and subgoals he has established. Let's say that an unmarried eighteen-year-old girl, Susan, comes to the coun- selor because of an unwanted pregnancy. The information/resource- seeking process has produced the following list of action programs to handle both the unwanted pregnancy and the anxiety and depression that accompany it.

> Join a counseling group consisting of unwed mothers-to-be, a group sponsored by a church agency in the client's home town.
> Read books on prenatal care.
> Leave town and live in a *crèche* in a large city some distance away until the baby is born.
> Stay at home and count on the care and support of family, relatives, and friends in facing this crisis.
> Get a job in town to help defray expenses.

Live with an aunt in a larger city until the baby is born; get a job there to help defray expenses.

Run away; get a job in some other city and have the child anonymously there.

Have an abortion.

Have the child secretly and abandon it once it is born.

Get married and keep the child.

Keep the child, but don't get married.

Commit suicide.

Have the child and put it up for adoption immediately.

Decide what to do about the child after getting used to the idea of being pregnant.

What is Susan to do? What should her strategy be? Which of these courses of action should she choose? A strategy is a plan for converting information and resources into action in the light of certain criteria such as personal values, probability of successful outcome, and so on. What criteria can Susan use to choose the most constructive courses of action to achieve her goal? She must respond to the crisis of an unwanted pregnancy. Notice that Susan has to face three interwoven issues: whether the baby should be born at all; if the baby is to be born, what to do to prepare for it; and what to do with the baby once it is born.

Help the client choose means (action programs) that are in keeping with his own personal values. The assumption is that the client is not interested in just any kind of solution, just as he is not interested in just any kind of life. If the action program goes counter to his value system, problems will be created that are perhaps worse than the one the client is trying to resolve. The values on which decisions are made should be those of the client, not those of the counselor merely imposed on the client. As I have noted, Stages I and II should do much to clarify the personal values of the client. However, if the values relevant to some proposed action program have not been clarified in Stages I and II, they should be clarified before the client acts. Values are necessary not only to help the client choose between action programs but to give temporal priority to one strategy over another.

A value, according to Raths and Simon (1966), is something that a particular person prizes and cherishes, even in public when appropriate —something that someone chooses freely from alternatives, after considering the consequences of these alternatives, and that causes a person to act (or to refrain from acting) in a repeated, consistent way. As such, values differ from opinions, interests, feelings, beliefs, and attitudes especially in that these, unlike values, do not always find their way into action. Values, then, are related to lifestyle. Another way of putting it is that my values constitute the ways in which I *commit* myself to myself, to others, and to the world about me. My values are extremely important, for my commitments constitute a significant part of my identity—the person I see myself to be.

Values determine how much time and energy the client is willing to invest in a given action program. Values give weight—positive or negative—to alternative courses of action. Ideally, the client should try to choose those action programs that are in accord with his highest values. Let's return to the case of Susan, the unmarried girl with the unwanted pregnancy. She looks over the list of possible courses of action and sees immediately that her values eliminate certain courses of action. For instance, she prizes human life wherever or in whatever form or condition it is found. Therefore, she immediately eliminates abortion, suicide, and abandoning the child once it is born. More positively, she chooses to *have* the child, for values are not merely instruments to be used to eliminate undesirable courses of action.

Let's consider another example. Bill has a two-year college scholarship, which is about to run out. His problem is how to finance the remaining two years of college. There are various possibilities. He has an extremely generous grandfather, who would "loan" (for all practical purposes, give) him all the money he would need for school. He could take out a low-interest government loan, but this loan would not cover all of his expenses. He could work part-time during the year and full-time during the summers and earn almost all the money he would need if he takes advantage of a state grant. He could use a combination of these means.

Exploration shows that it is important for Bill to be self-sustaining; but it is also important for him to engage in certain extracurricular activities (for example, being a volunteer at the university child-guidance center), which he considers an important part of his education. Therefore, Bill must balance his values. Ultimately, he chooses a combination strategy: he works during the summer, takes out a government loan, and accepts a small "loan" from his grandfather.

In our previous example, Susan may choose to stay in her home town to have the baby because family life is a high value for her and outweighs such considerations as the shame she might experience when her pregnancy becomes apparent.

In cases in which the client has no strong value system (he moves with the wind) or holds values that are actually destructive (for example, the belief that self-gratification must take precedence over every other consideration), then value education or re-education should become an important action program in itself. The client has to learn experientially that building a value system and acting consistently within it is a rewarding experience in itself.

Help the client choose practical action programs (means) that have a high probability for success.   First of all, help the client separate *practical* action programs from the merely possible. The brainstorming approach used in searching for means helps to discover action programs that might have been overlooked in a more practical search, but it obviously also produces means that, while possible, are not practical for this client in these circumstances. For instance, one way a client can stop drinking is to move to an isolated island where liquor is simply not available. However, choosing to move (literally) away from alcohol probably is not practical. It probably is more feasible to join Alcoholics Anonymous and count on the fellowship and social pressure of the group to help him stay dry.

Action programs are not practical if they ignore unbending environmental forces. Caplan and Nelson (1973) have noted the tendency of psychologists to emphasize "person-blame" over "systems-blame" or "environment-blame" in research on social problems. Since the research instruments that psychologists use to investigate problems get at personal variables more readily than at systems variables, there is an inherent "person-blame" bias in their research methodology. A similar failure to scrutinize the environment in a counseling situation can lead to a choice of action programs that prove useless in the face of opposing environmental forces. For instance, Susan might want to remain in her home-town community to have the baby, but she may also have to face the fact that she lives in a highly moralistic and punitive community. It may be better to move to a different community (for example, move into the *crèche* or live with her aunt) rather than face extreme psychological harassment in her home town.

Let's consider another example. Jeff is a young black resident of an extremely depressing ghetto. Although he has tried to find employment, the job market remains tight, and he is jobless. He has turned to "light" drugs, for drug use helps take the edge off the misery in which he lives and also is one of the requirements for belonging to the neighborhood gang. Jeff steals when he has to in order to support his drug habit. He is caught shoplifting and ends up with a counselor in a juvenile-delinquent program. An appreciation of the conditions of Jeff's day-to-day life will prevent the counselor from helping Jeff choose simplistic action programs that overlook environmental forces. For instance, although it may be possible for Jeff to join a volunteer program in a local hospital, this might be an ineffective way of helping him develop a sense of self-worth. Jeff's lifestyle is a reflection of the mores of the community in which he lives. If he is to live more effectively, he has to find some way of getting out from beneath his present environmental crush. He needs supportive human resources, a community within the community or neighborhood in which he lives. For instance, he might find an alternative community of friends in some of the programs sponsored by a neighborhood church—especially if he doesn't have to pretend to be religious in order to be accepted into these groups and if these programs draw their leadership from the community itself. At any rate, an indigenous counselor can help Jeff search out supportive human resources in the community or neighborhood in which he lives. It is evident that indigenous counselors and helping programs will do much more for Jeff than programs that come from "outside" and symbolize the forces that are the source of his oppression. Jeff has to be helped to choose action programs that are practical responses to his environment, not programs that ignore the environment and are merely good in themselves.

Try to help the client choose action programs that will not meet a great deal of environmental resistance. If increasing a facilitating or driving force merely results in a parallel increase in an opposing restraining force, it might be better to choose a different facilitating force or to work at reducing a restraining force. For instance, it is possible for Martha to try to get her husband to join Alcoholics Anonymous (she wants to increase a facilitating force), but if her attempt merely increases his opposition to taking *any* means to curb his excessive drinking, she needs a new strategy. She might stop trying to influence him directly and start instead with her own behavior, especially the behavior that sets the two of them apart. If she starts keeping the house in better order and prepares better meals (thus reducing a restraining force), her husband might see this as a sign of good will on her part and decrease his resistance to talking about his drinking problem. The direct assault, then, is not always the most practical approach.

In choosing an action program, the client should be helped to evaluate the risk involved and determine whether the risk is proportional to the probability of success. Estimating the risk involved in each alternative ties together personal values and the information gathered (Gelatt, Varenhorst, and Carey, 1972). Gelatt and his associates suggest four strategies that deal with the factors of risk and probability.

In the "wish" strategy, the client chooses courses of action that *could* lead to a goal he wants, regardless of risk, cost, or probability. For instance, if Susan values self-reliance very highly, she might flee to another city from her home town to try to get a job and support herself as she waits for the birth of the child.

In the "safe" strategy, the client chooses only safe courses of action, ones that have a high degree of probability of succeeding but that might not help a client achieve a goal in the way or to the degree he would like. For example, Susan might choose to live in the *crèche* in a large city away from her home town. This is the safest way of having her baby, for she will get proper prenatal care and will not have to risk the disapproval of her home town community.

The "escape" strategy lets the client choose means that are likely to help him *avoid* the worst possible result; it minimizes the maximum danger. Let's say that a client has had fits of violence. He commits himself to a mental hospital, for he feels that there he will be protected from his own violence. The greatest danger for him is harming another person. By placing himself in custodial care, he minimizes this danger.

The "combination" strategy allows the client to choose courses of action that, although they involve risk, both minimize danger and increase the probability of achieving a goal in the way and to the degree the client desires. This "combination" strategy is the most difficult to apply, for it involves the hard work implied in the comprehensive problem-solving methodology described in these pages: clarification of objectives, a solid knowledge of personal values, the ability to rank a variety of action programs according to one's values, plus the ability to predict results for a given course of action and to estimate the probability of success for a given course of action. Therefore, the counselor should be able to help the client estimate the risk, the probability of success, and the possible side effects of any action program. To do this, he must understand the client's inner resources well and have an understanding of the environmental resources available to the client. Returning to Susan, we see that marriages based merely on the fact of pregnancy have a very high failure rate. Since Susan is not highly committed to the young man, marriage should be ruled out. Susan wants what is best for the child, but she also wants to go to college to prepare herself for a career in nursing. In this case, then, it would probably be best for her to give the child up immediately for adoption.

Help the client order his action programs so that he moves gradually and systematically toward his goal. Moving toward a goal gradually, step by step, is one way of increasing the probability of reaching that goal. Most action programs are not simple, one-step processes; they can be broken down into a series of steps. The principle is not to let any one step be too complicated. If it is too complicated, break it down into simpler steps that the client can manage. For instance, before a client tries to establish closer contacts with people in his social environment, he might do well to learn human-relations skills in a good training group. But even in the training group he should start with the simplest skills, skills that are readily learned and yield immediate success (reinforcement). If he learns the simplest skill, attending, and feels rewarded, the probability increases that he will move on to learn more complex skills. Learning the simplest skill has two effects: it provides immediate reinforcement and it lays the foundation upon which more complex skills are built.

A very simple step can often ease the tension of a very serious problem. The person who enters an interpersonal-skills-training program and learns simply how to attend to another human being often changes his whole stance toward those he meets outside the training group. This simple skill gives him a new perception of others. Instead of moving into human contacts awkwardly or fearfully or belligerently, he now *pauses* and allows the other person to be present in his own way —a very simple but very important step. A first step for Susan might be a physical-training program as part of prenatal care. Step by step, she assumes a program of proper diet, rest, and exercise. She comes to enjoy the discipline introduced into her life; it makes her feel better and thus makes the implementation of other courses of action easier. Most goals, and even subgoals, look too formidable to the client when viewed all at once. But small steps, pursued consistently, are more easily faced by the client.

Let's consider an example all too familiar to the average college student. He usually gags at the thought of a term paper because he sees it all at once. The sting of writing a term paper could be removed if the student were to follow some systematic approach to writing it. The following program might not make the writing enjoyable (although even this is possible), but it can certainly reduce the pain.

> Choose a general topic (define the general goal).
> Delimit the topic (define the subgoal). Let the general goal ferment a bit in your mind. Perhaps do a little preliminary reading before settling on the delimited topic.
> Begin to read and think about the topic leisurely. Don't cram so much reading together that you get sick and tired of it. This will merely make the whole process a burden. The obvious implication here is: start early but leisurely.
> Whenever a relevant idea comes up in your reading or in your own musing on the topic or in a discussion with someone else about it, jot it down (a short quote, a summary of something longer, or an idea).
> Put only one idea or quote or summary on a sheet of paper or file card. If you put more than one idea on a card, you decrease your ability to move your ideas around and make them fit in with others.
> Give the idea a brief title at the top of the page or file card. It will enable you to identify the idea quickly.
> File your ideas in a general folder.
> As the ideas begin to congregate about certain topics, divide the folder into a number of subtopic folders. Don't force this process; let it grow naturally from the material gathered. However, if there are topics that must be covered in the paper, make folders for these and keep an eye out for relevant material.

Continue to read and discuss and muse, adding ideas, quotes, and sum-maries to the main-topic and subtopic folders as they occur.

Gradually begin to arrange the subtopic folders in logical order. Let the overall plan of the paper begin to take shape in your mind.

When the time comes to write the paper, put the folders in the logical order you have determined. Then, one after another, take each folder and arrange the papers or file cards in logical order. Begin to eliminate material that isn't relevant. This arranging will be quite easy, for there is only one idea on each paper or card.

Write a rough draft for each section. Write quickly, not trying to give what you're writing its final form. You will discover that it's easier to redo what is written roughly than to try to achieve perfection immediately.

Finally, polish up the rough draft where you need to. You will discover that much of what you have written need not be changed radically.

Most students I know hate to write papers and so put it off until the last moment. Then they are faced with the task of trying to create something out of nothing, ultimately handing in precisely that—noth-ing. The opposite is true if one follows the process just outlined. The task is spread out over time and the information-gathering process is comparatively effortless; when the time comes for writing the paper, it is usually a question of *eliminating* material rather than trying to create it. Eliminating irrelevant material will raise the quality of the paper considerably. Obviously, this systematic approach demands some de-gree of discipline from the student, but relatively little, and the rewards outweigh the effort involved. The student may even enjoy what he is doing and find the task worthwhile and intellectually stimulating. Simi-lar systematic approaches to a wide variety of educational tasks—both worthwhile and worthless—can result in the student's gaining time to pursue his own intellectual development in areas he finds stimulating. If systematic approaches to educational tasks can make education inter-esting, they are certainly worth trying.

6. Establish criteria for the effectiveness of action programs

Action programs must be concrete enough to measure in some way. If I am unable to measure and evaluate whether a given program is successful, either the problem or the solution, or both, have not been stated concretely enough. Tangible results form the backbone of the reinforcement process in counseling. If the client is to be encouraged to move forward, he must see results. Therefore, both counselor and client should be able to judge whether the action program is or is not being implemented, and to what degree, and the results of this implementa-tion. For instance, if a person joins a group in order to lose weight, the requirements of diet and exercise should be so clear that the client can say whether or not he is fulfilling the contract he made with the group and to what degree; and he should ultimately be able to measure the results in terms of weight loss, improved muscle tone, endurance, higher energy level, and so on.

Obviously, the client will not be able to measure change unless he can in some way measure his starting point. Measuring his starting point is called gathering *baseline* data. It is relatively easy to gather such data in physical-fitness programs. For instance, the client can find out how much he weighs before the program, how many sit-ups he can do, his pulse rate before and after some standard task involving a controlled degree of exertion, and so forth. Baseline data cannot always be collected so easily in other kinds of change programs, especially if problems and goals are not as concrete and operational as they could be. However, as the client learns to break down his behavior into its component parts, he soon sees that he can gather baseline data on almost any kind of behavior. If the client says "I'm shy," it is almost impossible to gather baseline data on shyness. However, if he spells out his shyness in terms of his behaviors (what he does and what he doesn't do), measurement is possible. For instance, one of the behavioral components of his shyness is his not volunteering to answer any questions or make any comments in class. Over a two-week period, he discovers that he volunteers some answer or opinion in class only twice. This is baseline data. The counselor, using role-playing and rehearsal techniques, teaches him to be more assertive in class. During the following two-week period, the client volunteers an answer or an opinion eight times. He is beginning to overcome his shyness in this area of his life, and he has some concrete measure of his success. He can then move on to acquiring and eliminating other behaviors centering around the theme of shyness or lack of assertiveness.

The ability to measure success is intimately related to reinforcement and motivation. In the beginning of many behavioral-change programs, much of the reinforcement a client gets must be social—that is, support and approval for fulfilling the demands of the program. For instance, in a physical-fitness program, the client is reinforced for attending meetings and fulfilling the requirements of the program contract regarding diet and exercise. Eventually, as the results of the program become more and more tangible (through weight loss, improved endurance, higher energy level, and so forth), reinforcement comes more and more from achieving goals that have been established. Motivation is sustained as the client sees himself bridging the gap between his present state of ineffectiveness and varying degrees of success.

7. Implementation: Use chosen means to achieve
established goals

The heart of the problem-solving process is the client's action itself:
his ridding himself of destructive behavior patterns, his enhancing current constructive patterns, and his instituting further constructive programs. If the action program has been carefully mapped out (that is, if
it is systematic and involves no step that is too complicated), the client
moves through the program step by step. If the client tries to do too
much too soon, he will lose heart and abandon his efforts. On the other
hand, the client might move too desultorily through the program. In this
case, the counselor should challenge his client to work more intently on
achieving the goals he has established. The counselor uses both Stage-I
and Stage-II skills to help the client through Stage III.

The function of Stage-I skills in Stage III.   Stage-I skills remain at the
core of the developmental model in Stage III. In Stage III, as the client
begins to act, problems associated with action arise.

The client experiences change as both growthful and painful: for
instance, the novelty of the discipline of a physical-fitness program soon
wears off. Or cravings for alcohol and other drugs persist and at times
grow very strong.

The client meets with both success and failure: for instance, he
makes headway in his struggle with drink but fails on occasion, or, on
occasion, he sees his world as a very empty place without alcohol. Or
another client works to change his negative attitude toward his employer but experiences no significant change in his employer's hostile
attitude.

Action uncovers new problems or further dimensions of problems
that have already been explored. For instance, a man improves his
relationship with his wife but begins to have trouble with his son. As
the one relationship improves, the other seems to deteriorate.

Stage-I skills are essential here because the problematic involved in
the execution of action programs must itself be listened to and understood. Sometimes action programs fail because the counselor abandons
the client to his own devices once an action program is initiated. This
is strange, since at this time many clients need a great deal of support.
While it would be ideal if this support were to come naturally from the
client's environment (support that will be discussed later in this chapter), this is frequently not the case. Stage-I skills, then, are important
instruments of reinforcement and support. The client's successes, too,

must be listened to, and the counselor should communicate "being with" the client as he experiences success.

The function of Stage-II skills in Stage III.   The developmental model is cumulative: the skills at each stage are necessary in each subsequent stage. In our discussion of Stage-II skills, the word "tentative" was used to describe the initial use of such skills as advanced accurate empathy, helper self-sharing, immediacy, and confrontation. It was stated that pains should be taken not to overwhelm the client, for Stage-II interactions can be "strong medicine." Stage II is geared to helping the client get a more objective view of himself and his world—that is, to help him understand himself in a way that lets him see the need for change. When the counselor uses these skills, he is aware that he is putting the client under pressure to get at the behavioral roots of his problems. Strong (1970), urging a social-influence model of counseling, suggests that ". . . action changes result from compliance to pressure applied by the counselor, not from the counselor's analysis of the client's attributes" (p. 398). Indeed, the entire developmental model puts the client under a great deal of pressure to change. But there is a certain progression in the application of this pressure. Stage I, skillfully executed, pressures the client to explore the problematic in his life freely and permits the counselor to apply further pressure associated with Stage-II interactions. As the relationship between counselor and client grows in trust and caring, it can support stronger and stronger interactions. Therefore, in Stage III, the Stage-II interactions of advanced accurate empathy, counselor self-sharing, immediacy, and confrontation are used more fully by the counselor *to the degree that they help the client formulate and implement action programs.* These interactions are not pursued for their own sake.

Advanced accurate empathy.   The counselor moves more deeply into the life of the client, helping him become aware of his deepest experiences and feelings. No implication of the client's lifestyle is overlooked if it is seen as relevant to his functioning more effectively. The counselor communicates his deepest understandings of the client openly and freely.

Counselor self-sharing.   The counselor holds back nothing from his experience that will help the client understand himself more deeply and act more effectively.

Confrontation.   The counselor, acutely aware of any discrepancies and smoke screens in the client's behavior, challenges them openly and freely, but still not punitively. He also challenges any reluctance he finds in the client to come to grips with the work of change.

Immediacy. The counselor deals openly and directly with what is taking place in the here-and-now of the counseling relationship. Since most clients need to grow in their ability to relate to others, the counseling sessions constitute a laboratory dealing with at least this interpersonal relationship. The counselor tries to help the client relate to him as effectively as possible.

Training the client directly in problem-solving methodologies

I have already suggested in several places that the helper can be, to a greater or lesser extent, a trainer—that is, one who teaches the client skills that will enable him to live more effectively. This same principle also applies to the skills of Stage III. If I can help a client live more effectively by "walking him through" some problem-solving methodology, then, at least in many cases, I can help him by training him in problem-solving and behavioral-change techniques directly. This training increases the probability that he will become a more autonomous problem-solver in his own life and, conversely, decreases the probability that he will become overly dependent on officially designated helpers when the inevitable problems of living do arise. As Thoresen and Mahoney (1974) note, we are constantly learning more and more about both the principles and the technology of self-control, and training clients in these principles and procedures is highly practical:

> If a person can be helped to manage his own behavior, less professional time may be required for the desired behavior change. Moreover, the person might be the best possible agent to change his own behavior—he certainly has much more frequent access to it than anyone else, particularly when the behavior is covert. Self-control strategies may also avoid some of the generalization and maintenance problems that often plague therapist-centered strategies. . . . Finally, training in self-control may provide an individual with technical and analytic talents that will facilitate subsequent attempts at self-control with different behaviors [p. 7].

In addition to the force-field-analysis problem-solving methodology outlined in this chapter, there are a variety of practical behavioral-change programs of varying degrees of complexity available that the helper can teach to the client (for example, Carkhuff, 1973; Gottman and Leiblum, 1974; Sydnor and Parkhill, 1973; Watson and Tharp, 1973). All of these are solidly based on the principles underlying the maintenance and change of human behavior. Furthermore, some of the behavior-modification techniques based on these principles can be taught to the client (see Sherman, 1973, pp. 132–149). For instance, Watson and Tharp (1973) outline a program for systematic self-desensitization (pp. 178–186).

Clients can be taught how to control their behavior by learning how to deal with both the antecedents and the consequences of behavior. Consequences refer to reinforcers, both positive and negative, and to punishment. Antecedents refer to all events, both internal (covert behavior) and external, that serve as cues or stimuli or prompts to trigger some kind of behavior. Therefore, physical circumstances (being confined to bed in a hospital with a broken leg), social settings (being a student in a classroom), the behavior of other people (a father nagging his son), and covert behavior (having a headache, feeling depressed, daydreaming, planning a vacation in one's mind) are all classes of antecedents that can serve as cues to trigger various behaviors. The person who learns constructive ways of controlling or relating to both the antecedents and the consequences of his behavior gains a great deal in freedom and autonomy.

Cautions concerning Stage-III programs

Balking at the mechanistic flavor of systematic behavioral-change programs. A friend of mine, after reading a short book dealing with a comprehensive problem-solving methodology even more extensive and complicated than the one outlined here, exclaimed: "Who would go through all that?" There is a problem inherent in any comprehensive problem-solving methodology: it can be overly analytic, and the unskilled person can get lost in detail. The unskilled person can be used by the methodology instead of using it. The caution given earlier in this chapter bears repeating here: this methodology is not an end in itself and should be expanded or abridged or laid aside in keeping with the needs of the client. This process should only be as detailed as is necessary to stimulate effective action.

Weick (1969) counsels against overplanning:

> The point is simply that planning can insulate members from the very environment which they are trying to cope with. Planning in the absence of action is basically unconstrained; the only actions available for reflective attention are the planning acts themselves. The members can learn more and more about how to plan and how they are planning, but they can lose sight of what they were originally planning for [p. 103].

Obviously, problem-solving procedures that become ends in themselves are counterproductive and "lose the name of action." There should be a balance between planning and action. Planning is putting order and reason into what is. Problem solving that is not based on a review of the "what is" of the client's ineffective behavior and of his resources, both inner and environmental, is doomed from the outset. Neither is problem solving an all-at-once process. Action produces reaction. When the client acts differently toward his environment in the execution of an action program, his environment reacts, often enough, in unexpected ways. When the client's environment reacts, it is time to put order and reason into this reaction—that is, to modify previously planned action programs. It can be wasteful to spend too much time trying to anticipate all future contingencies. Stage III demands a productive dialogue between planning and action.

On the other hand, another possible answer to my friend's question "Who would go through all that?" is: anyone who is interested in the work of living more effectively. At the minimum, problem-solving technologies provide the client with ways of looking at constructive action. While he might not follow each step, he does approach action more methodically. Counselor trainees should experiment with problem-solving methodologies in their own lives. These methodologies are not useless merely because most people avoid them. Most people live lives saturated with the "psychopathology of the average." If, in counseling, problem-solving methodologies seem overly logical and rational, it is up to the counselor to construct processes in which the feelings and aspirations of the client are dealt with humanly.

The client who chooses not to change. There is a kind of inertia and passivity in the makeup of many people that makes change difficult and distressing for them. Therefore, some clients who seem to do well in Stages I and II of the counseling program end up by saying, in effect, if not directly:

> *Client:* Even though I've explored my problems and understand why things are going wrong—that is, I understand myself and my behavior better and I realize the behavioral demands I should be making on myself —right now I don't want to pay the price called for by action. The price of more effective living is too high.

There are at least two kinds of client dropouts: the one with the low-level counselor who realizes he is going nowhere with him and the one with the high-level counselor who realizes that the price for change is too high. The question of human motivation seems almost as enigmatic now as it must have at the dawning of man's history. So often we seem to choose our own misery. Worse, we choose to stew in it rather than endure the relatively short-lived pain of behavioral change.

Never getting to Stage III.   Some low-level counselors stay in the safe waters of Stage I, exploring the client's problems in a rather circular way and hoping that the exploratory phase will suffice. The point is that such helpers are ineffective even in what they think they are doing well; for accurate empathy along with concreteness, when communicated genuinely and respectfully to the client, has a way of putting pressure on the client to move to deeper self-exploration—the kind of self-exploration that produces the kind of self-understanding that verges on action. The logic of the social-influence process is embedded in the interactions of the developmental model itself.

The high-level helper is himself a doer, an agent in his own life, and therefore at home with action programs. Some counselors are unable to help in the action phase of the counseling process because they themselves are basically passive people—nondoers. Therefore, in this respect, they are not living more effectively than their clients and cannot be expected to help.

Starting with Stage III.   Some counselors move to advice-giving almost immediately. They fail to see that, in most cases, action for the sake of action is rootless. Stages I and II ordinarily provide the roots for action. Moving too quickly into action programs satisfies the needs of the helper rather than those of the client, violating one of the primary principles of counseling: helping is for the client.

Conclusion

This problem-solving and action-program stage of the helping process is an exciting one to study. The current behavior-oriented revolution in helping has touched even those who have been reluctant to consider counseling an action-oriented process. While it is true that some debates still rage—behavior modification versus relationship therapy, insight versus action, helping as a social-influence process versus helping as a collaborative process—many helpers are opting for an integrated eclecticism that serves the needs of clients more effectively. New and more refined behavior-modification techniques, new problem-solving methodologies, and new approaches to action programs are being elaborated. The ultimate test is not whether these strategies fit into a theoretical system but whether they meet the needs of clients.

Chapter Seven

Epilogue

1. The developmental model is an open one. Effective helping is central; models and systems and schools should be subordinate to it.
2. Group approaches to helping and to training helpers are preferred. They provide settings for observing one's own behavior and that of others. They also provide a safe place in which the members can responsibly lower their defenses and are free to experiment with new behavior. Groups constitute laboratories for viewing such phenomena as social power, social-influence processes, social comparison and feedback, and reality testing. Group members provide both support and challenge.
3. Exercises and other structured experiences can be used in both training and helping groups to help members get an experiential feeling for a wide variety of human-relations skills.
4. A great number of people are helped today through peer self-help groups. These groups deserve our attention and study.
5. The high-level helper aims for reproducibility: he not only helps but trains others in the skills he possesses and teaches them a systematic methodology by which they, too, can train others to be helpers.

No attempt will be made here to summarize the developmental model, for this is the function of the overview given in Chapter 2. As you become more and more familiar with the model, you can use it as a tool to integrate helping research, theory, techniques, and practice. Conversely, you can use research, theory, techniques, and practice drawn from other models to expand, abridge, modify, refine, and criticize the developmental model. Effective helping should be central; schools and models should be subordinate to it.

I would like to repeat a caution here that has already been stated explicitly a number of times. Don't be overly rigid in the application of the developmental model. Once you have worked your way through the model and have begun to acquire the stage-specific skills, you will discover that the stages do not always follow one another in the logical and temporal sequence presented in these pages. For instance, you will find yourself, during the same counseling period, in different stages in dealing with different client problems. The model helps you develop a wide repertory of counseling skills. As you become more experienced, you will be able to draw on these skills with greater and greater facility, using whatever skills are necessary at a given moment to serve the needs of the client most effectively.

A final word on training-as-treatment and group approaches to helping

Carkhuff (1969b), Ivey (1971), and Kagan (1971), among others, suggest with varying emphasis that training clients directly in the human-relations and problem-solving skills needed for effective or "intentional" living is potentially one of the best forms of treatment. Although it is true that the high-level helper models all these skills and that modeling itself is a form of teaching or training, the best way to teach a skill is still to teach it directly (Downs, 1973).

For the following reasons, groups provide unique settings for training and treatment (Carkhuff, 1969b, Chapter 10; Lieberman, Lakin, & Whitaker, 1968).

Observing one's own behavior.   Because groups are composed of members with different interpersonal styles, each member has the opportunity to act out characteristic interpersonal behaviors with his fellow members. He is not limited to interaction with just the helper.

Observation skills.   Each trainee has the opportunity to develop observational skills as he watches the characteristic behaviors of his fellow trainees. The developmental model provides a structure that enables the trainees to categorize and evaluate interpersonal behavior.

Lowering defenses.   If the group becomes a working/learning *community* with a sense of caring and cohesiveness, the members can experiment with lowering customary but unproductive defenses. In a climate in which each member values and is valued by others, the lowering and investigation of defenses becomes practical.

Experimentation with interpersonal behavior and release of emotion. The group provides a controlled environment in which members can responsibly experiment with behavior, including the stimulation and expression of emotion.

Social influence. Social-influence processes are ubiquitous. The group allows for the distribution of interpersonal power and social influence and stimulates the examination of these processes.

Social comparison and feedback. The group provides a context for social comparison and feedback. The members become helpers to one another, sharing in the trainer's role of clarification and interpretation of behavior.

Helping. Each member has the opportunity not only to be helped but to help others.

Principles of behavior. The group has a great capacity to control behavior and to provide a system of rewards and punishments. It becomes a laboratory in which the members can study and experiment with these processes.

Learning helping skills through the group process enables the prospective helper to experience all of these advantages. Some helpers shy away from group approaches because they have no experience with groups. I am not suggesting that all helping must take place through the group process, but I do see the group process as a preferred mode of treatment. It is financially economical, it supplies clients with the advantages just listed, and it makes much fuller use of the helper's time.

The use of structured experiences in training and the helping process

Bednar, Melnick, and Kaul (1974), in discussing group therapy, review data suggesting that structure (for instance, the helper's initially identifying therapeutic goals and desired client behavior with the client) helps clients engage quickly in desirable but "high risk" behaviors (for instance, self-disclosure and interpersonal feedback in a group). Since it is the helper who sets up this facilitating structure, this initial client high-risk behavior is purchased at the price of what Bednar and his associates call "responsibility" (that is, initiative on the part of the client). Indeed, decreasing helper-initiated structure and increasing client responsibility are general goals of the helping process. In the training-as-treatment model, highly structured practice sessions provide the client with the kinds of skills he needs to increase his interpersonal initiative.

The developmental model is itself a structured approach to helping, especially when training in the skills of the model is part of the client's experience. The training manual designed to accompany this text has exercises that can be used not only with helper-trainees but also with clients themselves. The manual, however, in no way exhausts the exercises or "structured experiences" (Pfeiffer & Jones, 1969) that can be used. A great number of exercises and/or structured experiences have been developed. A partial list of sources would include: Albertson and Hannan, 1971; Gazda, 1973; Jones and Pfeiffer, 1972, 1973, 1974; Jongeward and James, 1973; Malamud and Machover, 1965; Mill, 1971; Napier and Gershenfeld, 1973; Pfeiffer and Jones, 1969, 1970, 1971, 1973; Sydnor, Akridge, and Parkhill, 1972; Sydnor and Parkhill, 1973. Although some counselors believe that the client (whether in a one-to-one relationship or in a group) works best in an unstructured situation (Rabin, 1970), my experience is similar to that of Bednar and his associates: the judicious use of structure in helping frees the client to use his resources in ways that facilitate skills acquisition and other kinds of learning.

For the sake of concreteness, let me describe one exercise that can be used to stimulate the learning of immediacy. This exercise can be used in any kind of group: training-as-treatment, helper-training, or human-relations training. This exercise should be used only after the group members have spent some time together and therefore have enough data to do the exercise. The exercise has several steps.

First, each member is asked to think of some secret that he would rather not reveal to the group. A minute or two is allowed for this. The members can be told that they will not be asked to reveal the content of their secrets.

Next, the group is given a few minutes of quiet time, during which each member is to picture or imagine himself revealing his secret to each of the other members of the group in successive one-to-one conversations. Each tries to picture in his mind as concretely as possible how he would feel telling his secret to each other member and how each would react.

Then the group members have a "round robin": the group breaks up into twos for a series of one-to-one conversations. At the end of a designated period of time (five or ten minutes), partners are switched and another round of one-to-one conversations takes place. This process is repeated until each member of the group has had a one-to-one conversation with every other member of the group (in a six-man group, there would be five rounds). In the one-to-one conversations, the members reveal to each other *not* the content of the secret but how they felt in telling this particular person the secret and how they imagined him reacting. Finally, they discuss their relationship to each other in light of what they reveal to each other.

Note that this is an exercise in immediacy, not in "secret-dropping" or self-disclosure. The exercise provides a structured experience through which the members can deal directly with their relationships to one another in the context of the training group. The issue of trust comes up quite often in the one-to-one feedback sessions.

> *Member A:* I tried to picture myself telling you my secret, but I couldn't do it. I feel that I am partially to blame for this, for I've done little to establish a relationship with you. But I also feel that you've been judgmental toward me from the beginning of the training experience. I haven't been able to trust you.
>
> *Member B:* You feel that we both have some responsibility in failing to establish working contact with each other. As for myself, I had no idea until now that you've been feeling this way. Let's see if we can begin to talk it out.

Note that Member B first tries to understand what A is saying before giving his own reaction. Because of the exercise, they are now ready to deal more concretely with their relationship and the issue of trust. Ideally, training groups are learning *communities,* in which direct mutual talk is encouraged.

There are certain cautions in the use of structured training experiences. First, these experiences are not ends in themselves. Some helpers and trainers become fascinated with exercises and use them constantly because they make things happen. Exercises are not substitutes for the helper or trainer's skill. When overused, exercises become gimmicks and cheapen the training process.

Second, the trainer should know precisely why he is using a given exercise at a given time. The exercise should fit into and promote the helping or training model. Trainees, also, should know why an exercise is being used.

Third, the excessive use of structure curtails the development of client responsibility or initiative. For instance, if clients or trainees engage in immediacy only when cued to do so by an exercise, they will not learn how to be spontaneously immediate with one another. Furthermore, no one is going to provide facilitating structure in day-to-day encounters.

In sum, use structured experiences in both training and helping to teach, exemplify, stimulate, highlight, refine, and provide practice, but don't overuse or abuse them. The training manual gives some idea of the kinds of exercises that might prove useful, but each helper should have a repertory that suits him, the needs of his clients, and the goals of the model he is using.

Peer self-help groups

Alcoholics Anonymous is an example of a peer self-help group familiar to most of us. The fully participating member admits to the group that he is an alcoholic, attends group meetings in which fellow group members openly share their histories of drinking, gives up drinking completely, shares with his fellows other problems in his life that seem to contribute to or aggravate his drinking, helps his fellows and is helped by them to deal with these problems, makes himself available day or night to help fellow members who are in trouble—especially if the crisis involves a temptation to start drinking again—and urges people who are having problems with alcohol to join the group. Over the years, groups composed of the spouses and children of alcoholics have also developed.

There are a great variety of peer self-help groups—Gamblers Anonymous, Recovery Incorporated, Schizophrenics Anonymous International, Neurotics Anonymous, Group Recovery Organizations of the World (GROW), Synanon, Daytop Village, Integrity Training, Parents Without Partners, and many more. These groups deal with such problems as overweight, addiction, child abuse, widowhood, divorce, old age, homosexuality (or, rather, the alienation consequent to professed homosexual identity), and many others. Some groups, especially initially, center around a specific problem (such as drinking or drug abuse); some (such as Synanon) have expanded to include lifestyle in general (Maillet, 1972; O'Quin, 1969; Yablonsky, 1965); and others deal more generally with emotional problems and character-building (Mowrer, 1973). Hurvitz (1970) describes the characteristics that quite diverse peer self-help groups have in common. He claims that in most cases these groups work better than professional approaches to helping: "And it is likely that more people have been and are being helped by [peer self-help psychotherapy groups] than have been and are being helped by all types of professionally trained psychotherapists combined, with far less theorizing and analyzing and for much less money" (p. 48).

Typically, peer self-help groups are staffed and run by noncredentialed professionals. A certain degree of mistrust and animosity exists between credentialed and certified professionals and the organizers and staff of peer self-help groups. Hurvitz (1970) decries the condescending and patronizing attitude of many conventional psychotherapists to the peer self-help group movement. Perhaps Carkhuff's notion of the "functional" professional (the *skilled* helper, whether credentialed or not) can help bridge the gap between the credentialed and the noncredentialed. In my opinion, credentialed professionals can learn a great deal from the peer self-help group movement and, conversely, this movement can learn much from functional credentialed professionals about systematic approaches to behavioral change and the learning of life skills.

If there is any truth to Hurvitz's claim with respect to the relative success rate of peer self-help groups, and if the research findings on the ineffectiveness of many credentialed professionals are valid (see Chapter 1), prospective helpers should familiarize themselves both cognitively and experientially with the peer self-help group movement. Peer self-help groups need not be limited to only those who are experiencing serious problems. For instance, a group of people who, after being initiated into the skills of the developmental model, get together every week or two in order to examine their current lifestyles and to provide challenge and support for one another would constitute a most useful kind of peer self-help group. Few of us would not benefit from such a group.

A final word: Reproducibility

A society in which the skills of the developmental model are widely distributed would certainly be a challenging and growthful one in which to live. Therefore, prospective helpers should not only learn these skills themselves so that they can help others effectively but also learn a training methodology so that they can train others in these skills. Each prospective helper is also a prospective trainer. The best helpers "reproduce" themselves through high-level training programs. Ideally, children should begin to learn these skills in school. Teaching these skills to adults is most certainly worthwhile, but there is something remedial about it. I can think of no more worthwhile task than promoting systematic skills-training programs in school systems.

Bibliography

Albertson, D. R., & Hannan, C. J. *Twenty interaction exercises for the classroom.* Fairfax, Va.: Learning Resources Corp./NTL, 1971.

Anthony, W. A. The relationship between human relationship skills and an index of psychological adjustment. *Journal of Counseling Psychology,* 1973, **20,** 489–490.

Archer, J., Jr. Undergraduates as paraprofessional leaders of integrated communication skills training groups using an integrated IPR (Interpersonal Process Recall) videotape feedback/affect simulation training model. Unpublished doctoral dissertation, Michigan State University, East Lansing, Mich., 1971.

Archer, J., Jr., Fiester, T., Kagan, N., Rate, L., Spierling, T., & Van Noord, R. New method for education, treatment, and research in human interaction. *Journal of Counseling Psychology,* 1972, **19,** 275–281.

Archer, J., Jr., & Kagan, N. Teaching interpersonal relationship skills on campus: A pyramid approach. *Journal of Counseling Psychology,* 1973, **20,** 535–540.

Bandura, A. Psychotherapy as a learning process. *Psychological Bulletin,* 1961, **58,** 143–159.

Bandura, A. *Principles of behavior modification.* New York: Holt, Rinehart, & Winston, 1969.

Bandura, A., & Walters, R. H. *Social learning and personality development.* New York: Holt, Rinehart, & Winston, 1963.

Bednar, R. L., Melnick, J., & Kaul, T. J. Risk, responsibility, and structure. *Journal of Counseling Psychology,* 1974, **21,** 31–37.

Beier, E. G. *The silent language of psychotherapy.* Chicago: Aldine, 1966.

Bercheid, E., & Walster, E. H. *Interpersonal attraction.* Reading, Mass.: Addison-Wesley, 1969.

Berenson, B. G., & Mitchell, K. M. Therapeutic conditions after therapist-initiated confrontation. *Journal of Clinical Psychology,* 1968, **24,** 363–364.

Berenson, B. G., & Mitchell, K. M. *Confrontation: For better or worse.* Amherst, Mass.: Human Resource Development Press, 1974.

Berenson, B. G., Mitchell, K. M., & Laney, R. C. Level of therapist functioning, types of confrontation and type of patient. *Journal of Clinical Psychology,* 1968, **24,** 111–113.

Berenson, B. G., Mitchell, K. M., & Moravec, J. A. Level of therapist functioning, patient depth of self-exploration, and type of confrontation. *Journal of Counseling Psychology,* 1968, **15,** 136–139.

Bergin, A. E. The evaluation of therapeutic outcomes. In A. E. Bergin & S. L. Garfield (Eds.), *Handbook of psychotherapy and behavior change.* New York: Wiley, 1971. Pp. 217–270.

Berkowitz, S. *The A-B-C's of behavior modification: Leader's guide.* Baltimore: Behavioral Information and Technology, 1972.

Blocher, D. H. *Developmental counseling.* New York: Ronald, 1966.

Boyd, J. D., II. Microcounseling for a counseling-like verbal response set: Differential effects of two micromodels and two methods of counseling supervision. *Journal of Counseling Psychology,* 1973, **20,** 97–98.

Brammer, L. *The helping relationship: Process and skills.* Englewood Cliffs, N.J.: Prentice-Hall, 1973.

Brammer, L., & Shostrom, E. *Therapeutic psychology.* Englewood Cliffs, N.J.: Prentice-Hall, 1968.

Bundza, K. A., & Simonson, N. R. Therapist self-disclosure: Its effects on impressions of therapist and willingness to disclose. *Psychotherapy: Theory, Research, and Practice,* 1973, **10,** 215–217.

Caplan, N., & Nelson, S. D. The nature and consequences of psychological research on social problems. *American Psychologist,* 1973, **28,** 199–211.

Carkhuff, R. R. Differential functioning of lay and professional helpers. *Journal of Counseling Psychology,* 1968, **15,** 117–126.

Carkhuff, R. R. *Helping and human relations.* Vol. I: *Selection and training.* New York: Holt, Rinehart, & Winston, 1969a.

Carkhuff, R. R. *Helping and human relations.* Vol. II: *Practice and research.* New York: Holt, Rinehart, & Winston, 1969b.

Carkhuff, R. R. *The development of human resources.* New York: Holt, Rinehart, & Winston, 1971.

Carkhuff, R. R. *The art of helping.* Amherst, Mass.: Human Resource Development Press, 1972a.

Carkhuff, R. R. The development of a systematic human resource development model. *Counseling Psychologist,* 1972b, **3,** 4–30.

Carkhuff, R. R. New directions in training for the helping professions: Toward a technology for human and community resource development. *Counseling Psychologist,* 1972c, **3** (3), 12–30.

Carkhuff, R. R. What's it all about anyway? Some reflections on helping and human resource development models. *Counseling Psychologist,* 1972d, **3** (3), 79–87.

Carkhuff, R. R. *The art of problem-solving.* Amherst, Mass.: Human Resource Development Press, 1973.

Carkhuff, R. R., & Berenson, B. G. *Beyond counseling and therapy.* Holt, Rinehart, & Winston, 1967.

Carkhuff, R. R., & Truax, C. B. Lay mental health counseling. *Journal of Consulting Psychology,* 1965, **29,** 426–431.

Chapin, F. S. Preliminary standardization of a social insight scale. *American Sociological Review,* 1942, **7,** 214–225.

Chinsky, J. M., & Rappaport, J. Brief critique of the meaning and reliability of "accurate empathy" ratings. *Psychological Bulletin,* 1970, **73,** 379–382.

Combs, A. *Florida studies in the helping professions.* Gainesville: University of Florida Press, 1969.

Combs, A., & Snygg, D. *Individual behavior: A perceptual approach to behavior.* New York: Harper & Row, 1959.

Corsini, R. J. (Ed.) *Current psychotherapies.* Itasca, Ill.: Peacock, 1973.

Cozby, P. C. Self-disclosure: A literature review. *Psychological Bulletin,* 1973, **79,** 73–91.

Culbert, S. A. *The interpersonal process of self-disclosure: It takes two to see one.* Fairfax, Va.: Learning Resources Corp./NTL, 1967.

Curran, C. A. *Counseling and psychotherapy: The pursuit of values.* New York: Sheed & Ward, 1968.

Danish, S. J. Film-simulated counselor training. *Counselor Education and Supervision,* 1971, **11,** 29–35.

Danish, S. J., & Kagan, N. Emotional simulation in counseling and psychotherapy. *Psychotherapy: Theory, Research, and Practice,* 1969, **6,** 261–263.

Dell, D. M. Counselor power base, influence attempt, and behavior change in counseling. *Journal of Counseling Psychology,* 1973, **20,** 399–405.

Dendy, R. F. A model for the training of undergraduate residence hall assistants as paraprofessional counselors using videotape techniques and interpersonal process recall (IPR). Unpublished doctoral dissertation, Michigan State University, East Lansing, Mich., 1971.

Deutsch, M. Field theory in social psychology. In G. Lindzey (Ed.), *The handbook of social psychology.* Vol. I. Cambridge, Mass.: Addison-Wesley, 1954. Pp. 181–222.

Dinkmeyer, D. C. *Developmental counseling and guidance.* New York: McGraw-Hill, 1970.

Downs, M. A comparison of two methods of human relations training for teaching communication skills to adults. Unpublished doctoral dissertation, Loyola University of Chicago, 1973.

Drucker, P. F. *The age of discontinuity: Guidelines to our changing society.* New York: Harper & Row, 1968.

Egan, G. *Encounter: Group processes for interpersonal growth.* Monterey, Ca.: Brooks/Cole, 1970.

Egan, G. *Encounter groups: Basic readings.* Monterey, Ca.: Brooks/Cole, 1971.

Egan, G. *Face to face: The small-group experience and interpersonal growth.* Monterey, Ca.: Brooks/Cole, 1973a.

Egan, G. A two-phase approach to human relations training. In J. Jones & W. Pfeiffer (Eds.), *The 1973 annual handbook for group facilitators.* San Diego, Ca.: University Associates Press, 1973b.

Erikson, E. H. *Insight and responsibility.* New York: Norton, 1964.

Eysenck, H. J. The effects of psychotherapy: An evaluation. *Journal of Consulting Psychology,* 1952, **16,** 319–324.

Eysenck, H. J. The effects of psychotherapy. In H. J. Eysenck (Ed.), *Handbook of abnormal psychology.* New York: Basic Books, 1960. Pp. 697–725.

Eysenck, H. J. The effects of psychotherapy. *International Journal of Psychiatry,* 1965, **1,** 97–178.

Ferster, C. B., & Perrott, M. C. *Behavior principles.* New York: Appleton-Century-Crofts, 1968.

Fiedler, F. E. A comparison of therapeutic relationships in psychoanalytic, non-directive, and Adlerian therapy. *Journal of Consulting Psychology,* 1950, **14,** 436–445.

Foote, N., & Cottrell, L. S., Jr. *Identity and interpersonal competence.* Chicago: University of Chicago Press, 1955.

Ford, D., & Urban, N. *Systems of psychotherapy.* New York: Wiley, 1963.

Frank, J. *Persuasion and healing.* Baltimore: The Johns Hopkins University Press, 1961.

Frank, J. *Persuasion and healing.* Revised edition. The Johns Hopkins University Press, 1973.

Garfield, S. L. Basic ingredients or common factors in psychotherapy? *Journal of Consulting and Clinical Psychology,* 1973, **41,** 9–12.

Gazda, G. M. *Human relations development: A manual for educators.* Boston: Allyn & Bacon, 1973.

Gelatt, H. B., Varenhorst, B., & Carey, R. *Deciding: A leader's guide.* Princeton, N.J.: College Entrance Examination Board, 1972.

Gendlin, E. T., & Rychlak, J. F. Psychotherapeutic processes. *Annual Review of Psychology,* 1970, **21,** 155–190.

Gergen, K. J. *The psychology of behavior exchange.* Reading, Mass.: Addison-Wesley, 1969.

Gibb, J. R. The counselor as a role-free person. In C. A. Parker (Ed.), *Counseling theories and counselor education.* Boston: Houghton Mifflin, 1968. Pp. 19–45.

Glaser, R. (Ed.) *The nature of reinforcement.* New York: Academic Press, 1971.

Glasser, W. *Reality therapy.* New York: Harper & Row, 1965.

Goldberg, A. D. A sequential program for supervision of counselors using the Interpersonal Process Recall (IPR) technique. Unpublished doctoral dissertation, Michigan State University, East Lansing, Mich., 1967.

Goldstein, A. P. *Structured learning therapy: Toward a psychotherapy for the poor.* New York: Academic Press, 1973.

Goldstein, A. P., Heller, K., & Sechrest, L. B. *Psychotherapy and the psychology of behavior change.* New York: Wiley, 1966.

Gordon, T. *Parent effectiveness training.* New York: Wyden, 1970.

Gottman, J. M., & Leiblum, S. R. *How to do psychotherapy and how to evaluate it.* New York: Holt, Rinehart, & Winston, 1974.

Grzegorek, A. A study of the effects of two emphases in counselor education, each used in connection with simulation and videotape. Unpublished doctoral dissertation, Michigan State University, East Lansing, Mich., 1970.

Haase, R. F., & DiMattia, D. J. The application of the microcounseling paradigm to the training of support personnel in counseling. *Counselor Education and Supervision,* 1970, **10,** 16–22.

Hackney, H. L., Ivey, A. E., & Oetting, E. R. Attending, island, and hiatus behavior: A process conception of counselor and client interaction. *Journal of Counseling Psychology,* 1970, **17,** 342–346.

Hackney, H. L., & Nye, S. *Counseling strategies and objectives.* Englewood Cliffs, N.J.: Prentice-Hall, 1973.

Hartson, D. J. Videotape replay and interrogation in group work. Unpublished doctoral dissertation, University of Missouri, Columbia, Mo., 1971.

Heiserman, M. S. The effect of experiential videotape training procedures compared to cognitive classroom teaching methods on the interpersonal communication skills of juvenile court caseworkers. Unpublished doctoral dissertation, Michigan State University, East Lansing, Mich., 1971.

Higgins, W., Ivey, A., & Uhlemann, M. Media therapy: A programmed approach to teaching behavioral skills. *Journal of Counseling Psychology,* 1970, **17**, 20–26.

Hobbs, N. Sources of gain in psychotherapy. *American Psychologist,* 1962, **17**, 741–747.

Hurvitz, N. Peer self-help psychotherapy groups and their implication for psychotherapy. *Psychotherapy: Theory, Research, and Practice,* 1970, **7**, 41–49.

Ivey, A. The intentional individual: A process-outcome view of behavioral psychology. *Counseling Psychologist,* 1970, **1**, 56–60.

Ivey, A. *Microcounseling: Innovations in interviewing training.* Springfield, Ill.: Thomas, 1971.

Ivey, A. *Microcounseling: Interviewing skills manual.* Springfield, Ill.: Thomas, 1972.

Ivey, A. Counseling: The innocent profession. Mimeographed paper, University of Massachusetts, Amherst, Mass., 1973.

Ivey, A., & Hinkle, J. The transactional classroom. Unpublished paper, University of Massachusetts, Amherst, Mass., 1970.

Ivey, A., Normington, C., Miller, C., Morrill, W., & Haase, R. Microcounseling and attending behavior: An approach to prepracticum counselor training. *Journal of Counseling Psychology,* 1968, **15**, Monograph Supplement, 1–12.

James, M., & Jongeward, D. *Born to win: Transactional analysis with Gestalt experiments.* Reading, Mass.: Addison-Wesley, 1971.

Janis, I. (Ed.) *Personality: Dynamics, development, and assessment.* New York: Harcourt, Brace, & World, 1969.

Jones, J. E., & Pfeiffer, J. W. *The 1972 annual handbook for group facilitators.* San Diego: University Associates Press, 1972.

Jones, J. E., & Pfeiffer, J. W. *The 1973 annual handbook for group facilitators.* San Diego: University Associates Press, 1973.

Jones, J. E., & Pfeiffer, J. W. *The 1974 annual handbook for group facilitators.* San Diego: University Associates Press, 1974.

Jongeward, D., & James, M. *Winning with people: Group exercises in transactional analysis.* Reading, Mass.: Addison-Wesley, 1973.

Jourard, S. M. *Disclosing man to himself.* New York: Van Nostrand Reinhold, 1968.

Jourard, S. M. *Self-disclosure: An experimental analysis of the transparent self.* London: Wiley-Interscience, 1971a.

Jourard, S. M. *The transparent self:* Revised edition. New York: Van Nostrand Reinhold, 1971b.

Jurjevich, R-R. M. (Ed.) *Direct psychotherapy: Twenty-eight American originals.* Vols. I, II. Coral Gables, Fla.: University of Miami Press, 1973.

Kagan, N. *Influencing human interaction.* East Lansing, Mich.: Michigan State University CCTV, 1971.

Kagan, N. Can technology help us toward reliability in influencing human interaction? *Educational Technology,* 1973, **13** (February), 44–51.

Kagan, N., Krathwohl, D. R., *et al. Studies in human interaction: Interpersonal process recall stimulated by videotape.* Educational Publications Services, College of Education, Michigan State University, East Lansing, Mich., 1967.

Kagan, N., Krathwohl, D. R., & Miller, R. Stimulated recall in therapy: A case study. *Journal of Counseling Psychology,* 1963, **10**, 237–243.

Kagan, N., & Schauble, P. G. Affect simulation in Interpersonal Process Recall (IPR). *Journal of Counseling Psychology,* 1969, **16**, 309–313.

Kanter, R. M. *Commitment and community.* Cambridge, Mass.: Harvard University Press, 1972.

Kaul, T. J., Kaul, M. A., & Bednar, R. L. Counselor confrontation and client depth of self-exploration. *Journal of Counseling Psychology,* 1973, **20,** 132–136.

Kaul, T. J., & Parker, C. A. Suggestibility and expectancy in a counseling analogue. *Journal of Counseling Psychology,* 1971, **18,** 536–541.

Kaul, T. J., & Schmidt, L. Dimensions of interviewer trustworthiness. *Journal of Counseling Psychology,* 1971, **18,** 542–548.

Kelman, H. C. Three processes of social influence. In E. P. Hollander & R. G. Hunt (Eds.), *Current perspectives in social psychology.* New York: Oxford University Press, 1967. Pp. 438–446.

Kennedy, E. C., & Heckler, V. J. *The Catholic priest in the United States: Psychological investigations.* Washington, D.C.: U.S. Catholic Conference, 1971.

Knapp, M. L. *Nonverbal communication in human interaction.* New York: Holt, Rinehart, & Winston, 1972.

Kopita, R. R. Preparing peer counselors. *Impact,* 1973, **2** (6), 59–62.

Kounin, J., Polansky, N., Biddle, B., Coburn, H., & Fenn, A. Experimental studies of clients' reactions to initial interviews. *Human Relations,* 1956, **9,** 265–293.

Krumboltz, J. D. Behavioral goals for counseling. *Journal of Counseling Psychology,* 1966, **13,** 153–159.

Krumboltz, J. D., & Thoresen, C. E. (Eds.), *Behavioral counseling.* New York: Holt, Rinehart, & Winston, 1969.

Lamb, D. H., & Clack, R. J. Professional versus paraprofessional approaches to orientation and subsequent counseling contacts. *Journal of Counseling Psychology,* 1974, **21,** 61–65.

Lassen, C. L. Effect of proximity on anxiety and communication in the initial psychiatric interview. *Journal of Abnormal Psychology,* 1973, **81,** 220–232.

Levy, L. H. *Psychological interpretation.* New York: Holt, Rinehart, & Winston, 1963.

Levy, L. H. Fact and choice in counseling and counselor education: A cognitive viewpoint. In C. A. Parker (Ed.), *Counseling theories and counselor education.* Boston: Houghton Mifflin, 1968. Pp. 57–84.

Lieberman, M. A., Lakin, M., & Whitaker, D. S. The group as a unique context for therapy. *Psychotherapy: Theory, Research, and Practice,* 1968, **5,** 29–36.

Lieberman, M. A., Yalom, I. D., & Miles, M. B. *Encounter groups: First facts.* New York: Basic Books, 1973.

London, P. *The modes and morals of psychotherapy.* New York: Holt, Rinehart, & Winston, 1964.

London, P. *Behavior control.* New York: Harper & Row, 1969.

London, P. The end of ideology in behavior modification. *American Psychologist,* 1972, **27,** 913–920.

Luft, J. *Of human interaction.* Palo Alto, Ca.: National Press Books, 1969.

Lynd, H. M. *On shame and the search for identity.* New York: Science Editions, 1958.

Maillet, E. L. Report on research visit to Synanon Foundation, Inc. Health Care Research Division, U.S. Army Medical Field Service School, Brooke Army Medical Center, Fort Sam Houston, Texas, June, 1972.

Malamud, D. I., & Machover, S. *Toward self-understanding: Group techniques in self-confrontation.* Springfield, Ill.: Thomas, 1965.

Maslow, A. H. Synanon and Eupsychia. *Journal of Humanistic Psychology,* 1967, **7,** 28–35.

Maslow, A. H. *Toward a psychology of being.* Second edition. New York: Van Nostrand Reinhold, 1968.

Maslow, A. H. *Motivation and personality.* Second edition. New York: Harper & Row, 1970.

Matarazzo, R. Research in the teaching and learning of psychotherapeutic skills. In A. Bergin & S. Garfield (Eds.), *Handbook of psychotherapy and behavior change.* New York: Wiley, 1971. Pp. 895–924.

Matarazzo, R., Phillips, J., Wiens, A., & Saslow, G. Learning the art of interviewing: A study of what beginning students do and their patterns of change. *Psychotherapy: Theory, Research, and Practice,* 1965, **2,** 49–60.

Matarazzo, R., Wiens, A., & Saslow, G. Experimentation in the teaching and learning of psychotherapy skills. In L. Gottschalk & A. Auerback (Eds.), *Methods of research in psychotherapy.* New York: Appleton-Century-Crofts, 1966. Pp. 597–635.

Matson, F. W. *Without/within: Behaviorism and humanism.* Monterey, Ca.: Brooks/Cole, 1973.

Mayeroff, M. *On caring.* New York: Perennial Library (Harper & Row), 1971.

McMahon, J. T. The working class psychiatric patient: A clinical view. In F. Riessman, J. Cohen, & A. Pearl (Eds.), *Mental health of the poor.* New York: Free Press, 1964. Pp. 283–302.

Mehrabian, A. *Tactics of social influence.* Englewood Cliffs, N.J.: Prentice-Hall, 1970.

Mehrabian, A. *Silent messages.* Belmont, Ca.: Wadsworth, 1971.

Mehrabian, A., & Reed, H. Factors influencing judgments of psychopathology. *Psychological Reports,* 1969, **24,** 323–330.

Menninger, K. *The vital balance.* New York: Viking, 1963.

Mezz, S., & Calia, V. F. Counseling the culturally different child: A black-white collaborative view. *Counseling and Values,* 1972, **16,** 263–272.

Mill, C. R. *Twenty exercises for trainers.* Fairfax, Va.: Learning Resources Corp./NTL, 1971.

Moreland, J. R., Ivey, A. E., & Phillips, J. S. An evaluation of microcounseling as an interviewer training tool. *Journal of Consulting and Clinical Psychology,* 1973, **41,** 294–300.

Mowrer, O. H. Loss and recovery of community: A guide to the theory and practice of integrity therapy. In G. M. Gazda (Ed.), *Innovations to group psychotherapy.* Springfield, Ill.: Thomas, 1968a. Pp. 130–189.

Mowrer, O. H. New evidence concerning the nature of psychopathology. In M. J. Feldman (Ed.), *Studies in psychotherapy and behavior change.* Buffalo, N.Y.: University of New York at Buffalo, 1968b. Pp. 113–193.

Mowrer, O. H. Integrity groups today. In R-R. M. Jurjevich (Ed.), *Direct psychotherapy: Twenty-eight American originals.* Vol. II. Coral Gables, Fla.: University of Miami Press, 1973. Pp. 515–561.

Murphy, K. C., & Strong, S. R. Some effects of similarity self-disclosure. *Journal of Counseling Psychology,* 1972, **19,** 121–124.

Murray, E. J., & Jacobson, L. I. The nature of learning in traditional and behavioral psychotherapy. In A. E. Bergin & S. L. Garfield (Eds.), *Handbook of psychotherapy and behavior change.* New York: Wiley, 1971. Pp. 709–747.

Napier, R. W., & Gershenfeld, M. K. *Groups: Theory and experience* (plus Instructor's Manual). Boston: Houghton Mifflin, 1973.

O'Quin, S. Close-up: Chuck Dederich, Mr. Synanon, goes public. *Life,* 1969, **66** (January 31), 36–38.

Patterson, C. *Theories of counseling and psychotherapy.* Second edition. New York: Harper & Row, 1973.

Patterson, G. P., & Gullion, M. E. *Living with children: New methods for parents and teachers.* Champaign, Ill.: Research Press, 1971.

Pfeiffer, J. W., & Jones, J. E. *A handbook of structured experiences for human relations training.* Vol. I. San Diego: University Associates Press, 1969.

Pfeiffer, J. W., & Jones, J. E. *A handbook of structured experiences for human relations training.* Vol. II. San Diego: University Associates Press, 1970.

Pfeiffer, J. W., & Jones, J. E. *A handbook of structured experiences for human relations training.* Vol. III. San Diego: University Associates Press, 1971.

Pfeiffer, J. W., & Jones, J. E. *A handbook of structured experiences for human relations training.* Vol. IV. San Diego: University Associates Press, 1973.

Phillips, J., Lockhart, J., & Moreland, J. Minimal encourages to talk. Unpublished manual. Amherst: University of Massachusetts, 1969.

Piaget, J. *Construction of reality in the child.* New York: Basic Books, 1954.

Pierce, R., & Drasgow, J. Teaching facilitative interpersonal functioning to psychiatric inpatients. *Journal of Counseling Psychology,* 1969, **16,** 295–299.

Pyle, R., & Snyder, F. Students as paraprofessional counselors at community colleges. *Journal of College Student Personnel,* 1971, **12,** 259–262.

Rabin, H. M. Preparing patients for group psychotherapy. *International Journal of Group Psychotherapy,* 1970, **20,** 135–145.

Rappaport, J., & Chinsky, J. M. Accurate empathy: Confusion of a construct. *Psychological Bulletin,* 1972, **77,** 400–404.

Rappaport, J., Gross, T., & Lepper, C. Modeling, sensitivity training, and instruction: Implications for the training of college student volunteers and for outcome research. *Journal of Consulting and Clinical Psychology,* 1973, **40,** 99–107.

Raths, L., & Simon, S. *Values and teaching.* Columbus, Ohio: Charles E. Merrill, 1966.

Raven, B. H. Social influence and power. In I. D. Steiner & M. Fishbein (Eds.), *Current studies in social psychology.* New York: Holt, Rinehart, & Winston, 1965.

Rimm, D. C., & Masters, J. C. *Behavior therapy: Techniques and empirical findings.* New York: Academic Press, 1974.

Rioch, M. Changing concepts in the training of therapists. *Journal of Consulting Psychology,* 1966, **30,** 290–292.

Rogers, C. R. *Counseling and psychotherapy.* Boston: Houghton Mifflin, 1942.

Rogers, C. R. *Client-centered therapy.* Boston: Houghton Mifflin, 1951.

Rogers, C. R. The necessary and sufficient conditions of therapeutic personality change. *Journal of Consulting Psychology,* 1957, **21,** 95–103.

Rogers, C. R. A theory of therapy, personality, and interpersonal relationships as developed in the client-centered framework. In S. Koch (Ed.), *Psychology: A study of science.* Vol. III. *Formulations of the person in the social context.* New York: McGraw-Hill, 1959. Pp. 184–256.

Rogers, C. R. *On becoming a person.* Boston: Houghton Mifflin, 1961.

Rogers, C. R. (Ed.) *The therapeutic relationship and its impact.* Madison: The University of Wisconsin Press, 1967.

Rogers, C. R., & Skinner, B. F. Some issues concerning the control of human behavior: A symposium. *Science,* 1956, **124,** 1057–1066.

Rogers, C. R., & Truax, C. B. The therapeutic conditions antecedent to change: A theoretical view. In C. R. Rogers (Ed.), *The therapeutic relationship and its impact.* Madison: The University of Wisconsin Press, 1967. Pp. 97–108.

Rokeach, M. *The nature of human values.* New York: The Free Press, 1973.

Roll, W. V., Schmidt, L. D., & Kaul, T. J. Perceived interviewer trustworthiness among black and white convicts. *Journal of Counseling Psychology,* 1972, **19,** 537–541.

Rosen, S., & Tesser, A. On reluctance to communicate undesirable information: The MUM effect. *Sociometry,* 1970, **33,** 253–263.

Rosen, S., & Tesser, A. Fear of negative evaluation and the reluctance to transmit bad news. *Proceedings of the 79th Annual Convention of the American Psychological Association,* 1971, **6,** 301–302.

Rosso, S. M., & Frey, D. N. An assessment of the gap between counseling theory and practice. *Journal of Counseling Psychology,* 1973, **20,** 471–476.

Saral, T. B. Cross-cultural generality of communication via facial expressions. *Comparative Group Studies,* 1972, **3,** 473–486.

Schmidt, L. D., & Strong, S. R. "Expert" and "inexpert" counselors. *Journal of Counseling Psychology,* 1970, **17,** 115–118.

Schmidt, L. D., & Strong, S. R. Attractiveness and influence in counseling. *Journal of Counseling Psychology,* 1971, **18,** 348–351.

Schofield, W. *Psychotherapy: The purchase of friendship.* Englewood Cliffs, N.J.: Prentice-Hall, 1964.

Shapiro, M., & Asher, W. Students who seldom discuss their post high school plans. *School Counselor,* 1972, **20,** 103–107.

Sherman, A. R. *Behavior modification: Theory and practice.* Monterey, Ca.: Brooks/Cole, 1973.

Simon, S. B., Howe, L. W., & Kirschenbaum, H. *Values clarification: A handbook of practical strategies for teachers and students.* New York: Hart, 1972.

Skinner, B. F. *Science and human behavior.* New York: Macmillan, 1953.

Skinner, B. F. Operant behavior. *American Psychologist,* 1963, **18,** 503–515.

Skinner, B. F. *Beyond freedom and dignity.* New York: Knopf, 1971.

Spivack, J. D., & Kagan, N. Laboratory to classroom: The practical application of IPR in a master's level pre-practicum counselor education program. *Counselor Education and Supervision,* 1972.

Standal, S. The need for positive regard: A contribution to client-centered theory. Unpublished doctoral dissertation, University of Chicago, 1954.

Stefflre, B. (Ed.) *Theories of counseling.* New York: McGraw-Hill, 1965.

Strong, S. R. Counseling: An interpersonal influence process. *Journal of Counseling Psychology,* 1968, **15,** 215–224.

Strong, S. R. Causal attribution in counseling and psychotherapy. *Journal of Counseling Psychology,* 1970, **17,** 388–399.

Strong, S. R., & Dixon, D. N. Expertness, attractiveness, and influence in counseling. *Journal of Counseling Psychology,* 1971, **18,** 562–570.

Strong, S. R., & Gray, B. L. Social comparison, self-evaluation, and influence in counseling. *Journal of Counseling Psychology,* 1972, **19,** 178–183.

Strong, S. R., & Matross, R. P. Change processes in counseling and psychotherapy. *Journal of Counseling Psychology,* 1973, **20,** 25–37.

Strong, S. R., Meland, J. A., & Keierleber, D. L. Resistance and opposition to influence in counseling. *Office for Student Affairs Research Bulletin, University of Minnesota,* 1972, No. 13.

Strong, S. R. & Schmidt, L. D. Expertness and influence in counseling. *Journal of Counseling Psychology,* 1970a, **17,** 81–87.

Strong, S. R., & Schmidt, L. D. Trustworthiness and influence in counseling. *Journal of Counseling Psychology,* 1970b, **17,** 197–204.

Strong, S. R., Taylor, R. G., Bratton, J. C., & Loper, R. G. Nonverbal behavior and perceived counselor characteristics. *Journal of Counseling Psychology,* 1971, **18,** 554–561.

Strupp, H. H. On the basic ingredients of psychotherapy. *Journal of Consulting and Clinical Psychology,* 1973a, **41,** 1–8.

Strupp, H. H. The interpersonal relationship as a vehicle for therapeutic learning. *Journal of Consulting and Clinical Psychology,* 1973b, **41,** 13–15.

Suinn, R. M. Training undergraduate students as community behavior modification consultants. *Journal of Counseling Psychology,* 1974, **21,** 71–77.

Sundland, D. M., & Barker, E. N. The orientation of psychotherapists. *Journal of Consulting Psychology,* 1962, **26,** 201–212.

Sydnor, G. L., Akridge, R. L., & Parkhill, N. L. *Human relations training: A programmed manual.* Minden, La.: Human Resources Development Training Institute, 1972.

Sydnor, G. L., & Parkhill, N. L. *Advanced human relations training: A programmed manual.* Minden, La.: Human Resources Development Training Institute, 1973a.

Sydnor, G. L., & Parkhill, N. L. *Behavior analysis: A programmed manual.* Minden, La.: Human Resources Development Training Institute, 1973b.

Szasz, T. S. *The myth of mental illness.* New York: Harper & Row, 1961.

Talland, G. A., & Clark, D. H. Evaluation of topics in therapy group discussion. *Journal of Clinical Psychology,* 1954, **10,** 131–137.

Tesser, A., & Rosen, S. Similarity of objective fate as a determinant of the reluctance to transmit unpleasant information: The MUM effect. *Journal of Personality and Social Psychology,* 1972, **23,** 46–53.

Tesser, A., Rosen, S., & Batchelor, T. On the reluctance to communicate bad news (the MUM effect): A role play extension. *Journal of Personality,* 1972, **40,** 88–103.

Tesser, A., Rosen, S., & Tesser, M. On the reluctance to communicate undesirable messages (the MUM effect): A field study. *Psychological Reports,* 1971, **29,** 651–654.

Thoresen, C. E., & Mahoney, M. J. *Behavioral self-control.* New York: Holt, Rinehart, & Winston, 1974.

Thorndike, E. L. Intelligence and its use. *Harper's Magazine,* 1920, **140,** 227–235.

Thorne, F. C. An eclectic evaluation of psychotherapeutic methods. In R-R. M. Jurjevich (Ed.), *Direct psychotherapy: Twenty-eight American originals.* Vol. II. Coral Gables, Fla.: University of Miami Press, 1973a. Pp. 847–883.

Thorne, F. C. Eclectic psychotherapy. In R. Corsini (Ed.), *Current psychotherapies.* Itasca, Ill.: Peacock, 1973b. Pp. 445–486.

Trotter, R. J. Peter Breggin's private war. *Human Behavior,* 1973, **2** (11), 50–57.

Truax, C. B. Therapist empathy, genuineness, and warmth and patient therapeutic outcome. *Journal of Consulting Psychology,* 1966, **30,** 395–401.

Truax, C. B. The meaning and reliability of accurate empathy: A rejoinder. *Psychological Bulletin,* 1972, **77,** 397–399.

Truax, C. B., & Carkhuff, R. R. Client and therapist transparency in the psychotherapeutic encounter. *Journal of Counseling Psychology,* 1965, **12,** 3–9.

Truax, C. B., & Carkhuff, R. R. *Toward effective counseling and psychotherapy: Training and practice.* Chicago: Aldine, 1967.
Tuckman, B. W. Interpersonal probing and revealing and systems of integrative complexity. *Journal of Personality and Social Psychology,* 1966, **3,** 655–664.
Vondracek, F. W. The study of self-disclosure in experimental interviews. *Journal of Psychology,* 1969, **72,** 55–59.
Walker, R. E., & Foley, J. M. Social intelligence: Its history and measurement. *Psychological Reports,* 1973, **33,** 839–864.
Wallen, J. L. Developing effective interpersonal communication. In R. W. Pace, B. D. Peterson, & T. R. Radcliffe (Eds.), *Communicating interpersonally.* Columbus, Ohio: C. E. Merrill, 1973. Pp. 218–233.
Ward, R. G., Kagan, N., & Krathwohl, D. R. An attempt to measure and facilitate counselor effectiveness. *Counselor Education and Supervision,* 1972, **11,** 179–186.
Watson, D. L., & Tharp, R. G. *Self-directed behavior: Self-modification for personal adjustment.* Monterey, Ca.: Brooks/Cole, 1973.
Weick, K. E. *The social psychology of organizing.* Reading, Mass.: Addison-Wesley, 1969.
Weigel, R. G., Dinges, N., Dyer, R., & Straumfjorn, A. A. Perceived self-disclosure, mental health, and who is liked in group treatment. *Journal of Counseling Psychology,* 1972, **19,** 47–52.
Weinstein, E. A. The development of interpersonal competence. In D. A. Goslin (Ed.), *Handbook of socialization theory and research.* Chicago: Rand McNally, 1969. Pp. 753–775.
Weitz, S. Attitude, voice, and behavior: A repressed affect model of interracial interaction. *Journal of Personality and Social Psychology,* 1972, **24,** 14–21.
Whaley, D. L., & Malott, R. W. *Elementary principles of behavior.* New York: Appleton-Century-Crofts, 1971.
White, R. W. Sense of interpersonal competence. In R. W. White (Ed.), *The study of lives: Essays on personality in honor of Henry A. Murray.* New York: Atherton Press, 1963. Pp. 73–93.
Whitely, J. Counselor education. *Review of Educational Research,* 1969, **30,** 173–187.
Williams, W. S. Class differences in the attitudes of psychiatric patients. *Social Problems,* 1956, **4,** 240–244.
Wittmer, J., & Lister, J. L. Microcounseling and microcounseling consultation via videotape. *Counselor Education and Supervision,* 1972, **11,** 238–240.
Yablonsky, L. *The tunnel back: Synanon.* New York: Macmillan, 1965.
Zimbardo, P., & Ebbesen, E. B. *Influencing attitudes and changing behavior.* Reading, Mass.: Addison-Wesley, 1970.

Author Index

Subject Index